# Technology and Transition

## The Maghreb at the Crossroads

*Edited by*

Girma Zawdie and Abdelkader Djeflat

## FRANK CASS
LONDON • PORTLAND, OR.

First published in 1996 in Great Britain by
FRANK CASS AND COMPANY LIMITED
Newbury House, 900 Eastern Avenue, London IG2 7HH, England

and in the United States of America by
FRANK CASS
c/o ISBS, Inc.
5804 N.E. Hassalo Street, Portland, Oregon 97213-3644

British Library Cataloguing in Publication Data
A catalogue record for this book is available from the British Library.

ISBN 0 7146 4745 4 (hbk)
ISBN 0 7146 4303 3 (pbk)


Library of Congress Cataloging-in-Publication Data



Technology and Transition: the Maghreb at the crossroads / edited by Girma
    Zawdie & Abdelkader Djeflat
        p. cm.
    Includes bibliographical references (p. ).
    ISBN 0-7146-4745-4. – ISBN 0-7146-4303-3
    1. Technological innovations – Economic aspects – Africa, North.
    2. Technology transfer – Africa, North. 3. Technology and state – Africa,
    North. I Zawdie, Girma, 1948-  . II. Djeflat, A.
    (Abdelkader)
    HC805.Z9T472  1996
338'.064'0961 – dc20                                                96-19696
                                                                          CIP

This group of studies first appeared in a Special Issue of
*Science, Technology & Development*, Vol.13, No.3 (December 1995),
Technology and Transition in the Maghreb

Printed in Great Britain by
Antony Rowe Ltd.

# Contents

# Introduction

The articles in this book are drawn from the proceedings of the First MAGHTECH International Conference on *Strategies Towards Science and Technology-Based Development and Transition in the Maghreb* (MAGHTECH '94), held in Sfax, Tunisia in December 1994. The Conference was organised by the UK-based Third World Science, Technology and Development (STD) Forum in collaboration with the University of Oran (Algeria), the Faculté des Sciences Economiques et de Gestion of Sfax at the University of Sfax (Tunisia), the David Livingstone Institute of Overseas Development Studies at the University of Strathclyde (UK) and the University of Lille I (France). The Conference was generously sponsored by the British Council, the Friederich Ebert Foundation (Germany), the Third World Academy of Sciences (Trieste/Italy) and the Centre d'Etudes et de Recherche sur l'Information Scientifique et Technique (Algeria).

The articles raise some of the major issues which Maghrebian researchers, planners and policy makers would need to address in the course of drawing up national and regional strategies for transition and development. Technological development is at the heart of long run growth, and the efficient management of science and technology offers the way forward for countries in the Maghreb, as indeed for other developing countries that now find themselves at the crossroads of rapidly changing global socio-political and techno-economic paradigms. Given this as the underlying theme of the book, the articles may be left to speak for themselves. The reader might nonetheless find it useful to have the overarching points emerging from discussions of the articles set in context. The remainder of this introductory note is an attempt to this end.

The Maghreb is a geo-economic entity in North Africa including mainly Algeria, Tunisia and Morocco (see map). Libya and Mauritania are also included in the wider Arab Maghreb Union, but have yet to be fully integrated. The Maghreb accounts for 25 per cent of the total area of the African continent, about 20 per cent of its population and 35 per cent of its production. The region is economically distinct from the sub-Saharan African region in that, with the exception of low-income Mauritania, all the other Maghrebian countries fall in the category of middle-income economies. Thus by African standards, the Maghreb, like South Africa, is relatively advanced in terms of the development of infrastructure, industrialisation and the development of technological capability. But as in most African economies, growth in the Maghreb has been deteriorating in

THE COUNTRIES OF THE MAGHREB

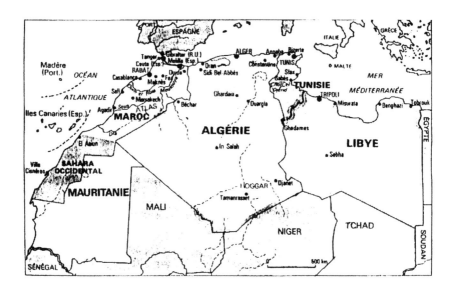

recent years. For instance, for the periods 1970–80 and 1980–90, the average annual growth rates of GDP per capita were, respectively, 1.5 per cent and zero per cent for Algeria, 3.2 and 1.6 for Morocco, and 4.1 and 1.3 for Tunisia (World Bank 1994). This deterioration in growth performance suggests that all is not well with the factors underlying long run growth in the Maghreb after all. More specifically, the strategy of industrialisation by import substitution and technology transfer from abroad, which for the most part determined the rate and direction of growth in the Maghreb over the last four decades since independence, is now fast running out of steam, casting doubt on the significance of the learning and innovative effects of the accumulation of industrial capacity in the region during this period.

The strategies the Maghreb countries opted for sought to promote growth through industrialisation, but delivered hardly any technological progress of significance. For instance, in Algeria, where the industrialisation effort appeared impressive for a good part of the post-independence period, the interventionist role of the state and the oil endowment have been crucial. Industrialisation thrived on the back of protection and the import of technology, and the oil boom of the 1970s provided sufficient elbow room for the acquisition of foreign technology. If the Algerian economy did well under the circumstances, its underlying orientation made it vulnerable to the so-called 'Dutch disease'. This is a phenomenon in which the oil boom during the 1970s induced contraction of the non-oil traded goods sectors (especially agriculture) and expansion of the non-traded goods sector including, *inter alia*, protected industry (Corden 1982, Neary and van Wijnbergen 1986, Fardmanesh 1991). The 'Dutch disease' took its toll in the 1980s when the collapse of the oil price dealt a heavy blow to the industrial growth effort in Algeria. Thus between 1970 and 1993, the share of industry in GDP expanded only marginally from 41 to 43 per cent in Algeria, while it grew from 24 to 31 per cent in Tunisia, and from 27 to 32 per cent in Morocco (World Bank 1995).

Today, though, all the three core Maghreb countries are facing the problem of technological obsolescence, as replacement of the existing technology stocks is becoming increasingly difficult in view of the economic problems they have been experiencing in recent years. The difficult economic position in which the countries in the region find themselves now is, in large measure, of their own making. Faulty policies begat poorly performing economies. The mission of the state was wrongly conceived and the economics of science and technology played second fiddle to the politics of industrialisation. In consequence, the economies of the region have been landed with macroeconomic, and – even more serious – structural deficits. Correcting these deficits in the light of changing global techno-economic circumstances constitutes a major transition agenda for the Maghreb countries.

For all the policy failures and misplaced priorities of the last four decades, the Maghreb countries are technologically and economically better placed than many other countries in Africa to take the challenge of transition head on. Indeed, the Maghreb is strategically significant for Africa – in economic terms, that is – in that like South Africa at the other end of the continent, it is potentially capable of serving as a growth pole with far-reaching spillover effects. All the three core Maghreb countries have, for instance, had a good measure of technological and scientific experience and have sought to develop national innovation systems over the last four decades. This and the industrial capacity created under the import substitution regime, however poorly integrated, provide the necessary basis on which to build the way forward for transition and development in the Maghreb.

Of particular concern for transition strategies is how well such strategies are adapted to rapidly changing global techno-economic circumstances. Recent trends in technological progress and, in particular, the generic character of new technologies have led to the progressive loss of traditional areas of comparative advantage bestowed by the relatively low labour costs of the region and by its rich natural resource endowment. These are no longer essential for accumulation and growth in the context of the unfolding global techno-economic paradigm. With the internationalisation of technology and production, the importance of policies fostering competition rather than protection is becoming increasingly apparent. Competitiveness would, however, be sustainable in a global framework as a derivative of the innovation process rather than as a product of the policy option for wage compression.

Contrary to the neo-liberal view which ascribes the deterioration of economic conditions in the Maghreb in recent years to the preponderance of macroeconomic imbalances and inadequate liberalisation – a point at the heart of structural adjustment programmes (SAPs) – it emerges from the discussions here that the Maghreb's techno-economic problem derives largely from policy-inflicted structural imbalances. These, it is argued, have made it difficult for the economies in the region to respond in a sufficiently flexible manner to the rapidly changing character of global production and market relations.

The market in the Maghreb economies – as indeed elsewhere in developing countries – is not so much inefficient as missing. But the roles played by the Maghreb states to fill this gap by providing the basis for the development of what Abramovitz (1989) calls 'social capability' – a necessary condition for innovation and technological progress at the firm, the industry and the national level – have been found wanting; and the economies in the region have been the poorer for all the missed opportunities due to the inefficiency of the state. An example of this is the sub-optimal level of technological capability development in the Maghreb consequent upon the passive role played by the state in reshaping the education and research and development systems, so that they could be effectively integrated with the production system of the economies in the region.

There is now consensus that the way forward for the Maghreb is through the promotion of innovation and technological progress and the adjustment of the Maghrebian economies to the rapidly changing trends of the global techno-economic system. In both cases, the role of the state is crucial. In the former case, the manner in which science and technology have evolved over the years in the Maghreb and the social, economic and political factors which have hitherto constrained their application as an engine of economic growth in the region have to be looked into in the context of a comprehensive science and technology policy. In the latter case, the Maghreb countries could derive substantial benefits in terms of increasing returns and technological spill-over effects from association with countries in the North (the European Union in their case) across the spectrum of economic activities. Indeed, in the light of the emerging techno-economic global framework, North–South link strategies would appear to be more grist to the mill of the South than to the North. This is because under the new techno-economic paradigm, the centre (North) has enough scope to accumulate and grow without the immediate need either for market expansion towards the periphery (South) or for sources of cheap labour and natural resources as in the past (Villaschi 1994).

In the light of the issues raised above, this volume is organised in three broad parts. The articles in the first part seek to set the issue of technology and transition in perspective from the vantage points of the world economy (Cooper and McRobie), the African economy (Yaker) and the Maghrebian economy (Djeflat). Those in the second part address some of the leading issues in technology and resource development drawing mainly on the Maghrebian experience. The articles in this part neatly fall into three sub-groups, covering aspects of technology transfer to the Maghreb (Saad and Oukil); the link between human resource development, research and development, innovation and technological progress (Alcouffe, Lehlou, Zawdie and Zghal); and agricultural and energy resource development (Mansfield and Riddell, and Twidell). The articles in the third part discuss lessons of experience in technology and transition for the Maghreb with reference to relevant cases from Mexico (Requier-Desjardins), China (Benyoucef) and Korea, India and Bangladesh (Huq).

No claim is made for this work to be comprehensive in its coverage of issues relating to technology and development in the Maghreb. It does, however, represent a first attempt at bringing into focus the issue of technology and transition in the Maghreb. For all its limitations, it is apparent from the authors' contributions that the Maghreb is now ripe for an S&T revolution. It is hoped that the broad issues discussed here will provide a useful frame of reference for setting the agenda for technology, transition and development in the region.

1996                                                                    GIRMA ZAWDIE
*(University of Strathclyde, UK)*

ABDELKADER DJEFLAT
*(University of Lille I, France)*

REFERENCES

Abramovitz, M. (1989), 'Catching Up, Forging Ahead and Falling Behind', in *Thinking About Growth,* Cambridge: Cambridge University Press.
Corden, W.M. (1982), 'Booming Sector and Dutch Disease Economics: a Survey', *Australian National University Working Papers,* No.079, Nov.
Fardmanesh, M. (1991), 'Dutch Disease Economics and the Oil Syndrome: an Empirical Study', *World Development,* Vol.19. No.6.
Neary, J.P. and S. van Wijnberger (eds.) (1989), *Natural Resources and the Macroeconomy,* Cambridge: MIT Press.
Villaschi, A. (1994), *The Newly Industrialised Countries and the Information Technology*

*Revolution: the Brazilian Experience*, Aldershot: Avebury.
World Bank (1994), *World Development Report: 1994*, Washington: Oxford University Press.
World Bank (1995), *World Development Report: 1995*, Washington: Oxford University Press.

# PART I
## PERSPECTIVES IN TECHNOLOGY AND TRANSITION

# New Technologies and Changing Trends in Development: Global Perspective I

## CHARLES COOPER

*Recent trends in technological progress and changes in the organisation of the world economy have transformed the objective conditions facing developing countries. Import substitution and protectionism are on the wane and successful industrialisation now depends on the capacity to learn to keep up with an unpredictable pattern of technological change and to switch from production the least efficient lines to those which promise the benefits of comparative and competitive advantage. Where industrialisation has been pursued without technological change, the desire to exploit price competitiveness has forced a downward pressure on real wages to maintain the share of profit in value added. On the other hand, industrialisation based on innovative competitiveness has shown that it is possible to have increases in real wages without reduction in the share of profits. The opening of developing economies to international competition has thus made technology more important for them now than ever before.*

## Introduction

Research and policy concern with the issue of technology and its role in development is not new. What is new is the immediacy and urgency the issue has assumed with regard to recent trends in technological progress. Why is technology more important now in the developing countries than it has ever been, or more precisely, since the early 1960s when we started thinking specifically about its role in economic growth and development and when the first UN Conference on Science and Technology for Development was held in Geneva?

To highlight the new urgencies about technology policy in relation to development, we shall in this article point to some significant economic

Professor Charles Cooper is Director of INTECH of the United Nations University, Maastricht. This article is an edited version of his keynote lecture delivered at the MAGHTECH '94 conference.

changes of the last five to ten years. We could call them *changes in the objective circumstances facing the South* which sharply accentuate the need for a new recognition of technological change. The first part of the article will describe two major areas of change. In the second part we shall try to bring out their importance for technology policy.

## Recent Trends in Development

The two areas of change in the objective circumstances facing the South are fairly obvious. They are:

- changes in the rate and direction of technological change in the productive and the service sectors of the economy; and

- the major changes in the organisation of the world economy since the late 1980s.

## The Rate and Direction of Technological Change

There are two main characteristics of technological change which are repeatedly described. One is that it has been accelerating; that the rate at which new technologies are incorporated into the system of production is higher than before, and that it seems to be increasing. This seems to be related to a much closer link between basic science or pure research and application. It is a new and remarkable phenomenon that university laboratories in fields such as biotechnology are successfully patenting technologies which, soon after their discovery, have been incorporated into production.

The other characteristic is that there has been a change in the patterns of technological change. Many describe new technologies such as biotechnology or microelectronics as generic. The term 'generic' is somewhat unclear, but what people have in mind when they use it is the fact that these new technologies have applications across many sectors. Computer technologies are an obvious case in point, and there are many others. This characteristic of wide applicability to production and service systems is, as it turns out, as important in its implications for developing countries as for the industrialised. What can we say about the implications for developing countries?

Until quite recently, the so-called traditional industrial sectors in the developing countries, such as textiles and garment production or food processing, were characterised as being by and large technologically stagnant. That, indeed, was sometimes given as a reason for their particular suitability for economies in which the technological capabilities were limited. But with the advent of generic technologies, this situation has changed perceptibly in recent years; for it is now clear that the application of new families of technology, and particularly of microelectronic control systems to production, has begun to affect the once 'stagnant' sectors very markedly. In textiles particularly, automation together with the development of new weaving and spinning equipment have created much more demanding technological conditions. In order to maintain competitiveness, enterprises in developing countries have sooner or later to come to terms with these more demanding technological conditions. Similar patterns of generic technological change are apparent in other 'traditional' sectors such as garments. So, while the shift towards free market conditions seems to simplify the concerns of technology policy from certain points of view – by restricting the possibilities of rent taking, for example – from the present standpoint of a rather general acceleration in the pattern and rate of technological change, the opening up of the market may result in some less expected difficulties. It remains true though that the newer types of technology in the traditional sectors are mainly available from machinery suppliers in the direct type of technology transfer.

We shall return to the implications of these changes in the pattern of technology. Now, however, we turn to the second set of changes mentioned at the outset: changes in the organisation of the international economy.

## The Changing International Economy

### Industrialisation under Protection

There have, of course, been many major transformations of the international economy in recent years. Here we shall focus on a particular set of changes which affect the developing countries especially. These are the sharp movements away from protectionist, closed economy approaches to economic development and the widespread espousal of various types of open economy approach.

Generally speaking, high levels of protection resulted in comparatively inefficient and uncompetitive industrial sectors in many developing countries. Industries were usually oligopolistic, with relatively few firms present in each market. And as industrialisation moved from the production of goods for local consumers on to intermediates and capital goods, such as plant and machinery, there was often a tendency for this inefficiency to grow. Local producers of these so-called producer goods were often protected by 'local content requirements', i.e., legislation which required that some specified proportion of the inputs used by firms established in the domestic economy should be from other domestic producers. In some countries, foreign direct investments in local industry were actually excluded by legislation, but in many, the transnational enterprises were notably present. In the vast majority of cases, they were there for the purpose of production for the local markets, not for export markets; and they, like all firms, were caught up in the cycle of inefficiency. The problem in protected 'industrial systems' is that inefficiency often results from conditions outside individual firms or industries because of a legislated requirement to use local machinery or highly priced local materials. As far as individual firms are concerned, these externally determined inefficiencies are added to the lack of inter-firm competition which itself creates conditions in which internally inefficient firms can survive.

These conditions had important influences on the technologies used in local industries. We now turn to this question and especially to the implications of protected industrialisation for technological change and the transfer of technology from abroad.

First, there is the influence industrial protection had on *technological change* within the industrial sector. In modern industry, technological change is in fact a central means of competition. It is the means by which firms reduce the costs of production for given outputs, and more importantly, it is also involved in the production of new outputs – for the search for new products is increasingly a central characteristic of inter-firm competition.

Insofar as protected industrialisation generally reduced the pressure of competition in local industries, it almost certainly lowered the rates of technological change. Firms were not required to find new technologies to survive: survival could be ensured by the high price levels for final outputs which were facilitated by protection and by the oligopolistic forms of market organisation in which relatively inefficient firms which would have disappeared under more open competition could coexist with market leaders, albeit with low profit margins.

The second effect of protected industrialisation relates to its impacts on the *transfer of technology from abroad*. In protected industries, policy towards technology transfer was driven by two main considerations. The first was the perception that the cost of foreign technology was very high. Policy makers were impressed by the fact that innovative technologies were usually in some degree monopolistically controlled by innovative companies, and that, especially in the protected markets, where market prices were much above world market levels, this could result in large outflows of technology rents.

The second source of concern related to the supposed 'perpetuation of technological dependency'. The idea was that use of foreign technology would tend to substitute for local technological capabilities, so that countries would remain permanently dependent on foreign technology suppliers.

The policy responses to these concerns were to bring into being rather heavy administrative systems. Looking back at these systems with advantages of hindsight, it is striking how much attention was devoted to preventing 'duplication' by the importing of technologies already available within the country, and, on the other hand, how little attention was given to ensuring that the technologies that were actually imported were properly integrated into the local production system; there was, in short, little attempt to ensure that enterprises learnt from imported technology.

Furthermore, now that we have had a chance to look back on the older system we must have doubts about its efficacy. Bureaucratic control of the costs of imported technologies had rather little effect on actual costs: the records show that royalty rates and the like were not changed to any great degree by the control system. And the attempts to prevent the importation of technology already available were similarly by and large ineffective.

Let us now pull together briefly the points made so far. First, trade-protected industrialisation produced uncompetitive and distorted environments, which in turn had some clear implications for technology. One was the effect on technology choices where protection was widely argued to result in inappropriate technologies in industry. A second implication was for the rate of technological change where it is argued that the uncompetitive environment undermined the rate of technological change, since firms did not have to bother too much about keeping up with international technological developments. The third implication was that tariff-protected industrialisation resulted in rather complicated institutional arrangements to control the monopolistic effects which were associated with the international transfer of technology.

*The Implications of Liberalisation for Technology Change*

In recent years, in repeated programmes of structural adjustment and the like, the protected industrial markets of developing countries have been opened up, sometimes very abruptly. In the process of liberalisation, many of the emphases in technology transfer policy which characterised the period of import-substitution have changed and new priorities have appeared. There have been three main changes, which will continue to be important for quite a long time to come in relation to industrialisation policies in developing countries.

The first major change is that the old concern with the rental or monopoly costs of imported technology – a notable feature of earlier Indian policy, and which was certainly a central preoccupation in many Latin American economies – has now more or less disappeared from the policy agenda. This is not all that surprising.

Once the domestic market is opened to international competition, licensee firms have to be concerned to meet internationally competitive prices in the home market and will mostly be concerned to export as well. This means that they are neither able nor willing to accept levels of royalty payment which might have been accepted as normal under tariff-protected industrialisation. There are competitive forces at work even in technology markets which set much narrower limits to the possibilities of rent taking behaviour than under conditions of protected industrialisation. Consequently, the opening of national markets to the international economy tends to take away one of the main concerns of technology policy makers in import-substituting industrial economies.

Second, the opening of national markets leads in a natural way to changes in the pattern of production. Basically, there is a shift away from the least efficient lines of production which prevailed under protection towards lines of production in which there is a comparative advantage – often in a narrow, short run sense.

Whatever the costs and benefits of the transition process, one thing is certain. The pattern of local industrial production changes, and the pattern of international transfer of technology changes along with it. So in many countries there has been a shift in industrial output away from the more sophisticated high income consumer goods and intermediate goods production towards the more 'traditional' sectors, such as textiles, garments, leather goods, food processing and industries based on local raw materials inputs. Accompanying this shift there is a move away from the 'indirect' licensing and foreign direct investment types of technology transfer, which tend to dominate in high income consumer goods sectors and in intermediates production, towards the more direct, 'supplier-dominated' technology transfers mediated by machine producers and engineering firms in the innovative, northern industrial economies.

The third and last change from a 'technological' point of view that is associated with the opening of domestic markets is that learning processes within local firms become much more important than under protected market conditions. Successful entry into international markets has to be followed, at the very least, by survival. And under conditions where technological change has plainly begun to affect even the erstwhile traditional sectors, survival requires that firms are able to maintain and improve productivity. The only alternative in the long run is to attempt to reduce costs by successive reductions in the real wage. The latter pattern is observable – for example in some of the export free zones appearing in developing countries – but it plainly has some quite strict limits.

This last point, about the need to generate technological learning processes within industrial enterprises – and increasingly even in enterprises in the so-called traditional sectors – is perhaps the most important implication of liberalisation for industrial policy.

## Why Does this Make Technology Questions More Important?

This paper started by putting forward the point that in the new technological and economic world the technological factor is truly more important than ever before. One way of making this point more explicitly is to categorise the different types of experience that countries have had in facing the opening of their economies to international trade and to distinguish between the different approaches they have taken to technology. It is possible to distinguish three groups of countries, at least:

- Some countries started industrialisation in technologically undemanding sectors, and then, after accumulating a wide range of capabilities, moved up to technologically more and more advanced sectors characterised by increasing intensity of innovative competition. The clearest example today is Korea. Japan went through a similar cycle. China, or at least parts of China, may be starting such a pattern. Korea illustrates the potential of this stepwise process: over the 20 years from 1969, exports by volume grew at an annual rate of 15 per cent. *Real wages* grew at 7 per cent per annum, as did real value added per worker. Thus the share of profit in value added was more or less constant. The increase in labour productivity was facilitated by a shift from low to high value-added types of production, characterised by increasing degrees of innovative competition.

- Other countries have entered manufacturing trade successfully, but have not achieved the step up to higher levels of innovative competition that Korea has managed. They have kept up with international technological change. Exports have grown but less rapidly and less sustainably than in Korea. Hong Kong is a case in point. There has been a much less spectacular growth in productivity and also in real wages. Wage pressure on the profit share has been a problem more frequently. There have been periods when real wages in Hong Kong have fallen, probably in response to a slow down in productivity growth.

- In yet other countries – the large majority of developing countries in all probability, where entry into manufacturing trade has been in sectors or subsectors with a low degree of innovative competition – competitiveness is based on low real wages and relatively low rates of productivity growth are required. Many countries have shifted into a pattern of this kind after adjusting out of the import-substitution policy. Chile seems a particularly clear example. Entry on these terms is evidently much less demanding in terms of technological capability than in the preceding cases, but the economic and social outcomes are less favourable.

This differentiated pattern of entry is not stable. In a world of innovative competition, matters do not stand still for long. There is a tendency for areas of production which were hitherto calm backwaters of steady technology and fairly predictable price competition to be caught up in new rounds of innovative competition. When that happens, success depends on whether existing producers possess the technological capabilities needed to imitate process and product innovations. If they do not, they may be forced out of international markets, or they may hang on by cutting costs through real wage reductions. This pattern seems to be present in a number of low-wage sectors in developing countries.

Successful industrialisation depends increasingly not only on efficient production at today's technology and relative price patterns but also on the capacity to keep up with an often unpredictable pattern of technological change. The success with which countries do this affects importantly the welfare implications of export-oriented industrialisation. High rates of technological change permit increases in real wages without adverse implications for profitability and the incentive to invest. Lower rates often imply that the only way to succeed internationally is by forcing the real wage down and turning the functional distribution of income against labour. The technological factor appears, therefore, to play a crucial role in determining the developmental outcomes of industrialisation, and this is a direct consequence of the way competition works within a more open world economy with high rates of technological change across most sectors.

## Conclusion

A crude summary to the foregoing discussion might be: industrialise without technological change and international competition will relegate the country to a low wage production zone, albeit putting continual downwards pressure on real wages to maintain the share of profits in value added. Industrialisation with high rates of technological change at least opens the option for increasing the level of real wages without necessarily reducing the share of profits. It seems that there is what might be called a productivity knife-edge: on one side, there is a virtuous world of growth with socially acceptable distribution; on the other, competitiveness, on which growth depends, which involves a vicious circle of declining real wages and an increasing maldistribution of income between profits and wages.

# Technology for Development – What Is Appropriate for Rich and Poor Countries: Global Perspective II

## GEORGE McROBIE

*Consider the auk, who became extinct*
*Because he forgot how to fly and could only walk.*
*Because he learnt how to fly and forgot how to walk*
*Before he thought.*

Ogden Nash

## Introduction

The choice of technology is one of the most critical issues that confronts any country, big or small, rich or poor. It is a choice with a pervasive influence. It determines what is produced, and how and where it is produced; where people live, who works, and the quality of working life; what resources are used, and what support systems, such as finance, education, transport, are required; and depending upon its environmental impact, it determines whether the economic system it has shaped is sustainable or not.

Because conventional ways of measuring economic growth ignore its environmental impact, there is today a wide gulf between the economic and the environmental interpretations of what is happening in the world. The business community feels that the world is in reasonably good shape: and it is axiomatic that the more economic growth, as measured by gross national product (GNP), the better. In contrast, on the environmental front, every major indicator shows deterioration. Forests are shrinking, deserts expanding, croplands vanishing, plant and animal species diminishing, air and water pollution accelerating.

It is of course possible to devise ways of measuring economic growth that take into account its environmental impact. One such measure, an index of sustainable economic welfare (ISEW), was recently published in Britain.

Dr George McRobie is Vice-President of the Intermediate Technology Development Group (ITDG), UK. This paper was read by the author at the MAGHTECH '94 conference in his capacity as a keynote speaker.

This shows a marked difference between the conventional index, GNP, and the new index, ISEW. For the past 15 years, while GNP per head rose by an average of 2.4 per cent a year, the ISEW fell by no less than 5 per cent a year. This reflects a rising toll of social and environmental costs and a falling quality of life. A large part of the decline in the ISEW is attributable to the growing impact of resource depletion and long-term environmental damage. Roughly similar conclusions have been reached by researchers in the USA and Germany.

Resource depletion and environmental damage are directly linked with the predominant technologies of the industrialised countries. There is also the human cost of technologies which substitute capital and energy for human skill. The spectre of jobless economic growth is now haunting Europe and North America. Few would deny that the most urgent task of both rich and poor countries today is to discover and introduce technologies that are sustainable: technologies that respect the human need for useful and satisfying work, that minimise damage to the environment, and that conserve the world's resource base.

**A New Direction**

It was in relation to the needs and resources of the developing world that the deficiencies of rich-country technologies first became evident. The critical role of technology in economic development was first brought into focus by E.F. Schumacher in the early 1960s. He argued that Third World countries were relying on rich-country technologies at their peril: that the large-scale, capital- and energy-intensive industries of the rich countries would do more to exacerbate than to solve the problems of the poor countries. Such technologies were singularly inappropriate because they:

- offer relatively few, very expensive workplaces whereas the poor countries, with their masses of un- and under-employed, desperately need, large numbers of relatively inexpensive workplaces;

- are located chiefly in cities, which offer the mass markets, scarce skills and infrastructure facilities not found in rural areas where the majority of the poor live;

- in many instances, compete out of existence traditional non-farming activities formerly carried on in rural areas;

- accelerate the migration of people from rural areas to metropolitan centres;

- make the developing country increasingly dependent upon rich countries for loans, spare parts, skills and markets; and

• distort the cultures, as well as the economies of poor countries by concentrating economic activity in cities and social elites, breaking down rural structures – technology is not culturally neutral.

## Intermediate Technology

In 1965, a group of us helped Schumacher to start the Intermediate Technology Development Group in London. Our starting point was that mass unemployment and rural misery could be overcome only by creating new workplaces in the rural areas themselves; that these workplaces must be low-cost so that they can be created in large numbers without calling for impossible levels of savings or imports, that production methods and associated services must be kept relatively simple, and that production should be largely from local materials for local use.

We used the term 'intermediate' to indicate that, in terms of cost per workplace, the technology appropriate to a poor country would lie somewhere between the almost nil cost of a primitive hand tool, and the (say) £20,000 cost of a combine harvester. Thus if a developing country insisted on technologies which needed £20,000 for each new workplace, obviously (being short of capital) they would be able to create relatively few new jobs. But with a technology costing, say, £500, they could create 40 times as many. The best engineering talent available, we argued, should be engaged on the task of creating or discovering low-cost technologies: tools and equipment that could be owned and controlled by the rural and urban poor, and with which they could work themselves out of their poverty.

Our purpose was to demonstrate that technologies appropriate to the needs and resources of the rural poor could be developed and introduced, and then, by helping to create an international network of like-minded organisations, to change the whole emphasis of aid and development towards small-scale technology really capable of bringing industry into the rural areas.

At first, and for several years, the Group did not get a very warm welcome either in rich or in poor countries. But then the conventional strategy of development, based on large-scale capital intensive industries, came to be increasingly challenged by development economists and planners. Many of the large industries proved to be very inefficient, kept going only by protection and subsidies. They did not generate the hoped-for surpluses and they did nothing to raise the living standards of the majority, the rural and urban poor.

By the mid-1970s the accumulating evidence of the failure of the large-scale industry strategy was accompanied by the dawning recognition that small-scale, localised industry and agriculture can reduce transport costs, decelerate city growth, produce goods and services efficiently, and are the best way of distributing incomes. Then came the failure of African agriculture; the vast and unrepayable Third World debt; and the relentless growth of unemployment in developing countries. These, largely man-made, disastrous developments served to underscore the fact that encouraging the poor to behave as if they were already rich only compounded their problems.

The direct transplanting of rich-country technologies into the South has already done much damage to the interests of the poor. Mushrooming cities (whose growth is closely associated with cheap oil) continue to grow apace. On UN projections, Mexico City, Sao Paolo, Calcutta, Cairo and Jakarta will all have more than 15 million inhabitants by the end of the century, and some of these will have between 20 and 30 million. While in 1950 there were only six cities with more than five million, within the next decade there are likely to be no fewer than 60. The prospects in terms of energy and food supplies alone are daunting.

Employment prospects are no better. 'During the next 10 years, another 1.2 billion will enter working age ... About a quarter of them will find some form of work in agriculture, industry or services. The remaining 900 million people will be unable to find a regular source of income...' (de Wilde *et al.*1991). According to the International Fund for Agricultural Development (IFAD), more than one billion people are already below the poverty line in the rural areas of developing countries, and this could become 1.3 billion by the end of the century, thus representing misery on an unprecedented scale.

The attempt to transplant Northern technologies into the South has in general been a disastrous failure. This is not perhaps surprising in view of the prevailing demand in developing countries for Northern lifestyles and, therefore, for Northern technologies and the kind of economic growth they bring in their train. So, is not the task that of adapting Northern technologies, so that they may be absorbed more gradually, equitably and efficiently? On this view, small-scale, low-cost appropriate technologies are considered to be not really an alternative but simply a stepping stone to the conventional technologies and lifestyles of the North.

## The Economics of Impermanence

I am certainly not alone in believing this to be a dangerous misconception. In their predominant form, Northern technologies and their associated institutions are not sustainable. This is true both of industry and agriculture.

There is, first, the virtually total dependence of the North upon oil, which has decisively ceased to offer a low-cost, reliable or long-term energy supply; cheap oil has in fact proved to be an environmental disaster.

Secondly, conventional industrialisation is on a collision course with the environment. We now see the pollution of groundwater, air and food by industrial and agricultural chemicals, and the appalling prospect of living – if that is the right word – with what are to all intents and purposes permanently lethal radioactive wastes; the destruction of forests and the erosion of arable land; ruthless overfishing, and the prospect of permanent climatic change.

There are, above all, the human consequences of large-scale and highly centralised technology. The alienation and de-skilling of working people by mass production, the substitution of capital and energy for human skill – these have long been recognised but ignored in the interests of economic growth. But unemployment is now haunting both Europe and North America, and unemployment and alienation will continue so long as we treat labour merely as a cost. The growing centralisation of economic power also poses a threat to democratic processes.

We can no longer assume, in short, that conventional technology is appropriate for the purposes of environmental protection, for the responsible stewardship of scare resources, or for the human need for useful and satisfying work. We must increasingly find ways of asking and demanding answers to these questions about technological development. What does it do to the resource base, renewable and non-renewable? What does it do to the environment? What are its social and political implications?

Thanks largely to a growing number of voluntary organisations on both sides of the Atlantic, the policies required to create a more sustainable industry and society are now widely agreed, though not yet by governments and their paymasters. These policies include:

- a determined programme of energy conservation: the elimination of nuclear power; the development of renewable energy sources;

- the progressive introduction of product standards and specifications leading to long-life products which can be readily repaired, renewed and recycled;

- a transport policy that rapidly diminishes the damage done by the internal combustion engine; and the promotion of public transport, especially rail;

- a rapid transition towards organic (non-chemical) agriculture; and

- the localisation of economic activity, and the promotion of democratic forms of ownership and control, e.g., by workers and communities.

The technologies that would emerge from such policies, and the values that inform them, would be very different from those which dominate the North – and which hold out no long-term future for anyone, anywhere.

## AT as a New Approach to Development

There is now a considerable body of experience of appropriate technologies (ATs) in developing countries, and in what follows I try to highlight some of the salient features of this experience, and to put AT in context as an essential component of a new development strategy – a strategy aimed at mobilising the labour power of the rural poor.

Because most poor people in the world make a living by working on small farms, in small family businesses or as artisans, technologies appropriate to their needs and resources will generally be small, relatively simple, inexpensive and (to be sustainable) non-violent towards people and the environment. But experience has shown that it is not by any means enough to produce and field-test such technologies. Devising or adapting the right hardware is part of a package which includes identifying the specific needs and resources of the community; developing a technology that can meet their needs – that raises their income on a sustainable basis; and getting the technology, widely introduced under operating conditions. Obviously, to be appropriate the technology should be capable of local operation and maintenance, and local or at least indigenous manufacture; it should be owned and operated by its users, and result in a significant increase in their net (real or money) income; it should utilise to the maximum extent local and renewable raw materials and energy; and it should lend itself to widespread reproduction by the use of indigenous resources and through the medium of local markets.

There are today at least 20 organisations around the world with a significant capacity for identifying needs and undertaking practical research and development work. In the industrialised countries there are the pioneer organisations, ITDG, VITA, Brace Research, more recently joined by AT International in the USA, TOOL in Holland, GATE in Germany, GRET in France. Among international organisations UNICEF, the ILO and IDRC, UNIFEM and IFAD are major supporters of AT work in developing countries. The World Bank has steadfastly resisted becoming involved in appropriate technology.

In the developing countries, there are now dozens of AT organisations, ranging from technical R&D teams to information networking groups. There is also a large number of voluntary organisations working at grass-roots level, mostly with the rural and urban poor and often collaborating with AT groups in the field.

The growth of indigenous voluntary agencies, including IT groups, in the developing countries is one of the reasons for a major shift towards decentralisation by the Intermediate Technology Group. It has recently set up six country offices, under local staff, in Bangladesh, Kenya, Peru, Sri Lanka, Sudan and Zimbabwe. These centres will become increasingly independent of the parent body in Britain, thus opening the way for country offices to be started in other countries. In this way decisions about appropriate technologies, and the action needed to promote them, will be taken, as they should be, by people in the developing countries themselves. The accompanying table shows a summary of the Group's current activities in a number of countries.

| Country | Activity |
| --- | --- |
| Bangladesh | Agro-processing and textiles |
| India | Inshore fisheries, textiles, household energy |
| Kenya | Transport, stoves, building materials, animal husbandry |
| Nepal | Micro hydro |
| Peru | Agro-processing, mining, building mats., micro-hydro |
| Sri Lanka | Rural workshops, transport, stoves, ag. processing |
| Sudan | Food security |
| Zimbabwe | Transport, mining, agricultural processing, building materials |

Today appropriate technologies are available over a wide range of human activities, especially those related to basic human needs. Small-scale, low-cost technologies exist in farm equipment and food processing, water supply, building materials, textiles, small-scale manufacturing, energy and transport. What is beyond question is that technological choices may now be created for all practical purposes across the board. When high-quality engineers turn their minds to devising small-scale, capital and energy-saving technologies, they can produce some remarkable results (Carr 1985). But it is also true that while many ATs have achieved local success, few have spread widely through the market. To discover why, AT International compiled a series of case studies of high-impact ATs, which included the following examples (Fricke 1985).

*Mark II Handpumps in India*

The Mark II deepwell handpump (18 to 50m.) is now the basis of widespread community water supply in India. More than 600,000 are installed, serving 120 to 150 million villagers. Some 38 firms employing 8,500 people are now engaged in making these pumps at the rate of about 156,000 a year. Some 50,000 people are employed in well drilling or maintenance of existing installations. At village level, there is a pump caretaker equipped with a set of tools; at sub-district level, there are roving mechanics; at district level, mobile maintenance teams. The per capita cost to the users (covering the well, pump and maintenance costs) is less one dollar a year. During the past five years, an estimated 15,000–20,000 pumps have been exported.

Implementing organisations are: UNICEF, the Government of India, State Governments, villages and communities, private and public pump manufactures.

### Oral Rehydration Therapy

This is a simple inexpensive and effective way of treating diarrhoea in young children. Over the past 15 years ORT has spread to virtually every developing country, and about 100 million packets of ORT sales are produced and distributed annually. There is a growing number of local production units in developing countries, and a home preparation of a basic unit is now envisaged.

Implementing agencies are: UNICEF, Red Cross, WHO, Government and non-government health services, communities and families.

### Water Pumping Windmills in Argentina

About 60,000 water-pumping windmills are currently in use in Argentina and annual production is 1500 to 2000. About 300,000 people get water for livestock or own use. Implementing agencies are private manufacturing companies.

### Bamboo-Reinforced Concrete Water Tanks in Thailand

More than 24,000 tanks have been installed since 1979. Villagers contribute their labour, pay materials costs and a small surcharge into a revolving loan fund; up to 10,000 more tanks are likely to be build in the next three years.

Implementing agencies are community-based appropriate technology and development services with some funding from ATI, the Ford Foundation, IDRC and CUSO.

### Bamboo Tubewells, India

Work on bamboo tubewells started in 1967. By 1980, there were some 100,000 wells in Bihar and Uttar Pradesh. A mobile pump services five or six tubewells, which operate at depths of 30 to 36 m; work is now in hand on a bullock-powered pump. The technology was developed by farmers and small contractors. Its cost is one-third to one-half that of steel tubewells.

Implementing agencies are: Deen Dayal Research Institute, Governments of Bihar and Uttar Pradesh and local entrepreneurs.

### Rural Access Roads Programme, Kenya

An example of the AT approach applied to civil engineering. Competitive with capital-intensive methods, the programme established more than 40 field units and completed some 7,000 km of rural roads. It incorporates a technical service unit and a training programme and employs about 8,000 labourers.

Implementing agencies are: Ministry of Transport, Kenya, IBRD, ILO and UK and other bilateral donors.

*Women's Pappad Processing Co-operative Enterprises, India*

This started 25 years ago when seven women invested 80 rupees in a low-cost, nutritional, snack food venture. Today the business generates sales of 30 million rupees and provides income for more than 6,000 co-op members. Raw materials are bought in bulk and distributed to the co-operative's 21 centres, which operate with a good deal of autonomy and are run entirely by women.

Implementing agency is Lijjat Pappad Women's Co-operative.

*Rural Small Farm Implements Components Manufacture, Tanzania*

A decentralised approach to the production of ox-drawn implements (ox carts and toolbars) for small farmers. Two small factories are in production and two others are planned. In two years more than 2,000 ox-carts and 2,500 toolbars have been sold. The equipment pays for itself in a matter of months rather than years, as it enables more land to be cultivated. Surveys indicated that only a small fraction of the demand for this equipment has yet been met.

Implementing agencies are: Tanzania public and private implement manufactures and USAID.

Other projects with similar potential are not hard to find. The local manufacture of *fibre-reinforced roofing tiles*, an ITDG project in Kenya, is one such case. From a pilot project of ten production units this is envisaged as 50 production units after four years. By then, local income generation from the project would amount to 2 million Kenyan Sh. annually. Low-cost, local manufacture of FCR roofing tiles has potential in practically every developing country. Another example is the small-scale, locally-made *sorghum and millet dehuller*, developed and funded by the International Development Research Centre of Canada in collaboration with several African countries. Some 35 dehullers are in commercial operation in Botswana, 40 are planned in Zimbabwe, ten are working in the Dominican Republic, and pilot schemes are starting in India and the Gambia.

A programme which is well past the pilot stage is ITDG's introduction *of plywood fishing boats* in south India. At least 2,000 fishermen are earning a good living from 400 plywood boats operating along the south-west coast of India. There is now a firm base for a decentralised, capital-saving, skill and labour-using industry there, for boat-building and repairs. (It should be added here that it is far better to 'unroll' a huge mango tree into plywood which can make many boats than to use the same tree to make one dugout canoe and a heap of wood chips).

Some of the projects of AT International are analysed in detail by de Wilde *et al.* (1991). Six case studies (small-scale maize mills in Cameroon; appropriate wheelchairs in Colombia; glazed pottery in rural villages in Tanzania; improved *jikos* in Kenya; small-scale production of pigs in the Dominican Republic; and shrimp farming in Indonesia) demonstrate a non-traditional approach to economic development. Along with introducing ATs, these projects create markets by financing both production and consumption: financing potential buyers, enhancing the product quality of small enterprises, and giving small-scale producers access to markets and inputs that would have been denied them if only market forces prevailed. Thus the project on maize milling in Cameroon involved the technical development, production and maintenance of a locally-made maize mill; identification of people who would buy and operate the mills; and a financial mechanism – a lease/purchase scheme – that would give the poor access to ownership and new income. Women's groups buy the mill from the profits made by operating it.

### Reasons for Success

Some of the technologies noted above – especially the high impact ones – have been going long enough to become widespread; others, more recent, show potential for being widely taken up. What are the ingredients of success?

First, the technologies themselves have been thoroughly field-tested and refined before going into production – the history of handpump failures is impressive, for example, and tens of thousands of man-hours have been spent on getting animal-drawn equipment right. The technologies lend themselves to local manufacture wholly or in part and to local maintenance; and they are low-cost enough to be afforded by individuals or working groups of the 'target' population.

Secondly, the users or beneficiaries of the technologies are closely associated with the processes of selection, introduction and use of the technology or product; and from the standpoint of the users, the advantages (in the form, for instance, higher real income or life enhancement) significantly outweigh the costs incurred by them.

Thirdly, the technologies are disseminated through the mechanisms of the market; but in practically every case the market alone would be inadequate – it has to be supplemented in several ways. Thus R&D and testing are preconditions of a product making its appearance in the market.

But neither its appearance nor detailed information about it puts it in the hands of the rural poor. The poor have no money, or none to spare; their needs must be translated into effective demand, that is demand backed by purchasing power. This requires that the poor have access to credit enabling them to buy the new equipment. They can then, as in the case of the maize mills in Cameroon, repay the loan out of the income they get by using the new technology. Credit that enables the poor to become more productive lies at the heart of the process of rural development, of capital accumulation and income generation by the rural poor.

Careful attention must also be given to such matters as quality control, training, extension and demonstration, and the creation of new local institutions to ensure continuity of user control and benefit. In all instances, that is, the hardware part of the technology is part of a package which empowers local people to choose what suits them best; gives them access to a low-cost, good quality product over which they have a good measure of control; and which enables them, by using it, to raise their standard of living. Essentially, this is investing in people by making them more productive.

One important reason for the widespread adoption of these technologies is that they have either had support at government level or that they have in some way overcome or bypassed the formidable obstacles that inhibit ATs in most developing countries. These are familiar enough – development strategies based on top-down, large-scale programmes and projects, and financial policies, administrative procedures and rules that favour the big over the small, the urban over the rural, the rich over the poor. If such obstacles could be lowered or removed, the disastrous consequences of the conventional large-scale technologies would be clearly revealed, and cost-effective AT's would be widely adopted through the market.

The importance of government policies in fostering or inhibiting the spread of ATs was explored in Stewart (1987). She showed that in most developing countries there is a hostile environment for appropriate technologies: legal, financial, fiscal, administrative and other barriers effectively prevent their widespread adoption through the market. The analysis was extended and amplified in Stewart *et al.* (1990). Changes in government regulations and practices that favour capital-intensive and inhibit small-scale enterprises would remove one major set of obstacles preventing the spread of ATs.

But there are also deficiencies in the market that must be made good, especially in the allocation of credit and foreign exchange. Small-scale activities are generally denied access to the formal sector and have to go to the informal sector, where interest rates may be ten or more times as high. This is one of the reasons why proponents of appropriate technology would argue for a 'structured market' in place of the unregulated market which is currently much in vogue. Other reasons are the failure of the unregulated market to meet social needs (which include both primary income and services such as health) and its failure to provide such external inputs to industry as public purchasing and other market supports, physical infrastructure, R&D and training facilities, some or all of which, experience shows, may be needed to kick-start industries into a process of self-generating growth.

**Towards a New Strategy**

The structured market is one where the state provides a structure to guide the market towards the achievement of economic and social goals. Within this structure the market operates freely. The object is to avoid the failures of the unregulated market but retain the market as an effective way of allocating resources. 'The aim of structuring the market is to promote the achievement of three objectives which are poorly served by the unregulated market: economic growth, social justice (and especially the elimination of poverty), and environmental sustainability' (Stewart 1993). The structured market thus offers both the goal of a new development paradigm and the action needed to implement it.

Essentially the same strategy is spelt out in some detail by Jazairy *et al.* (1992), who state the objective as participatory and environmentally sustainable growth based on poverty alleviation. The targets of this goal include environmental conservation, enhancing the productivity of the rural poor and maximising their resources, strengthening the institutional framework for the rural poor and the economic role of poor rural women.

Appropriate technology is one of the most important tools needed to carry through a policy of mobilising the poor to achieve economic growth and poverty alleviation. For more than 30 years, aid and development programmes have excluded and marginalised the rural poor, who form a very large part of the development world's population. How much theoretical justification is needed before the poor are given a real chance to work themselves out of their poverty?

REFERENCES

Carr, M. (1985), *The AT Reader*, London: IT Publications.
Fricke, T. (1985), *High Impact AT Case Studies*, Washington, DC: AT International.
Jazairy, I., T. Alamgir and T. Panuccio (1992), *The State of World Poverty*, London: IT Publications (for IFAD).
Stewart, F. (ed.) (1987), *Macro Policies for Appropriate Technology in Developing Countries*, London: Westview.

Stewart, F. (1993), *Why We Need a Structured Market*, Oxford: Queen Elizabeth House.
Stewart, F., H. Thomas. and T. de Wilde (eds.) (1990), *The Other Policy: the Influence of Policies on Technology Choice and Small Enterprise Development*. London: IT Publications.
de Wilde, T., S. Schrews and A. Richman (1991), *Opening the Market Place to Small Enterprises*, London: IT Publications.

# Science and Technology-based Development and Transition: The African Perspective

## LAYASHI YAKER

*This article reviews the problem of African development, indicating science and technology oriented strategies as the way out of the poverty and dependence syndrome. Africa is richly endowed with natural resources but remains undeveloped in most parts mainly for lack of the scientific and technological capability to transform these resources into economic goods at competitive rates. Africa currently contributes only two per cent to world trade, which is less than the share of South Korea. This shows, inter alia, the marginalisation of scientific and technological services in Africa. Science and technology constitute an agenda which has yet to be addressed in earnest in Africa as an engine of development. The paper discusses the international context within which Africa could launch its strategy for the development of science and technology capability and the role of the United Nations Economic Commission for Africa in particular in this regard.*

## Introduction

North Africa has an important weight in Africa, representing 25 per cent of the total area, which, excepting South Africa, constitutes the most developed region in the continent, accounting for 18 per cent of its population and 30 to 35 per cent of its production. In the field of science and technology, it has an experience which may be emulated by and/or transferred to the other regions of Africa. The problems of education, science and technology are common to all countries in the continent and the Maghreb experience could help to instruct others in Africa as to how to get round these problems. For example, the Maghreb Arab Union created in 1989 gives particular importance to the Maghrebian co-operation in the field of science and technology through the exchange of teachers and students and the establishment of common university and research

H.E. Mr Layashi Yaker is former Undersecretary-General and Executive Secretary of the United Nations Economic Commission for Africa (UNECA) in Addis Ababa. This article is adapted from his keynote address delivered at the MAGHTECH '94 Conference.

institutions. The existence of a Maghrebian University and of a Maghrebian Academy of Sciences are signposts of promise, even if their activities have not really begun. In Africa, in general, development in science and technology could benefit significantly from the experience of regional co-operative initiatives in the Maghreb. The aim of this article is to set out a continental perspective for placing the Maghreb agenda in context.

## The Problem of African Development

Africa's deepening economic and social problems are now well known. The hope that the long period of stagnation in production, of financial distress and of institutional weakness would draw to a close has been dashed by the fact that Africa is now operating in a world which is characterised by acute geo-economic asymmetry. The rationale for promoting the role of science and technology lies therefore in the recognition and acknowledg-ment of Africa's developmental problem, namely, the presence of acute poverty compounded by the continent's failure to break its developmental gridlock.

The reality of poverty in Africa is now well established. There is little evidence that absolute poverty is generally on the decline. It is clear that in Africa the reverse is, in fact, the case. Per capita incomes have fallen by almost 25 per cent during the last decade; investments have fallen by almost 50 per cent and are now, in per capita terms, lower than they were in the middle of the 1960s. The division of the world into exporters of primary products on the one hand and exporters of manufactures (goods) on the other, which has led to the almost perpetual adverse terms of trade for the products of the developing countries, has been particularly irksome for Africa. Most African economies are oriented towards the production of primary commodities (agriculture, forestry, fuel, and other raw materials) as opposed to secondary (manufacturing) and tertiary (service) products. These primary commodities account for over 92 per cent of total export earnings of Africa, and yet real commodity prices fell by almost 50 per cent between 1957 and 1992. Such declines in commodity terms of trade have hurt Africa the most, since the continent relies greatly on these products. In addition to this, Africa's external debt had grown to a staggering US$275 billion in 1993. The capacity to service it has not kept pace, thus creating an unmanageable situation for most African countries.

This dependency on primary commodity trade has led to the inability of African countries to diversify their economies and establish core industries, such as metallurgical, engineering and chemical manufacturing, that would provide essential and strategic inputs to other industries and economic activities, particularly food and agriculture, the sector which was accorded the highest priority in the Lagos Plan of Action for the Economic

Development of Africa, 1980–2000. The identification and establishment of engineering-based core industries, as well as resource-based core industries, by African countries would reverse economic decline by: (i) providing wide linkages with other industries and economic sectors, particularly agriculture, mining, transport, building and construction, and energy; (ii) contributing to the creation of a self-reliant and self-sustaining industrial base; (iii) reducing dependence on external factor inputs; and (iv) earning the necessary foreign exchange for use in developing other sectors, including the service sector.

## The Role of Science and Technology in Development and Transition

Africa's underdevelopment and the structural weaknesses of its economies are largely attributable to its inability to apply science and technology to add value to its raw materials and commodities. Over the years, Africa has depended heavily on the export of basic raw materials and minerals, the international market price of which has been constantly tumbling with the advent of new materials and products manufactured in developed countries through the development and application of new and advanced science and technology. Along with political stabilisation and enhanced co-operation among the member states, the development and application of relevant science and technology offer the only hope for the teeming masses that are now groping in humiliating poverty and underdevelopment. Given economically and socially appropriate domestic and international environment, science and technology can raise the value of Africa's exports, and bring the revenue necessary to promote development and improve the living standards of the people.

Undoubtedly, the development gap between the industrialised countries and the developing countries of Africa is essentially a science and technology gap. The newly industrialising countries, many of which have hardly any natural resources in the form of raw materials, are showing the way by this masterly appropriation of science and technology and thus achieving a high degree of competitiveness in the manufacturing field. There is an immense pool of knowledge and technology that is there for the taking or the buying. There is no need to reinvent the wheel. What is required is foresight and vision, sound policies and strategies, short-term and long-term planning, hard work and sacrifice, and an openness and pragmatism that allow a people to capitalise on global trends and achievements. In the last 30 years, the world has changed tremendously but African development policies have not favoured indigenous growth. Science and technology policies have been conceived too narrowly, without any integration of them with economic and development policies. Science and technology have been, and will remain for a long time, the main locomotive to shape world development, and Africa has to adopt them to catch up and forge ahead, lest it falls further behind.

It is to be noted that Africa has the richest potential in terms of natural resources. Its population, currently growing at the rate of 3.1 per cent per annum, has reached the 700 million mark and is expected to double in 23 years. For all that, Africa can become self-sufficient in food by applying science and technology. It must, however, transform its mineral resources and develop and modernise its infrastructure, so that it can become a real and strong partner in the world economy. Presently, it contributes to only 2 per cent of the world trade, which is less than the share of South Korea. This shows the level of its marginalisation in industrial production and technological services. Only the large-scale development and application of science and technology can reverse this trend. The Economic Commission for Africa (ECA) is working towards this goal. As well as providing the chairman of the Task Force on the Implementation of the United Nations New Agenda for Development of Africa in the 1990s, it is also working with the Organisation of African Unity (OAU) and the African Development Bank (ADB) as a joint secretariat towards the realisation of the African Economic Community ushered in by the Abuja Treaty of 1991.

## The Uruguay Round Agreement and the New International Context for the Transfer of Technology

The issue of the transfer of technology raises questions about technical co-operation, but relates first to economic and trade problems. The link with trade in particular is strong because of the increasing transformation of new ideas into marketable products and processes. The significance of this trend is strongly reflected in the Uruguay Round Agreement signed in Marrakech in April 1994. The Marrakech Agreement particularly contains new disposals on trade-related aspects of intellectual property rights (TRIPs), disposals which will deeply affect the conditions of the acquisition and transfer of technology.

The Uruguay Round Agreement will, in the short-term, have a generally negative impact on African economies and consequently also on technology. This impact will be positive only in the medium- and long-term if appropriate measures are taken to increase the diversification, competitiveness and productive efficiency of African economies. African countries would nonetheless face some difficulties in adapting to the new trading environment emerging from the implementation of the Uruguay Round Agreement.

The Agreement does not make any special and lasting treatment in favour of the developing countries. The TRIPS agreement deals with minimum standards to be respected for patents, copyright, trademarks, industrial designs, geographical indications and protected information. However, viewing intellectual property protection exclusively from the angle of trade would amount to ignoring its paramount role in technological innovation and in access to technology. In consequence, the price of imported technologies will tend to grow. In fact, the new rules may extend the monopolistic abuses by suppliers of technology in the name of 'profit' and 'struggle' against counterfeiting practices. Therefore for African enterprises, which in some cases use technical specifications for products without verifying whether these products are protected by intellectual property rights, there is limited scope for the application of appropriate technology because their exports may expose them to suits for damages for the infringement of intellectual property rights. In all cases African states have to amend their intellectual property legislation and to enact new laws in order to comply with the TRIP obligations.

However, defenders of the Uruguay Round Agreement argue that this agreement on intellectual property rights could increase access to technologies insofar as it can convince firms that their ideas are safe from copiers. This access is essential if Africa wants to foster new industries that could compete in liberalised international markets.

All this means that African economies will need to reorient their industrial, agricultural and other sectoral strategies and programmes with the view to achieving science- and technology-based development. They have in particular to promote research and development activities in areas such as food technologies and product development and to build capacities for enhanced productivity; to increase standardisation and quality control; to establish networks and links in the field of technology, marketing and human resource development for economic activities.

### The Prerequisites for Science and Technology-Driven Development and Policy Orientations

Science and technology cannot, on their own, open the gates of sustainable development. Science and technology would need to be applied in the context of inter-sectoral linkages in order to serve as an engine of growth and development. The major prerequisite for this is the articulation of a well-defined social and economic policy which has science and technology at its centre. Thus national social policies should foster:

• mass literacy and education campaigns and high quality of educational services;

• social consensus through popular participation and political pluralism;

civic sense, discipline and stability;

- consideration of socio-cultural factors in technological development, and

- promotion of an indigenous science and technology culture.

These are essential prerequisites. It is not possible to implant foreign science and technology in an environment which is not prepared to absorb or receive them and where local norms and beliefs are not conducive to the process. The rapid dissemination of ideas through modern communication media can greatly alleviate the problems of mass education and popular participation.

The adoption of appropriate economic policies is also crucial to the process. These policies should favour the development of strong entrepreneurial community through: (i) financial, fiscal and institutional incentives to entrepreneurs and (ii) risk-venture capital for the commercialisation of R&D results.

Financial incentives should be given to entrepreneurs undertaking projects that will develop technological capacity, say, in the form of low-interest loans. Such an approach will encourage the enhancement of the local capacity to develop and promote technologies.

The necessary fiscal incentives should include the reduction of import duties on products that are necessary for R&D such as computers, laboratory equipment, and materials required for enhancing the domestic manufacturing capacity of consumer items locally. Such incentives should also allow, *inter alia*, accelerated depreciation of capital investment with respect to R&D laboratories and reduction in capital gains tax applying to venture capital companies.

In the past, undue attention was given to the formulation of policies that favoured high level research and training, and the setting up of institutions and mechanisms to support these. The popularisation of basic science and technology with the view to creating a science and technology culture in Africa was very limited. In the last ten years, African member states have come to realise that they have to give science and technology a proper orientation in order that they may be effective in providing solutions to their socio-economic development problems. In the context of developing and least-developed countries, the very concept of science and technology has to be different, however. Science and technology should not be construed merely as high level R&D and training at the tertiary level. In Africa, the stress has to be laid on the application of available off-the-shelf science and technology, as a start, and research should follow this application, based on the needs arising from it. Even here, there should be more stress on the 'D' component of R&D, so that research results can be readily commercialised.

## The Role of UNECA and Other International Organisations in the Promotion of Science and Technology for Development

It is in the global context set out above that the United Nations Economic Commission for Africa (UNECA) seeks to promote the development of science and technology in Africa along with its sister organisations within the United Nations system. Thirty years ago, the first UN conference on the application of science and technology was held to examine ways and means of accelerating development through the application of scientific and technological innovations in less developed countries. This was followed by important international conferences that led to the World Plan of Action and the African Regional Plan for the Application of Science and Technology to Development and, in 1979, to the Vienna Programme on Science and Technology for Development. The Lagos Plan of Action of 1980, CASTAFRICA II of 1987 and the UN World Summit on Environment and Development of 1992 recognised science and technology as prime engines of development.

The ECA has been instrumental in establishing the major intergovern-mental institutions in the field of technology, standards, intellectual property, mapping and remote sensing and aerospace surveys. These institutions have contributed towards the relevant training, advising African governments on suitable policies and strategies. However, over the last decade, since many member states were unable to pay their annual contributions, these institutions have had to retrench to the extent that they can barely survive. Indeed, at the present rate they could be closed down before too long for lack of funding support.

More recently, the UNECA sub-programme on science and technology for development laid emphasis on establishing and strengthening structures at national, sub-regional and regional levels for the development and application of science and technology programmes and for facilitating processes for science and technology policy making and planning. It looked into the issue of the role of sub-regional and regional technological associations and professional institutions in the management of science and technology and proposed recommendations for making them more effective. In view of the perceived importance of science and technology, it has been recommended that member states create an enabling environment through such measures as subsidies and tax exemptions to allow these structures to play their role fully and effectively. At the same time, it is assumed that these professional associations and institutions would exercise their own initiatives to raise the funds they would need. As regards institution building, studies have led to the recommendation that science and technology institutions in member states should review their orientation and emphasise the wider application of science and technology through the marketing of research results, thus creating job opportunities for trained manpower. In view of the close linkages between science, technology and the economic operators, it has been stressed that the implementation of science and technology policies will need the removal of structural impediments in trade, fiscal and immigration policies, all of which need to be reviewed. Commercial institutions and the private sector should be encouraged through policy incentives to participate in the funding of science and technology.

With a view to easing the ever growing food crisis in many African countries, the UNECA sub-programme undertook a study on the acquisition and transfer of nuclear science and technology, and proposed measures to enhance national capacities to acquire and utilise nuclear science and technology in the development of agriculture, food processing and preservation. Additionally the UNECA has felt the need to encourage the setting up of funds to promote applied scientific research, which will act as channels for the mobilisation of funding for science and technology and the commercialisation of research results. Its ultimate objective is to have functional organs in Africa for creating an interface of R&D with national and regional development in key areas of public policy such as agriculture, environment, education, health, culture and industrialisation.

## Conclusion

A major way forward for promoting technological development in Africa would call for the creation of a network of links between universities or research centres and industry. In many African universities the coalition between university, science and technology and industry is still weak, despite recent attempts to redesign university programmes to meet the immediate needs of local industry. A framework for promoting university–industry dialogue should be established, so that a desired synergy in the moulding of university graduates and the development of an endogenously strong, stable and dynamic industry may be expected to be forthcoming. This task would be facilitated if research sought to show how science and technology-based development should be promoted for the benefit of rapid socio-economic development in the African countries including those of the Maghreb Union.

# Strategies for Science and Technology-based Development and Transition: the Maghreb Perspective

## ABDELKADER DJEFLAT

*'Globalisation' has had its effect widely felt in the Maghreb socially and economically. The forces of dynamism, however, remain constrained by the legacies of the culture of import substitution which continue to thwart the emergence of innovative tendencies. The mechanism for channelling science and technology towards the development of innovatively competitive industrial systems is hardly in evidence in the region; instead, the economic burden due to high-cost industries which thrived on the back of protection is apparent. The application of structural adjustment programmes (SAPs) in recent years was sought to provide the way forward for transition. In the event, this missed the point by marginalising the role of the state in the promotion of science and technology as the crucial basis for development in the region.*

## Introduction

After three decades of repeated, if vain, attempts to join the group of advanced countries, the Maghrebian countries have come to realise that the way forward lies in the mastery of scientific and technological knowledge and its efficient application to the production of goods and services. They have still a long way to go on this, however. In comparison with the science and technology policy experience of the newly industrialising countries (NICs) such as Korea and Brazil, and also in relation to the challenges of development confronting the region itself, the science and technology effort made by the Maghrebian countries over the years since independence has generally been far from satisfactory. This relative shortfall in technological performance may in large measure be attributed to the incongruity of policy with the imperatives of sustainable development. A consequence of this has

Professor A. Djeflat is at the University of Oran (Algeria). He is currently Visiting Professor at the University of Lille (France). He is also Co-ordinator of the MAGHTECH network.

been the failure of the education system in the Maghreb to deliver science and technology that is capable of being translated into innovation and technological progress.

There are not many public and private initiatives directly aimed at the application of science and technology to the process of socio-economic development in the Maghreb. Nor have the Maghrebian countries acted in concert in this respect. The significance of regional science and technology research and policy programmes is, however, generally felt in the wake of the global transition to the development of competitive national economies. In the Maghreb, as indeed elsewhere, the process of transition would involve the active role of the state aimed at promoting scientific and technological innovation as a basis for the development of a market-driven competitive economy.

The efficiency of the market in allocating resources is enhanced with the supply of more and better information about new 'combinations'. New combinations assume the vision of the entrepreneur as well as the flair for innovation. The emergence of the enterprise culture cannot, however, be expected to occur in a policy vacuum.

To date, though, the state in the Maghreb has been far from effective in promoting technological progress, so that a major agenda for transition would now be the institution of regional initiatives to explore new policy trajectories based on a sound synthesis of theory and experience. In this article, we seek to highlight some of the major issues concerning the relationship between technology and development in general, and structural adjustment and transition in particular. What, for instance, are the mechanisms that have to be put in place before the provision of science and technology may be expected to expedite the transition process in each of the Maghreb countries?

## Towards a Maghreb-Wide Initiative for Transition through Innovation

Policy models for transition in the Maghreb, as in most parts of the developing world, would assume structural adjustment of the national economies. Success in structural adjustment effort would, however, depend on how effectively the state conducts itself in removing structural bottlenecks and facilitating the emergence of market forces. In the Maghreb, the inward looking, import substitution-based strategy of development has done more to deepen than to remove the constraints on growth, mainly because import substitution involved protective policies often at high social cost. A question at the heart of the transition agenda is how technology transfer practices, which hitherto provided the basis for import substitution, may now be managed to provide the basis for innovation and competitiveness on a global scale.

Cooper (1994) addresses this question at the level of the firm and also at the level of the world economy. In view of the emerging global trend of competition through innovation, development strategies in the Maghreb, hitherto based on the liberal provision of protection, will need to be science and technology-based if economic transformation and sustainable development are to be achieved (Djeflat 1994).

Structural adjustment programmes appear to have paid off in Tunisia where growth rates are observed to have been impressive. Elsewhere in the Maghreb, though, the socio-economic crisis precipitated by these programmes has been overwhelming. The social and political troubles that erupted in Algeria constitute a transition problem aggravated in part by the rough edges of the adjustment programmes dictated by the IMF and the World Bank. The Maghreb experience with structural adjustment indicates that the short term orientation of policy has not been favourable to the achievement of the long term objectives of growth and development. Thus, for instance, programmes relating to science and technology, education and research have been underrated in spite of – or indeed, as some would argue, because of – the structural adjustment policies pursued by the Maghrebian countries.

The process of structural adjustment of national economies has to be placed in a global context to see the extent to which adjustment policies foster – or else undermine – long term development objectives. A major feature of recent global trends in technological progress is the ascendancy of biotechnology and microelectronics. These have given rise to generic technologies which when applied to a wide spectrum of industries, including the traditional ones, make them innovatively competitive and efficient, thus taking them well beyond the narrow confines of protected national markets. There is, however, little in the competitive performance of developing countries to suggest that generic technologies have made sufficient inroads to transform the industrial and technological landscape of a good part of the Third World where the problems of the non-mastery of technology and the virtual absence of innovation still prevail. This raises the question as to how well structural adjustment programmes are implemented or else how well the technological preconditions of transition have been incorporated into such programmes in the first place. Let us deal with these in the Maghreb, taking the latter issue first.

## Technology and New Economic Factors

Economies in transition would seek to employ technologies which can protect employment while at the same time increasing productivity; but the traditional view that these are better served by labour-intensive than by capital-intensive technologies does not appear sustainable in view of developments which have been transforming the global technological landscape since the 1970s, during which time some, among the developing countries, have grown fast, catching up on the technology leaders while others have simply lagged behind. All countries may will the end of innovation and technological progress, but not all are clear as to what strategies they should adopt to promote economic and technological progress to a level that would qualify them as newly industrialising.

Proponents of intermediate technology would argue that the adoption of simple, if demand driven, technologies could have the far-reaching effect of putting 'a grain of economic power into the hands of the poor' by enabling them to master the instruments of their work and to innovate without obliterating the fabric of their culture and environment (McRobie 1994). Recent studies covering the case of some rural zones in Morocco suggest that intermediate technologies indeed provide the basis for the development of innovative culture and technological progress (Guerraoui 1994).

The concept of intermediate technology is not, however, without its limitations. First, there are technologies such as aeronautics and gas liquefaction which do not have an equivalent in the range of intermediate technology that would match market size, as studies in Algeria have shown (Djeflat 1981). Secondly, left unqualified, the concept of intermediate technology would convey the idea that there can be a world division of technology appropriation – namely, technology for the rich and technology for the poor. This, however, is pre-emptive and, what is more, is suggestive of the technology tail wagging the economic dog. In a world where supply does not create its own demand, it would be only proper to start with the question as to what is to be produced and then proceed to explore how efficiently it is to be produced. Thirdly, the Maghreb's geographic proximity to and economic interaction with Europe means that decision makers in technology choice would be open to marketing influence that would make them opt for more advanced technologies. Whether the Maghreb economies would be the better in terms of competitiveness for this neighbourhood effect is, however, a different matter. But it is suggestive of the growing significance of new technologies in the region *vis-à-vis* the case for intermediate technology.

Hydrocarbons in Algeria, textiles in Tunisia and phosphates in Morocco involve advanced technologies. A common feature of these industries is, however, that they are all in the export sector and have only a limited diffusion impact on the rest of the regional economy. Moreover, there is the question as to the efficiency performance of these advanced technologies.

For instance, in the case of Algeria, industrial capacity utilisation rates are known not to have exceeded 50 per cent of the installed capacities during the 1970s and the 1980s. The evidence derived from the experience of industrialisation in the region appears to suggest that advanced technologies, though appropriate to some activities, cannot be applied across the industrial spectrum without involving high cost to the economy.

The Maghreb region has the distinctive feature of having experimented with different strategies. It thus has varied experience regarding the technology issue. This is reflected, *inter alia,* in the multiplicity of sources of technologies as well as in their character (El Aoufi 1994). Behidji (1994) investigates this point with respect to the railway sector in the Maghreb and draws the conclusion that for technology acquisition to be growth effective, it is crucial that technology choice is matched with local capacity and circumstances. The 1980s saw a massive supply of technology – particularly locomotives and passenger carriages – to the railway sector in the region. These, however, turned out to be high cost technologies for the most part, offering limited scope for integration with local industries. Moreover, the technologies acquired from French suppliers, such as the Inox and Corail carriages chosen for the network and the diesel electric locomotives used in Morocco, were outmoded and technically inefficient.

## Competitiveness and Structural Adjustment Programmes (SAPs)

Structural Adjustment Programmes (SAPs) have been applied over a longer duration in Morocco and Tunisia than in Algeria. To what extent has the application of these programmes helped to promote the development of scientific and technological potential of these countries? Studies based on the Moroccan case (Lehlou 1994, El Aoufi 1994) indicate that the implementation of SAPs was, if anything, counter to technological progress. It, for instance, resulted in the increased unemployment of skilled people, suggesting apparently that the Moroccan economy would settle well with the adoption of technologies that do not make an exacting demand on skill development. If this makes sense in the context of the neoclassical paradigm, it flies in the face of evidence provided by the experience of the NICs. The short term orientation of SAPs thus does more to undermine than to consolidate prospects for long term growth.

For instance, a consequence of the implementation of SAPs in Morocco was the disappearance of firms consequent upon the liberalisation of the local markets. As a response to inefficient industrialisation by heavy protection, the liberalisation strategy has, however, little to be said against it. The problem with SAPs – particularly those of the early generation – is that in their assiduous pursuit of liberalisation, they have, if inadvertently, thrown out the baby with the bath water. In the Moroccan case, the loss of firms due to SAPs meant the loss of organised crews of workers and the loss of capital and experience gained through 'learning by doing', thus interfering with the process of endogenous technological progress. According to El Aoufi (1994), the rate of birth of firms was not enough to compensate the number of lost firms, so that, on balance, the 'learning by doing' effect of SAPs was negative.

Recent generation SAPs have consequently sought to take the long term into account while providing the policy basis for the development of competitive national economies. Hence, for instance, the creation of the African Capacity Fund (ACF) at Harare by the World Bank. The aim of ACF is to develop local capacities in economic management and in science and technology – or human resource development in a nutshell. This would necessarily call for the active role of the state since the promotion of science and technology, education and research and development initiatives, among other factors, cannot be left to the jurisdiction of the market which would preclude long term options in favour of short term gains. Policies aimed at strengthening the efficiency of the market do not have to rule out the role of the state in the long term. In the context of developing countries, in particular, the latter is absolutely necessary for the realisation of dynamic, comparative advantage. The Moroccan experience, revealing the disappearance of firms in the wake of the SAP-driven liberalisation process, clearly shows that while the market is capable of eliminating small and non-viable firms it is on its own incapable of creating others. The scope for technological expansion and diffusion is bound to remain limited without the active role of the state to provide the basis for capacity building, as is also apparent from the Algerian experience (Mezaache 1994).

Also, the size and growth of the national and regional markets are crucial for the development of technological capability, as capacity building involves increased production and increased investment; and small national markets, however protected, are not of much help in this respect. In their proximity to Europe, however, the Maghreb countries could expect to benefit in the same way as Mexico benefited from its proximity to the United States. Exposure of local investment and production initiatives to wider regional and international markets would require firms to be competitive in order to survive and grow. Competitiveness is expressed in two major forms, namely, through the compression of real wages and through innovation. Competitiveness assumes the capacity not only to maintain and expand one's share in traditional markets but also to create market niches through the introduction of new and improved, quality-sensitive products.

*Competition through Wage Compression*

The prevalence of low wages was in large measure a crucial factor behind the economic success of the south-east Asian countries, at least at the initial stage of their growth spurt. Low wages provided the basis for price competitiveness and hence for the expansion of export markets. In Morocco, the pressure of competition in the international export market has forced a reduction in real wages to levels 20 to 30 per cent of what they were in the 1960s. For all that, Morocco has seen its share in all the traditional markets declining, while competitors like Turkey and Korea have forged ahead, increasing their shares even in carpet making in which Morocco traditionally had a competitive edge. While Turkey and Korea opted for competition by productive gains and by raising the qualification standards of the labour force, Morocco adopted the strategy of competition by, for instance, a continued compression of real wages and child labour, thanks to SAPs (Lehlou 1994). In this respect, the social clause of GATT, which precludes options for competition by wage compression or exploitation, is invoked by some as the most important clause of the Marrakech Agreement.

*Competition by Innovation*

This form of competition is independent of changes in price and wage levels. It is referred to in the literature as multidimensional competitiveness (Porter 1990); structural competitiveness (Chesnais 1986) or technological competitiveness (Cooper 1994). In this context, liberalisation cannot be dissociated from the capacity to master technology and, in particular, to innovate following changes in the profiles of demand (Cooper 1992, Fagerberg 1988).

Quality competitiveness is of central concern in the Maghreb at present. Affes (1994) shows, by using the Tunisian case, that quality competitiveness depends not merely on a single firm at the downstream end of the chain of production, but also on all subcontractor firms upstream. Tunisia, which has been particularly conscious of the importance of quality competition since 1983, has adopted measures such as the creation of the National Institute of Standardisation and Industrial Promotion (INNORPI), and the publication of a National Plan aimed at promoting the quality of export products. These have proved to be significantly advantageous (Boudarbala 1994).

Overall, the technological problems of the Maghreb countries may be summarised as twofold. On the one hand, the low degree of technological mastery limits the propensity of these countries to apply competition on the basis of technological innovation. On the other, the struggle for survival in the face of sharp competition in the international market, simply because firms do not have the wherewithal for maintenance of machinery and equipment, means that they would either give in or else resort to the policy option of depressing real wages, as observed in the case of Morocco, to be able to compete.

With regard to the first problem, new technologies obtained through transfer arrangements, were adopted for lack of local innovation, but the rapid change in market behaviour sets a limit beyond which technology transfer would cease to be a viable option, particularly for developing countries. Many Maghrebian firms, however, suffer from the inertia that rent-seeking behaviour breeds, and this, more often than not, inhibits the introduction of new technologies. This problem is apparent from the study on the hydrocarbons sector in Algeria (Mezaache 1994). With respect to the second problem, the short term orientation of policy has resulted, *inter alia,* in the maintenance function of firms being progressively replaced by casual 'repairs' (Tandjaoui 1994). Moreover, the technological potential of the maintenance function is forfeited: the maintenance function is said to have played a significant role in the technological development of the present developed countries as a powerful instrument of technical change, notably in connection with ergonomics, new materials and the rationalisation of equipment from the time of their conception.

The neoclassical belief that R&D initiatives may be efficiently superseded by the mechanism of capital and labour substitution or increment in both factors leaves much to be desired in the context of countries such as those in the Maghreb where factor constraint operates and the scope for development and active participation in the international market is, in the final analysis, conditional on the existence of opportunities for technological progress. For instance, the traditional sectors such as textiles and farming in which the Maghrebian countries are known to have comparative advantage are being increasingly penetrated by new technologies as a result of the advent of generic technologies. This means that for exports from the Maghreb countries to continue to be competitive in the future, the important factor to consider would be not the policy enforcement of low wage regimes, as has been the case hitherto, but rather the incorporation of innovation in national and regional export functions.

## Technological Learning in the Maghreb

The issue of technological learning is of a particular importance to the Maghreb and especially in Algeria, where policy has for long been geared to developing local skills and reducing dependence on foreign technical assistance (Oukil 1984). This 'deficit of inventiveness' (Abbou 1994) is found also in the case of Morocco and Tunisia.

Expenditure on R&D in Morocco amounts to 2 dollars per inhabitant per year. Expenditure as a whole is 300 million dollars per year for a population of 27 million inhabitants, of which 95 per cent goes towards wages.

Regarding personnel for R&D functions, Morocco trains 11 engineers per 100,000 inhabitants, Tunisia trains 60 engineers per 100,000, whereas a country such as Singapore trains 360 engineers per 100,000.

In terms of publications, out of 1229 articles published by Maghrebians during 1981-86, only 5.1 per cent of them were concerned with engineering and technology (Alcouffe 1994). It is necessary to add that many of the Maghrebian authors who manage to publish either live outside the sub-region or publish as co-authors with researchers from the North. This pattern finds itself also repeated in the field of industrial research. An empirical study based on a survey of electronics firms in Algeria showed that, in the majority of cases, the research themes dealt mostly with the large electronics multinational companies rather than with the problems infant, national firms (Dahmane 1994).

These weaknesses are also shared by many other developing countries. How do they arise?

*Absence of Links Between R&D Centres and Industry*

The lack of communication between research carried out in universities and research centres and that carried out in industry blocks development prospects in certain sectors, notably in the domain of new technologies (e.g., biotechnology) where intense communication and proximity are crucial for success (OECD 1992, Cooper 1994). An alternative to pure R&D in the Maghrebian countries would be the adoption of old patents which are now in the public domain, as in the case of the pharmaceutical industry in India, with the aim of improving on them through incremental innovation.

*Academic versus Applied Research*

There is a lack of clear vision regarding the role of the university in the promotion of scientific and technological research. Views, however, differ between those who favour research within universities and those who prefer to see applied research conducted by autonomous organisations. The traditional split between academic research and applied research still prevails. It shows the need for close relationships between research institutions and industry and institutions in charge of promoting the transfer of technologies and which are non-existent at the present moment in the Maghrebian countries (Zghal 1994, El Aoufi 1994). About a dozen research institutions have been reorganised over the last decade and a half in Algeria. The innovation effect of this exercise has, however, been marginal.

*R&D Funding*

R&D initiatives in the Maghreb are constrained by the lack of adequate financing. The issue of financing is a relatively old one in the advanced countries. If it takes a renewed importance in the LDCs, there are several reasons for that, including: involvement of private capital in the process of transfer of technology; the withdrawal of the state from some sectors following the privatisation of the public enterprises; and, the fact that the prospects for innovation in LDCs are better now than before and that NICs such as Brazil, India and South Korea have emerged on the world scene as credible competitors. The question of financing is asked in connection with the mobilisation of capital for R&D. This is constrained by the weakness of domestic savings and the problem of chronic budget deficits, and the 'mercantile' character of Maghrebian entrepreneurs who are least inclined to devote funds to industrial activities involving high risk. The lack of risk or venture capital therefore constitutes a major handicap in the short and the medium term. Resort to foreign financing would be facilitated by domestic financial reform, covering the organisation and management of financial projects, as illustrated by studies of cases from Morocco and Tunisia (El Borgi 1994).

*Radical versus Incremental Innovations*

Discussions on R&D have focused more on radical innovations than on incremental innovation. The latter, however, is often within reach of developing economies, both technically and economically and is, in fact, the stuff of which technical progress is made in such countries, as shown by studies on the textiles industry in Algeria, although they have not featured prominently in policies at the macro level as well as at the level of firms (Tandjaoui 1994).

*Innovation as a Social Phenomenon*

In the Maghreb, even if there exist innovative individuals or institutions, they are constrained by the absence of mechanisms – social and economic – for developing and diffusing innovations (Zghal 1994). Strategies for transition would consequently need to develop the capacity to mobilise and organise social forces, with the view to enhancing the same for the realisation of the scientific and technological potential in the region. The status of knowledge and its development remains one of the issues at the heart of the Maghrebian societies.

In spite of all these problems, innovation there thrives for the most part on informal R&D, although the extent of this is not fully documented. Some empirical studies of the iron and steel sector have, for instance, demonstrated the existence of a non-negligible innovational dynamism (Djeflat 1985). These would, however, need to be integrated with the formal R&D systems to provide a sound basis for technological promotion in the region.

## Integration of Science and Technology into the Maghreb Economies

Two agents are considered to be crucial for the understanding and effective management of technology, especially as regards choice, adoption, innovation and adaptation (Foray and Freeman 1992). One of these, the firm, holds a central position in the 'Maghrebian dynamism'. The other agent is the individual and his scientific and technological environment and, in particular, the education system within which knowledge and skills are developed.

The importance of private and public enterprises varies from one country to another in the Maghreb. Traditionally public enterprises have been perceived as being productive and private enterprises as merely speculative. In effect, both have lived in the comfort of protectionism and guaranteed income as a result of the import substitution policy pursued by the three countries. However, this has not helped to promote innovation and competitiveness. Instead, business behaviour has been averse to risk-taking and long term investment. This behaviour has been reinforced by industry's limited exposure to the forces of competition in the world market. The challenge for Maghrebian enterprises now is to produce a sufficiently broad range of goods while keeping costs down, as the Tunisian experience has shown (Ben Alaya 1994). The adoption of new management systems could help to reconcile the imperatives of variety, flexibility and economies of dimension, while continuing to benefit from economies of scale (Watanabe 1983, Sciberras and Payne 1985). The question is to what extent can enterprises in the Maghreb be expected to adjust to conditions of competitiveness and innovation? A look at the present situation and at some recent experiences would show the potentials and difficulties.

*The Problems*: the difficulties result primarily from the Fordist or Taylorist organisational structure of enterprises. The Taylorist structure created multiple shields between the different categories of personnel (Clark *et al.* 1987) which constrained innovation as studies of Tunisian firms have shown (Zghal 1994). Fordism gave way to 'Toyotism' in many cases (Boyer 1991), but the coexistence of archaic and modern processes owing to the multiplicity of suppliers and the absence of technology policy, the systematic application of capital and labour intensities across industrial firms (El Aoufi 1994) and the prevalence of wages too low to stimulate local demand militated against innovative tendencies. This is apparent in the experience of Moroccan enterprises (Lehlou 1994). Even when the wage level is relatively high, as in the case of Algeria, there is a 'diversion of demand' towards foreign manufactured products often imported through smuggling. In Morocco, small and medium enterprises (SMEs) do not have a sufficient financial base to allow them to undertake R&D (OECD 1992: 119). Moreover, unlike the SMEs of south-east Asian countries, which thrive on innovation, SMEs in the Maghreb are often short termist in their outlook and risk averse in their behaviour (Guerraoui 1994). In Algeria, the large, capital intensive public enterprises have been mostly devoted to investment and the covering of overhead costs for huge projects that often proved difficult to manage, rather than to R&D.

*The Potentials:* for all the factors which have militated against innovation in the Maghreb, the introduction of information technology and electronics appears to have enabled enterprises to face up to these challenges of competition and growth. Thus, for instance, the firm Valeo Embrayag Tunisie has introduced the principles of 'total quality' and 'just in time', in order to improve its competitiveness by adopting three precision rules from Japanese industrial culture: to produce 'what is needed', 'when it is needed' and 'with the needed quality'. Some notable improvements have consequently been registered in terms of performance. They include the optimal use of space, optimal stocks, optimal manufacturing time and effective participation of workers in the decision making process (Ben Alaya 1994). This success story, though limited, shows that there exists a large potential for adopting new technologies by operatives in Maghreb enterprises and hence for broadening the scope for innovation.

**Conclusion**

The post-colonial generation of governments in the Maghreb have had to face up to the challenges of illiteracy, restore cultural identity through *arabisation* and provide the infrastructural bases for national development. University education, initially aimed to produce high level manpower to administer national construction, is now also called on to respond to the challenges of innovation and creativity and hence to enhance competitiveness in the world market.

The issue of education and human resource development and their liaison with technological development has recently become the object of policy concern in the Maghreb. This has been prompted by factors including the success of Asian countries and notably Japan (a country with meagre natural resources but with brains); the sharp rise of the unemployment rate, the emergence of a relatively new phenomenon, namely graduate unemployment, and the incapacity of a good number of those trained locally to demonstrate any kind of dynamism in terms of the mastery of technology and innovation.

In Tunisia, for example, the School of Engineering produces approximately 500 student projects, of which 100, at least, can be valorised in industry each year. In the event, only two or three find their way to industry (Ben Alaya 1994). In Morocco, graduate unemployment has increased by 30 per cent (100,000 graduates in 1990) in the last two decades, while, ironically, the non-graduate unemployment rate has been on the decline. The firm has consequently been 'turning its back' on training and the acquisition of advanced knowledge (Lehlou 1994, Amrani 1994). The application of structural adjustment programmes does not seem to have improved the situation. The conception of these programmes and their implementation account for much of the prevailing problem of educated unemployment and the remoteness of the university system from innovative activities.

From the conceptual point of view, structural adjustment programmes have to consider the theory of human capital. This would see education as investment and would prescribe any further investment superfluous on grounds that human resources are overqualified in relation to the countries' needs and the type of technology used (Lehlou 1994). From a more general point of view, the question of the effectiveness of investment in education and its liaison with economic growth and development is subject to debate. And at a time when capital is rare, SAPs find it proper to question the viability of supporting the education sector and especially higher education which is investment-intensive. SAPs would rather settle for the rationalisation of resources.

At the empirical level, the view taken of over-qualification has had direct implications for the education system and training. In the case of Morocco, for example, the annual budget for education has been sharply reduced from 33 to 25 per cent of the total since the application of SAPs; 50 per cent of the population are illiterate and only 40 per cent have been provided with schooling and there is under-schooling of the population as a whole. Korea produces 300,000 graduates, including 50,000 engineers, annually for a population of 40 million people, while Morocco, with 27 million inhabitants, produces fewer than 16,000 graduates per year and 500 to 1000 engineers.

Moreover, SAPs have reinforced individualism and have dislocated the old system of social solidarity resulting from religious and traditional values, especially as a result of the heterogeneity of the education system.

SAPs have also seen the emergence of private sector education, which, while promoting the virtues of the market place in education, has had the long term effect of weakening the coherence of a strategy for teaching (Lehlou 1994).

The Korean experience clearly shows that technological mastery is linked to a successfully performing education system and especially to a higher education system that seeks to thrive on interactive links with the productive sector. The role of the state there has been significant to the extent that technological progress has been state-led. The central issue in the Maghreb relates, not simply to the magnitude of investment in higher education and training, but equally importantly to the type of approach adopted and the extent to which university–industry links are promoted.

## REFERENCES

Abbou, M. (1994), 'Système Educatif et Impulsion Scientifique et Technique en Algérie', Conférence Internationale MAGHTECH sur le thème 'Technologie et Transition au Maghreb' [MAGHTECH'94], Sfax, 7–9 Dec.

Amandola M. and J.L.Gaffard (1988), 'La Dynamique Economique de L'Innovation', *Economica.*

Alcouffe, A. (1994), 'Etudes des Systèmes Nationaux de RD, le cas de l'Union du Maghreb Arabe', Note de synthèse. Université des Sciences Sociales de Toulouse.

Affes, H. (1994), 'Innovation Technologique et son Impact Socio-organisationel dans le Secteur Textile en Tunisie', MAGHTECH'94.

Amrani, M. (1994), 'Les Réformes de la Recherche Scientifique au Maroc', MAGHTECH'94.

Ben Alaya, L. (1994), 'La Performance Industrielle par le Juste à Temps', MAGHTECH'94.

Bendhia, H. (1994) 'Place de la culture et des sciences humaines dans la formation des ingenieurs en Tunisie', MAGHTECH'94.

Behidji, K. (1994), 'Industrialisation et Management de la Technologie au Maghreb : le cas des Entreprises de biens d'Equipement Ferroviaire', MAGHTECH'94.

Boyer, R. (1991), 'Nouvelles Tendances de la Gestion des Entreprises et de l'Organisation du Travail', OECD, Paris.

Bouderbala, R. (1994), 'L'enjeu de la Qualité : Différentiation ou une Exigence?' MAGHTECH '94.

Chesnais, F. (1987), 'Science, Technologie et Competitivité', *STI Revue*, No.1, OCDE, Paris.

Clark, B., B. Chen and T. Fujimoto (1987), 'Product Development in the World Auto Industry: Strategy, Organisation and Performances', MAGHTECH'94.

Cooper, C. (1992), 'Integrating Science and Technology to Third World Economies', STD Forum, University of Strathclyde, Glasgow, April.

Cooper, C. (1994), 'The Role of New Technologies in Development', MAGHTECH'94.

Dahmane, A. (1994), 'La relation Université-Recherche-Enterprise: Approche par le Paradigme de la Communication', MAGHTECH'94.

Djeflat, A. (1981), 'Limitations to Technology Policy Implementation in the Arab World: the Case of Algeria', Proceedings of the International Conference on Technology Policy, UNESCO–NECWA, Paris, Dec.

Djeflat, A. (1985), 'Industrialisation and Technology Acquisition in the Steel Industry in Algeria', *Cahier du CERMAC,* No.38, Louvain-la-Neuve.

Djeflat, A. (1994), 'Transition et Technologie: les Dimensions de la Problematique', MAGHTECH'94.

El Borgi, A. (1994), 'Impératifs de la Recherche et Développement dans le Secteur Agricole

Tunisien et son Financement', MAGHTECH'94.

El Aoufi, N. (1994) 'L'Enterprise Marcoaine entre la Révolution Technologique et le Bricolage Organisationnel', MAGHTECH'94.

Fagerberg, J. (1988) 'International Competitiveness', *The Economic Journal,* Vol.98, No.391.

Foray, D. and C. Freeman (1992), 'Technologie et Richesses des Nations', *Economica.*

Guerraoui, D. (1994), 'Quelle Recherche Economique dans une Phase de Transition?', MAGHTECH'94.

Lehlou, M. (1994), 'Systéme Educatif, Entreprises et Difficultés de la Transition au Maroc', MAGHTECH'94.

McRobie, G. (1994), 'Technology for Development: What Is Appropriate for Rich and Poor Countries', MAGHTECH'94.

Mebarki, M. (1994), 'Relations Formation-Emploi et le Défi Technologique dans les Pays Avancés (France): Quel Defi pour le Maghreb?' MAGHTECH'94.

Mezaache, A. (1994), 'Assainissement des Entreprises et Problématique Technologique dans le Secteur Public en Algérie', MAGHTECH'94.

OECD, (1992), 'La Technologie et l'Economie: des Relations Déterminantes', Programme TEP.

Oukil, M.S. (1989), 'The Function and System of Industrial Research and Development in Algeria', PhD thesis, University of Strathclyde, Glasgow.

Porter, M.E. (1990), *The Competitive Advantages of Nations,* London: Macmillan.

Sciberras, E. and B.Payne (1985), *Technology and International Competitiveness: the Machine-Tool Industry,* Longman, London.

Tandjaoui, R. (1994), 'Maintenance Industrielle en Algérie et les Perspectives de son Intégration dans une Nouvelle Dynamique Technologique de Maîtrise et d'Innovation', MAGHTECH '94.

Watanabe, S. (1983), *Market Structure Industrial Organisation and Technological Development: the Case of the Japanese Electronics Based NC-Machine Tool Industry,* BIT, Geneva.

Zghal, R. (1994), 'Science, Technologie et Société', MAGHTECH '94.

# PART II

## ISSUES IN
## TECHNOLOGY AND DEVELOPMENT
## IN THE MAGHREB

# Transfer and Use of Advanced Technology in Less Developed Countries and Impact on Organisational Change and Learning: Evidence from Algeria

## MOHAMMED SAAD

*This article examines the growth effectiveness of the application of advanced manufacturing technologies transferred to developing countries with reference to the experience of two Algerian firms. The relatively under-examined body of technology transfer related to learning, organisational and managerial adaptations is also explored. Both firms under study are state-owned monopolies. One of them is responsible for the development of electronic activities and the other for agricultural machinery. This article is divided into two main sections: a presentation and analysis of the strategies adopted by the two firms in the transfer and the use of advanced technologies, and an analysis of the impact of these strategies on the learning curves of the firms.*

## Introduction

The growth effectiveness of technology transfer to developing countries is largely reflected by its impact on the learning and innovation processes. These are generally constrained by managerial capability and the mode of organisational framework within which technologies are selected, installed and operated. Incompatibility between imported technologies and the organisational context in which they are used precipitate – as they have done in the case of the two Algerian firms discussed below – a series of difficulties such as bottlenecks, breakdowns and delays; poor and inadequate maintenance; waiting for parts, tools and fixtures; low rate of capacity utilisation, high rate of scrap and low quality; high inventory levels; unreliable deliveries; long production lead times; low productivity; shortage of in-house skill; poor worker involvement; absence of autonomy

Dr Mohammed Saad is Head of European Business Culture, Director of Research, European Regional Studies Unit, Faculty of Languages and European Studies, University of the West of England, Bristol.

leading to excessive paper work and lack of managerial commitment; and absence of good and long-term relationships with suppliers. The remainder of this article will explore strategies adopted in developing countries for the transfer and use of advanced technologies and the implication of these strategies for the learning curves of firms, with particular reference to two cases from Algeria.

## The Strategy Adopted by the Electronic Firm

Developing countries may be classified into three broad groups according to their capability in the management and development of the electronics industry. The first group includes those countries which have no electronics industry at all. The second group comprises a large number of developing countries where the electronics industry is implemented through investments of multinational firms. In this case, the electronics industry is essentially limited to assembly activities. The third group includes countries such as South Korea, Brazil and India which have successfully attempted to develop an electronics industry as a national, independent and export-oriented industry. In this group, activities are more concerned with electronic component manufacturing rather than simple assembly activities.

Algeria belongs to the third group. The firm selected for examination in this study is engaged in research and development, production, maintenance and the importing and distribution of equipment and components of electronic appliances, electronic components themselves, medical electronics, computing and professional electronics.

This firm has 18 plants including eight devoted to maintenance and after-sales service, two training centres, one engineering and construction plant, one research and development plant and five manufacturing plants. The firm's strategy is based on the idea that assimilation of assembly techniques is associated with assimilation of machinery used in the whole process of the assembly line (insertion, welding, testing) as well as the assimilation of components manufacturing. This explains the construction of a large sized plant characterised by an important vertical integration.

The whole process of production, starting from the manufacturing of components to the assembly of end-products is executed in this plant. It was initially constructed to produce TV sets (colour and black and white), radios, radio-cassettes, music centres, car-radios, indoor and outdoor TV aerials, as well as a wide range of electronic and non-electronic components to be integrated in the assembly of end-products. Such an approach meant the use and assimilation of raw materials and sub-components, the design and development of new products; and the assembly  and testing of end-products.

This has implied the use of a large number of techniques and technologies (over 20 different technologies), 5000 different machines and tools, 30,000 different parts and approximately 1000 sub-components. Most of this plant's supplies (92 per cent) come from abroad, and as a consequence the firm deals with 2000 different suppliers.

The data gathered in this study indicate the complex dimension of this plant. Because of this complexity and the shortage of in-house skills, assimilation was very low. As a consequence, its foreign constructor was asked to run the department of materials and supplies for two years (1978–79) as a part of the contract package.

The variety of products, activities and supplies has made the co-ordination between the different departments and workshops extremely difficult for the inexperienced Algerian workforce. This has also made it difficult to make products on schedule meeting satisfactory quality and cost criteria. The complex interactions between the different departments and workshops have made it impossible to optimise the utilisation of production capacities.

In line with the initial strategy of developing a national and independent electronics industry, the aim of the Algerian firm has been to strengthen its assimilation of assembling techniques as well as techniques for component manufacturing. The objective was to limit this large and complex plant to the manufacturing of major electronic components including, cathode-tubes; semi-conductors; condensers; resisters and potentiometers; metallic and plastic components; and printed circuits.

This action is known as the 'redeployment' of the plant. After this process the average increase in production capacity for all activities of component manufacturing was 230 per cent. However, this figure is lower than the increase of the areas (267 per cent) to be utilised for the manu-facturing of these components. This clearly indicates that augmentation in production is the result of the acquisition of new hardware rather than rationalisation and the better use of existing capacities.

The evolution in the field of assembly activities has followed a different pattern to the one put forward for the activities of component manufacturing. An average increase of 97 per cent in production capacity for the assembly lines was carried out with a 29 per cent reduction of the total assembly areas. Three major reasons are cited for this achievement:

• use of machinery requiring smaller raw material consumption and less time for adjustment;

• optimisation of existing areas of assembly activities; and

• improvement in learning.

These reflect the utilisation of automatic and semi-automatic machinery in the assembly lines as well as a better assimilation of the assembly techniques. The pattern of evolution of production capacities in component manufacturing does not lead, however, to the same conclusion as far as the assimilation of the manufacturing of electronic components is concerned. The low assimilation of manufacturing techniques, as explained by the workers and managers of the firm, is a consequence of the following elements:

- complexity of technologies used in the plants;

- nature of the contract in the construction of the electronic plant which has led to the non-involvement of local management; and

- poor availability of documentation regarding the utilisation and maintenance of machines, the specifications of products, the components and materials, the nomenclature of products and the specifications of tests.

To these points, it is important to add the incompatibility between the strategy adopted to develop electronics in Algeria and the low availability within the firm under study and throughout the country of in-house skill and industrial experience. The large scale of the plant and the variety of techniques and activities within it has made this incompatibility more significant. To overcome this problem the firm started questioning the approach that considers technological change as merely related to importing the physical hardware of the technology. Indeed, substantial investment has also been carried out in order to acquire the software. For each dollar spent on the acquisition of machinery, 66 per cent of it is spent on the acquisition of knowledge and information regarding this machinery. In reality, this rate comes to a higher figure as a consequence of the high recruitment of graduates and a skilled workforce.

There is a clear tendency to recruit more graduates in the science-oriented activity of components manufacturing in which changes are frequent and rapid. This new approach, based upon capital knowledge, is motivated by the requirements of new technology in terms of high skill and is aimed at avoiding errors such as those made in the past with respect to the nature of the contract and the choice of products and techniques adopted and their impact on the firm's performance and organisation.

The complexity and the large dimensions of the plant have led to a schedule of construction spread over six years. The full operation of the plant was achieved in 1982. The contract with the foreign partner was signed in 1974. This means that most of the techniques and technologies used in this plant correspond to those available in the market at that period which were developed and launched in the early seventies. This time lag has inevitably led to obsolescence which has occurred at the level of finished products as well as in the electronic components. For instance, the audio products (radios, cassette players and record players) chosen at that period were of mono-function character and, as soon as the plant started operating, these were already obsolete and in fierce competition with products with combined functions. These products were also obsolete in their design. The electrical design was based on the use of discrete components, leading to the utilisation of a large number of them. Some of these components have even disappeared from the international market. The mechanical design was also based on the use of several cases and disconnecters on printed circuits. This gave large and heavy printed circuits.

In addition to the cases of technical obsolescence, another example concerns the structural organisation which will be addressed later.

## Performance of the Electronic Firm

From the review of the performance of the firm under study, it is possible to assess the firm's strategy to develop the electronics industry and to improve its learning curve.

The plant was designed with a capacity for 4000 employees, with 280 workstations and seven hierarchical levels. Its operation, however, proved to be difficult to manage. Its size was the major factor militating against efficient management.

The current organisational system is based on Fordist principles with a high level of hierarchies and a strong division between departments and activities that make the co-ordination and integration of the activities of the different workshops extremely difficult. The necessary interaction and exchange of information between the commercial, technical and production functions was slow as a consequence of the organisational system currently in operation, which is based on a strong separation between these functions.

The average capacity utilisation achieved by the firm in 1992 was 62.5 per cent. After more than ten years of operation, full utilisation of the capacity installed had not been reached. This can certainly be accounted for by the following factors:

- the strategy adopted by the firm whose aim was to implement, use and learn simultaneously different technologies; and

- the poor level of locally available skills.

It is clear that the availability of in-house skills has never been neglected by the firm, but the approach adopted has not enabled it to achieve its objectives with respect to the transfer of technology and assimilation.

The presentation of the firm's strategy and performance cannot be considered as a positive achievement. The clear evolution of the production volume was attained, but full capacity utilisation has not yet been achieved since the current capacity utilisation is no higher than 65 per cent. The increase of the total overheads is significantly higher than the increase of the output volume.

The firm is overstaffed as a result of the decision imposed by the central government to create as many jobs as possible. The workforce is underqualified and has a limited experience in an industry characterised by rapid technological changes.

The strategy adopted by the firm was aimed at developing an electronics industry as a national, independent and export-oriented activity. According to this strategy, the assimilation of assembly techniques is associated with the assimilation of machinery used in the whole process of the assembly line, as well as the assimilation of components manufacturing. This choice has led to the construction of plants in which the entire process of production, starting from the manufacturing of components to the assembly of end-products, is executed.

Thus this strategy based on vertical integration means the assimilation of various techniques regarding (i) the raw materials and sub-groups integrated as inputs in the manufacturing process, (ii) the electronic components, (iii) the design and development of new products, and (iv) the assembly process and testing of the end-products.

This, however, requires the availability of a local stock of capability. For this reason, the negative result identified above is accounted for by the incompatibility between the complex strategy adopted by the firm and the lack of in-house skills. Both factors inhibit diffusion and learning.

## The Agricultural Machinery Firm

This firm was allowed the monopoly of the farm machinery industry and was therefore given charge of the following activities: (i) research and development; (ii) production; (iii) distribution; (iv) maintenance; and (v) imports and exports of farm equipment and agricultural machinery. The production range of this firm comprises three types of tractor, four types of engine (tractors, lorries, combine-harvesters and mechanical appliances), agricultural vehicles (trucks and trailers), ploughs, sowing machinery, fertilisation machinery, agricultural treatment machinery and parts.

In 1990 the farm machinery firm had five manufacturing plants, four sites for distribution, one research unit, and a plant located abroad and owned jointly with a foreign company.

As with the electronics firm, the plants of the farm machinery firm may be divided into two major groups. The first consists of two large plants which were constructed in the 1970s. The second comprises three small-to-medium plants which were established in the 1980s by the firm itself as a result of an attempt to have the large sized companies specialise in a limited range of production. This difference in plant size is explained by the strategy adopted by the firm.

## The Agricultural Machinery Firm's Strategy

In the international context, the production of farm machinery equipment is distributed as follows:

| | |
|---|---|
| Developed countries | 66 % |
| Ex-socialist countries of eastern Europe | 27 % |
| Developing countries | 7 % |

The pace of technological change and the heavy investment required has led to an important concentration in this sector as a result of merger and take-over initiatives. Farm machinery equipment is, in fact, undergoing considerable change as a result of the introduction of micro-electronics and automation. This is seen in the proliferation of computer numerically-controlled machine tools as well as the use of robots in welding and spraying and of automated assembly lines. This explains the small participation (7 per cent of world production) of firms from developing countries in this industry. As far as this participation is concerned, developing countries fall into three groups:

• those carrying out only assembly activities;

• those with manufacturing capacities and in which 20 to 30 per cent of local components are integrated into their production; and

• those with manufacturing capacities in which more than 50 per cent of local components are integrated into their production. South Korea, Mexico, Argentina, India, Brazil, Yugoslavia and China are in this group.

The objective of the Algerian firm was to adopt the strategy of the third group. This explains the large diversity of activities available in the two major plants. Three separate phases may be identified in the strategy adopted to develop the Algerian mechanical and farm equipment industry:

• high investment to introduce the industry through construction of large plants with a high level of integration;

- rationalisation of the capacities installed, and

- renewal of production capacities in order to update the technology used and to be competitive in the international market.

The first phase corresponds to the introduction of this industry during the 1970s through product-in-hand contracts. As a result, the engines and tractors plant and the farm machinery plant were installed by foreign contractors. Both plants are large and were designed to manufacture a wide range of products. One of these two farm machinery plants was initially meant to produce ten different products as well as the parts to be integrated in these.

The second farm machinery plant was also designed to manufacture 33 different products belonging to the four following groups: (a) farm machinery, (b) sowing machinery, (c) fertiliser machinery, and (d) treatment machinery and a wide range of parts to be incorporated in the finished products. This gave a plant running with 300 machine tools and making from 10,000 to 12,000 components. The combine harvester, for instance, requires 7000 different components, of which 2000 are manufactured in the same plant. In comparison, to produce the same combine harvester, the foreign constructor and owner of the licence draws upon five different plants which do not produce more than 30 per cent of the required components. The rest are provided by sub-contractors.

Consequently, several technologies of high complexity were implemented in these two plants, for which the level of qualification and experience of the workforce was not adequate at all. These firms had also to cope with a diversified number of imported supplies. This has inevitably led to a high frequency of production stoppages, bottlenecks and under-utilisation of capacities (35 per cent). This is why the second phase of this strategy was aimed at rationalising the current potentialities through the specialisation of existing manufacturing plants and the optimisation of their production processes.

Seven to ten years of practice has enabled the two plants to reach the designed volume of output. This has been achieved gradually. However, there is still considerable idle capacity in them. The two examples also prove that the more highly integrated and complex the plants are in terms both of size and the technologies used, the more difficult it is to run them efficiently. This confirms that the level of qualification of the workforce of these plants is low and not adequate for an efficient use of the technology implemented.

In 1986, although 90 per cent of the machinery used by the agricultural machinery plants was of conventional type, the rate of capacity utilisation in these plants was less than 60 per cent and the scrap rate was as high as

30 per cent. The management of this firm explains poor performance with reference to the 14-year old machine tools and the difficulties of maintaining them. This, according to these managers, is the reason for the numerous production stoppages, bottlenecks, the high scrap rate, and the poor quality of the products.

The third phase of the farm machinery firm's strategy is aimed at enhancing performance by the use of new equipment based on information technology.

## Acquisition of Advanced Manufacturing Technology

Significant emphasis is placed on automated finished lines in order to improve the assembly, control and testing of products. With the use of new technology, the management of this firm expected to increase the output volume by as much as 42 per cent and to raise the capacity utilisation from 53 to 85 per cent in 1992. This was to be achieved through better integration and better organisation of work. These organisational changes were to lead to a reduction in bottlenecks and lead time in the production lines. The use of new technology equipment was also motivated by the desire to achieve better accuracy in production. It was therefore forecast that reductions in lead time and scrap rate would inevitably lead to drastic decreases in production costs.

However, an assessment of the first experience in the acquisition of new technology machine tools by the farm machinery firm shows a difficult integration of the new tools and, as a consequence, a persistence of considerable bottlenecks in production lines. These are due to the speed of the new tools while the other machines cannot proceed at the same pace. This leads to overstocking waiting in the production sequence, suggesting the lack of a total organisation approach when investing in new technology acquisition. New machine tools were introduced in manufacturing and assembly with the objective of replacing conventional technology and hence increasing the speed and the quality of production. The impact of new technology on the entire process of production seems to be neglected. Maintenance, which still gives rise to production stoppages, may be interpreted as evidence of incompatibility between the level of in-house skill and the new technology used.

In the international context, the pace of technological change in agricultural machinery and the heavy investment it requires have led to the concentration of firms through mergers and take-overs. However, in Algeria, the strategy to develop farm machinery has been built with the intention of integrating more than 50 per cent of local components. This has led to the construction of large, complex plants designed to manufacture several different end-products as well as the parts to be integrated in these. In these plants, various technologies are used by an underqualified and inexperienced workforce. As a result, even after almost two decades of operation, there is still considerable idle production capacity. In 1992, the increase in production costs per worker was higher (61 per cent) than the increase of production volume per worker (58 per cent).

**Learning and Managerial Implications**

The strategy adopted by the firms under study is based on technological dissimilarity and is extremely difficult to implement with success in a developing country such as Algeria where in-house skill and experience are lacking (Dahmani 1985, Hoffman and Girvan 1990). This is confirmed by the unsatisfactory rate of production capacity utilisation by small plants in which very simple technologies are adopted (for example, the manu-facturing of trailers and tracks). Even within the large-scale plants, the simple manufacturing process for hay-makers is better assimilated than that of combine-harvesters. Thus the more highly integrated and complex plants are in terms of both physical dimensions and technologies used, the more difficult it becomes to run them efficiently. The incompatibility between the complexity of the technology used and the local environment, characterised by lack of in-house skill and competence, may be aggravated by the acquisition of advanced manufacturing technology.

As pointed out above and highlighted in Cooper's study of developing countries (1980), the Algerian firms have placed emphasis upon the acquisition of the hardware aspect of technology (conventional as well as advanced technology) with meagre thought for the best management practice that is essential for its success and which can come from the matching of organisation and technology (Saad 1991).

The incompatibility discussed above and its negative impact on firms' performance and learning curve is aggravated by the organisational structure which is characterised by:

- separation of complementary functions such as production and techniques or inventory and supplies;

- existence of several levels of hierarchy and decision-making centres; and

- fragmentation of tasks, such as methods and work organisation.

Organisational development plays an important part in the way technologies are selected, installed and operated. Indeed, the incompatibility between the imported technology and the organisation and the context in which this technology is being used has led to a series of difficulties that both firms are faced with, such as breakdowns, delay, poor and inadequate maintenance, waiting for parts, tools and fixtures, time wasting in adjusting tools, bottleneck operations, low machine utilisation downstream of bottlenecks, high rate of scrap and low quality products, high inventory levels, unreliable deliveries, long production lead time, low productivity, shortage of in-house skills, poor worker involvement, absence of autonomy leading to excessive paper work and a lack of management commitment, and absence of good and long-term relationships with suppliers. Schonberger (1982), in his study of Japanese manufacturing techniques, came to the conclusion that the main reason for Japanese effectiveness in quality and productivity lies in the approach to organisation and management of production rather than technological change.

Dempsey (1982) suggests that most of these problems are typical of firms neglecting organisational adaptations. Ebrahimpour and Schonberger (1984) and Bessant (1990) consider these difficulties as typical of firms from developing countries which can be dealt with via a systematic approach based on rationalisation and simplification of work. Such an approach based could also, as Dempsey (1982) has suggested, create a motivated and committed workforce that knows it is trusted. The strong dependence upon the central government limits initiative and is more likely to lead to frustration and a lack of commitment in managers. This dependence also suggests that the Algerian firms are operating in a predictable and stable environment and hence do not need to be aware of market reality or to be attentive to market changes and requirements.

**Conclusion**

Examination of the use of an advanced technology system in developed countries has indicated difficulties surrounding the implementation of new technology. The problem is indeed further complicated in developing countries where technology is often viewed as an item or a piece of hardware bought and transported from one place to another regardless of the cultural, social, economic and organisational context of the host company/country.

The present study has clearly indicated that the transfer and the use of advanced technology in both Algerian firms has led to the persistence of considerable difficulties which derive from lack of technical as well as managerial experience. This study has also shown that, when the technology is simpler and local managers are given the opportunity to use their potential in the process of selecting and implementing the imported technology, the achievement rate is significant. It is therefore vital for firms from developing countries to seek a market niche in an environment where business strategies are increasingly oriented towards globalisation with merger and take-over initiatives where market needs and requirements are changing constantly and rapidly, and where the industry is characterised by a high proliferation of advanced technology. This market niche strategy ought to be built on the strengths of the firm. It may, therefore, be suggested that the determination of the market niche strategy could be associated with the transfer and use of a more appropriate and simpler technology. The adoption of such technology may also generate more jobs. The use of advanced technology should not be neglected but should be conceived with a good and lasting collaboration with foreign partners and with more appropriate learning and transfer mechanisms.

This study has also given a clear evidence that both Algerian firms have followed a similar pattern of development. There is, indeed, a tendency to generalise about firms and employees' behaviour and to ignore differences. It is often assumed that organisations and people will respond in the same way to the same set of conditions. Greater autonomy and responsibility should, therefore, be offered to firms as well as to individuals in order to take into consideration all relevant specifics and to release their potential, creativeness and initiatives (Saad 1993 and 1994).

## REFERENCES

Bessant, J. (1990), *Fifth Wave Manufacturing: Management Implications of Advanced Manufacturing Technology*, Blackwell, Oxford.
Cooper, C. (1980), 'Policy Intervention for Technological Innovation in Developing Countries', *World Bank Staff Working Paper No 441*, Washington, DC, Dec.
Dahmani, A.M (1985), *L'Engineering dans la Maitrise Industrielle et Technologique*. Office des Publications Universitaires, Algiers.
Dempsey, P. (1982), 'New Corporate Perspective in FMS', in Rathmill, K. (ed.) *Proceedings of FMS-2 Conference*, Kempston, IFS Publications.
Ebrahimpour M. and R. Schonberger (1984), 'The Japanese Just in Time/Total Quality Control System of Production: Potential for Developing Countries', *International Journal of Production Research*, 22, pp.421–30.
Hoffman, K. and N. Girvan (1990), 'Managing International Transfer. A Strategic Approach for Developing Countries', *IDRC*, Apr.
Saad, M. (1991), 'The Transfer and the Management of New Technology – the Case of Two Firms in Algeria', University of Brighton, PhD thesis, Sep.
Saad, M. (1993), 'Innovation and Culture', paper presented to the Second International Conference on *The Culture of the Artificial*, Ascona, Switzerland, May.
Saad, M. (1994), 'The Role of Culture in the Design of New Forms of Organisation (Post-Fordist) Conducive to Innovation and Creation', paper presented to the International Conference on *New Visions of the Post-Industrial Society*, University of Brighton.

# Transfer of Technology to Algeria by Nationals Living Abroad

## MOHAMMED SAID OUKIL

*Transfer of technology can take place by different means. In Algeria, the potential contribution to the transfer process of Algerian scientists and technologists who work abroad is least explored. Rather, the focus has been on the 'brain-drain' aspect. Various factors induce scientists and technologists to emigrate and stay abroad. While the emigration trend is on the increase, the question is whether the brain drain effect can be reversed to the benefit of the home economies. Some governments of developing countries have recently begun to address the issue seriously as a strategy for promoting their capacity building programmes. This article notes the significance of the case for Algeria and considers ways and means by which Algerian nationals abroad could be mobilised to contribute to the national scientific and technological capability development effort.*

## Introduction

Technological development[1] is a process which involves an extensive use of scientific and technical capabilities in the several sectors of an economy. Unfortunately, many developing countries have been doomed to bad management of their scientific and technological stock.[2] In some, if not all of these countries, scientists, technologists, inventors and innovators[3] find themselves under-utilised in terms of their potential capabilities; alienated from participation in decision-making; discouraged and frustrated upon return from abroad[4] or forced to emigrate.

In the case of Algeria[5] the last two points in particular seem to have recently captured the attention of the authorities.[6] This is apparent from the deliberations of the official organisation of the first international forum on the question.[7]

As regards the broader issue of science and technology (S&T), the main questions to ask are the following. First, is, for example, the response by the

Dr Mohammed S. Oukil is Researcher and Senior Lecturer in Economics at the University of Algiers, Algeria.

Algerian government a simple political gimmick – a flash in the pan – or is it a serious decision reflecting good vision and long-term policy concern? Second, is there evidence to suggest the commitment of the government to serious management of the national S&T policy? In other words, has research and development (R&D) in Algeria been properly managed at both the macro- and the micro-economic levels? Third, has technology transfer (TT) been undertaken within the context of an intelligently elaborated system and strategy? Fourth, as the Algerian economy is moving towards a market economy, what does that imply in terms of S&T in general and R&D and technological innovation in particular?

The remainder of this article is an attempt to answer these questions. The first part will explain why it is crucial for any country, including Algeria, to use all available human resources, wherever they may live or work. The second part will show the weaknesses of the Algerian research system and its weak impact on growth effectiveness. The third part will suggest ways and means to maximise the socio-economic benefits accruing from nationals abroad and will discuss conditions for a successful, practical transition.

**Residents and Non-Residents, Unite!**

There are many reasons why the involvement in the development process of all nationals with scientific and technological capabilities – whatever their levels of capability and wherever they may live and work – is quite essential. First, the development of human resource is crucial for economic growth. Neglect of this resource or loss of it through the mechanisms of the 'brain drain' therefore represents opportunities lost. Policies aimed at reversing the 'brain drain' would help countries such as Algeria to bolster their human resource bases for the development of local capabilities and enhance the prospects for technological progress and economic growth. Secondly, nationals abroad are, generally speaking, more aware of and knowledgeable about local conditions and hence local needs than foreigners. Thirdly, the majority, if not all, of the skilled labour force living abroad have at one time or another benefited from the provision of public funds for their education. It is consequently natural to expect a return from the investment made in them. Education in Algeria has since independence been free to all nationals at all levels, and the great majority of educated Algerians abroad are beneficiaries of national grants and scholarships. Fourthly, nationals abroad represent a 'hidden' source of scientific and technological knowledge, information and experience, so much needed for problem-solving and decision-making. A case in point is the example of Algerians working in the automobile industry in France. The experience of those who have returned home since 1990 is said to have had a significant positive impact on the mechanical engineering industry in Algeria.

However, a major constraint on policy which seeks to involve nationals abroad in the development process would be whether, for example, the research problems which nationals established abroad worked on or their skills were of any relevance to the needs of the economy and local firms. In general, foreign scientists and technologists who are engaged by universities and industries in the developed countries often work on issues and problems closely related to conditions in these countries. For instance, Algerian post-graduate students studying abroad would take up research themes that are often of interest either to their supervisors or to industry in the countries where they study. This is particularly true in engineering and chemistry. No less at fault is also the general tendency for developing countries to copy the industrial world, irrespective of the relevance of whatever is copied to the socio-economic circumstances of developing countries. This uncritical attitude to technology transfer practices has been a major source of problems for developing countries which gave rise to the well-known 'appropriate technology' debate.

The issue of technology transfer to developing countries is not new. What is new here is the proposition that nationals of developing countries resident abroad would do it better – they would select and 'send'; they would not simply 'transfer'. But this is easier said than done. It is, for instance, important to understand what should be transferred and how, and which projects would be useful and relevant. This, in fact, could be controversial and could end up driving a wedge between the national scientists/technologists and their governments. A project could be useful and appropriate from the point of view of engineers and managers but may not necessarily be so from the vantage point of the government.

## Effectiveness of the Algerian R&D System

The infrastructure for Algeria's R&D was in existence well before independence. There were R&D initiatives in the fields of energy and health, such as the Centre Nuclèaire and l'Institut Pasteur. After independence, the choice of a socialist road for socio-economic development led to the establishment of a large public sector including R&D. All pre-independence scientific research institutions were nationalised after 1967. A major post-independence objective in Algeria was to create the ability to emulate research efforts in the successfully industrialised countries with the view to quickly catch up with them and rapidly close the 'technological gap'.

In 1971, the basis for a national S&T policy was laid down. The main driving elements of this policy included: (a) engagement in programmes of scientific research, both fundamental and applied; (b) recourse to the massive transfer of up-to-date technologies from several countries, mainly the developed ones; and (c) substantial investments in education and training, locally and abroad, particularly at post-graduate level.

A critical view of these elements would indicate that the S&T policy was far removed from the economic concern of promoting productivity. For a long time, industry and scientific and technological institutions were set quite apart from each other. The flow of petro-dollars and the politically distorted economic visions of the then authorities made that possible. The political influence on policy making was so overwhelming that science and technology institutions would be opted for not so much for their economic consequences as for the political agenda they would serve. 'Go for S&T', advisers would point out, 'the linkages and interactions between S&T and economic sectors will come about later on in the future automatically.' In the event, this proved far-fetched.

Later on in the 1980s, some positive reforms occurred but mainly on the administrative side. Scientific research and higher education were administratively differentiated, and the S&T sector passed through various appellations: HCR (Haut Commissariat à la Recherché), SER (Secrètariat d'Etat à la Recherché), MDR (Ministère Délegué à la Recherché) and latterly MESRS (Ministère de l'Enseignement Supérieur et de la Recherché Scientifique). The structure of the S&T system evolved gradually, giving rise to the establishment of many research centres, units and laboratories at both the macro- and the micro-economic levels. Add to that, the large amounts of equipment and tools which were imported and allocated to these structures. Nationally ambitious programmes were also adopted, elaborated and opportunities were created for a large number of post-graduate students to be trained both locally and abroad.

However, against all that, the conditions in which research has been carried out have been alarmingly unsatisfactory. To start with, the reluctance to recognise the professional credibility of Algerian researchers increased the threat of alienation. This was more than a 'teething' problem, with the result that many highly qualified people were in the end forced to emigrate. Besides, there was hardly much communication between the researchers themselves. It is ironic that contacts between Algerian researchers often took place abroad for lack of the provision of venues for local scientific opportunities. Linkages between research centres and industry are also too remote or non-existent (Oukil 1989). Add to that the scientific equipment and tools that are technically and economically obsolete and inappropriate. The local research environment certainly left a lot to be desired.

In brief, the policy for S&T has been too ambitious with little or no appeal to the direct and immediate needs of the economy. R&D made no impact on productivity. Instead it alienated the accumulated experience of the local industrial labour force. The R&D network also involved poorly integrated components that account for the dysfunctioning of the system. All this points to the fact that the R&D sector in Algeria has been resource-intensive but grossly inefficient.

## Capturing Emigrant Capabilities

Emigrants are generally unpopular in the eyes of governments because they constitute for the most part a population of *refusniks*. Liberally minded governments would, however, be least exclusive with regard to their respective nationals living and working abroad. In Algeria, for example, politicians and administrators in charge of higher education and scientific research invited a sample from the national scientific community living abroad for discussions with some of their local colleagues. The agenda aimed at strategies for:

- allowing local and outside participants to exchange ideas;

- creating an official institution for Algerian scientists and technologists;

- making the invited participants aware of the problems facing research, higher education and the economy at large; and

- urging them to make suggestions that would facilitate the machinery, tools and the transference of knowledge to Algeria.

The gathering, which lasted for a few days, resulted in the creation of an important institution: the 'Association of Algerian Scientists'. This, it is generally hoped, will help in promoting the scientific and technological contribution of Algerians living abroad to technological development in Algeria.

Such actions on the part of the government seem to reflect a naive way of dealing with the question of S&T development in the country. Making S&T economically productive and socially useful cannot simply be a matter of setting up organisations and providing funds for importing technology. There is also a real need for coming up with carefully designed strategies and the appropriate framework for sound macro- and micro-economic management. On this point, the views and recommendations of scientists and specialists should necessarily be taken into account.

## Conditions for Enhancing Effectiveness of Technology Transfer

A major problem of S&T policy is that when there are gaps between the products of local R&D and the importing of technologies and scientific education on the one hand, and the socio-economic environment on the other, successful results can neither be expected nor realised. Hence a basic condition for eliciting a useful and serious contribution of national scientists and technologists working abroad is for the government to make the existing research system work properly (Oukil 1992, Bessalah 1994). This would involve, *inter alia*, the provision of incentives in the form of competitive remuneration; conducive working conditions, including the provision of infrastructure and funding for research and development, and freedom of thought. These could be built as part and parcel of a policy framework for the promotion of R&D. No less important is the legal aspect concerning technological innovation and the importing of technologies and knowledge. In various sectors, the absence or inadequacy of laws and administrative procedures (Riehl 1992, Hamdi 1993) and lack of managerial consciousness (Oukil 1993) operate as a major source of constraint militating against the effective application of S&T policy.

If local scientists and technologist suffer from lack of access to up-to-date knowledge, it will be necessary to create new conditions or procedures for recycling. The creation of a review for S&T, involving particular fields and specialties needed for local use would consequently be of great help. Such a review would also help to resolve another critical problem – that of the 'equivalence' of degrees held by nationals coming from abroad. At present, apart from degrees obtained from France, all other foreign degrees are subject to reassessment and vetting. Until recently this procedure took a very long time.

On the external front, it is essential to identify countries or groups of countries – both developed and developing – with which relationships must be forged or reinforced.[8] Such government-driven initiatives would also include an inventory of all contributors, potential and actual, in different areas of S&T and explore channels, mechanisms and ways of transferring technologies to Algeria and building on their positive contribution to the economy and society.

## Conditions for the Useful Reintegration of Nationals Abroad

Generally, success in socio-economic development depends on the good use of technology, wherever the technology comes from (Djeflat 1991). In this context, the transition of the Algerian economy into a competitive environment would not be successful short of efficient management of technology and strategies for restructuring the economy to create conditions for real competitiveness[9] and for attracting investment flows and enhancing factor mobility in general, and technical and professional skills in particular.

Transition to a competitive economic environment would thus call for changes both in the public and the private sector of the economy.

Within the public sector the provision of incentives including competitive rates of remuneration and of mechanisms for the effective application of skills in supply is necessary. The profile of the private sector could be improved through the encouragement of investment in the field of S&T, provision of financial assistance for nationals to exploit their patents, and incentives to import technically and economically appropriate technologies.[10]

## Conclusion

The benefits which may be gained by the Algerian economy from the contribution of nationals abroad cannot be straightforward. This calls for a whole range of policy provisions and revisions. Nationals abroad and particularly those with scientific and technological skills may be well placed to identify and develop opportunities that would enhance the development of technological capability in Algeria. They would not, however, respond when policies defining socio-economic conditions in Algeria are restrictive and taxing. Hence the need for the reform of policies.

If local socio-economic conditions and the management of the economy remained without reform for long, the transition towards a market economy based on an innovatively competitive model of growth and the active participation of nationals abroad in such a transition effort would be unduly delayed and Algeria would be the poorer for that.

### NOTES

1. In the sense used by Dahlman, Ross-Larson and Westphal (1987), which refers to the building of four types of capability: investment, production, innovation and engineering.
2. Including tangible ones such as officers and staff, and non-tangible ones such as knowledge and experience.
3. Both formal and informal ones.
4. Not necessarily in the country where they did the post-graduate studies.
5. We make particular reference to this country as one of the five of the Maghreb Union. Some facts as well as conclusions would apply to the other four: Morocco, Tunisia, Mauritania and Libya.
6. Including mainly the Ministry of Foreign Affairs which has played a key role.
7. First Forum of Algerian Scientists: 14–16 Aug. 1994, Algiers.
8. Note here that in Toulouse (France) a team of researchers has been commissioned by the CEE to study the national R&D systems in the integration zone of UMA: Maghreb Arab Union.
9. The process of liberalisation has led to the emergence of an important force of speculators and a spate of commercial activities. In theory, competitiveness is real when it involves technological innovation; see Porter (1990) and Cooper (1993).

10 The 'Code des Marchés' of 1966, which stipulates that only new (not above three years old) are allowed, should be revised.

## REFERENCES

Bessalah, H. (1994), 'Le Système National de Recherché Scientifique et de Développement Technologique, Etat et Perspective'. Forum des Scientifiques Algeriens, Algiers, Aug.

Cooper, C. (1993), 'New Technologies and Development', keynote lecture, Glasgow International Conference, Apr.

Djeflat, A. (1991), 'Resources Humaines, Recherche et Développement, et Problèmatique de L'Intégration Maghrébine', Actes de la Deuxième Session de l'Université d'Hiver, Marrakech, pp.257–67.

Freeman, C. and B.A. Lundvall (1988), *Small Countries Facing the Technological Revolution*, Pinter, London.

Hamidi, H. (1993), *Reforme Economique et Propriété Industrielle*, Office des Publications Universitaires, Algiers.

Dahlman, C.L., B. Ross-Larson and L.E.Whestphal (1987), 'Managing Technological Development: Lessons from the Newly Industrialisation Countries', *World Development*, Vol.15, No.6.

North, D.C. (1994), 'The New Institutional Economics and Development', guest editorial, *Forum*, Vol.1, No.2, May.

Oukil, M.S. (1989), *The Function and System of Industrial Research and Development in Algeria*, PhD thesis, University of Strathclyde, Glasgow.

Oukil, M.S. (1993), 'Technological Innovations and Industrial Property Issues in Developing Countries: a Case Study of Algeria', Conference Proceedings, Glasgow, 5–7 April.

Porter, M. (1990), *The Competitive Advantage of Nations*, Free Press.

Riehl, C. (1992), 'Aspects Juridiques du Transfer de Technologie et al Propriété Intellectuelle dans les Accords Internationaux', *Journées d'Etudes Algéro-Francaises*, Algiers, 22–24 June, pp.39-42.

# National Innovation Systems:
# The Case of the Arab Maghreb Union

## ALAIN ALCOUFFE

*The article addresses the issue of research and development (R&D)
in the context of national innovation systems (NIS) in the Maghreb.
The components of NIS including the productive system (industrial
structures), the training and education system and the R&D
systems are discussed. The article indicates training and human
resource development to be crucial for the quality and direction of
research and for innovation and technological change in industry.*

## Introduction

Research and development (R&D) activities are, generally speaking, skill
and scale sensitive. This would make the role of the state in providing the
framework for the development of relevant skill and industrial structures
absolutely crucial for such initiatives to thrive. The Maghreb countries –
Algeria, Tunisia, Morocco, Mauritania and Libya, which together constitute
the Arab Maghreb Union (AMU) – would be keen to build on their
respective national innovation systems (NIS) through integration of effort to
exploit the synergy in co-operative R&D. This, however, is a daunting
challenge – the AMU has yet to evolve in economic, social and political
terms, while the NIS will have to be strengthened to provide the basis for
the long-term development of regional R&D strategies. Hence the need for
policy focus on NIS in the AMU. This would, needless to say, benefit from
recourse to theoretical and empirical knowledge about NIS.

## The NIS Concept

The literature in this area is vast and varied. Freeman (1972) has shed light
on the role of R&D departments in firms. Von Hippel (1976) has worked on
the interactions between firms in the process of technological innovation.
Gilles (1978), explores the concept of the 'technical system' based on the

Alain Alcouffe is Professor of Economics at the Université des Sciences Sociales de Toulouse,
Toulouse, France. This article is a translated and edited version of the paper presented in French
at the MAGHTECH'94 conference.

important historical works of science and on the experience of capitalist firms. The role of science was discussed equally extensively by Mowery and Rosenberg (1979), while Nelson (1982 and 1984) has shown the role of the state in promoting technological innovation to be positively significant. Also, Niosi and Faucher (1991) identify the state as the principal purveyor of the most important factor of production in the history of modern industry, namely, scientific and technological knowledge. Finally, in the 1980s many writings have corroborated that of Von Hippel in showing the importance of technical alliances and co-operation agreements among countries.

Figure 1 indicates the different, interdependent components which make up the NIS in principle:

- the economic context and the industrial structures: the productive system;

- training and the quality of human resources (HR): the training and education system; and

- cooperation between firms and the centres of public research.

In these relationships, the international aspect cannot be neglected particularly when the role that the most industrialised countries (MIC) play in influencing R&D trends is significant. However, for the inventor of the concept of NIS, 'the national aspect is central insofar as technological development and their flows between firms appear more frequently within national boundaries than outside them'(Niosi *et al.* 1992). Also, Freeman like Nelson specifies social and political institutions and economic policies as factors behind the homogeneity of behavioural patterns of national agents of innovation.

FIGURE 1

NATIONAL INNOVATION SYSTEM (NIS)

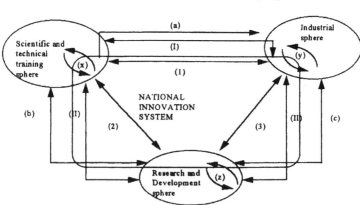

## The Productive System

*General Data*

Table 1 presents basic socio-economic data for the five countries in the Arab Maghreb Union (AMU). These data are set against corresponding data for Brazil and the European Union (EU), as a group for comparative purposes. The countries of the AMU together cover a total area of more than 6 million square kilometres, which is close to 2.5 times that of the EU and 67 per cent that of Brazil. The discrepancies between the EU and the AMU are weak if we consider the cultivable agricultural land (CAL), where the AMU would come per head 100 million hectares (1 million km2 per head) in front of the EU and Brazil.[1]

TABLE 1
PHYSICAL AND DEMOGRAPHIC DATA

| | | ALG | TUN | MAR | MRT | LBY | BRA | EU |
|---|---|---|---|---|---|---|---|---|
| Area ($km^2$) | | 2381.7 | 164.0 | 710.9 | 1030.7 | 1759.0 | 8475.0 | 2300.0 |
| CAL% | | 16 | 50 | 53 | 1 | 9. | 8 | 31 |
| CAL ($km^2$) | | 381.1 | 82.0 | 376.8 | 10.3 | 158.3 | 669.5 | 713.0 |
| Population | 2000 | 32.7 | 9.8 | 31.7 | 2.7 | 6.4 | 172.8 | 350 |
| (millions) | 1990 | 25.6 | 8.2 | 25.7 | 2.1 | 4.7 | 151.6 | 345 |
| | 1960 | 10.8 | 4.2 | 11.6 | 1.0 | 1.3 | 72.6 | 290 |
| Pop/$km^2$ | | 13.7 | 59.8 | 44.6 | 1.0 | 2.7 | 17.9 | 150.0 |
| Pop/$km^2$CAL | | 85.8 | 119.5 | 84.1 | 97.0 | 29.7 | 226.7 | 483.9 |
| Life | 1990 | 65.1 | 66.7 | 62.0 | 47.0 | 61.8 | 65.6 | 75.9 |
| expectancy | 1960 | 47 | 48.3 | 46.7 | 35.3 | 46.7 | 54.6 | 69.7 |
| Variation | | 18.1 | 18.4 | 15.3 | 11.7 | 15.1 | 11 | |
| Rate of total fertility | | 5.0 | 3.6 | 5.5 | 6.5 | 6.5 | 2.9 | 2.0 |
| Rate 91/rate 60 | | 69 | 50 | 86 | 100 | 92 | 47 | 65 |

ALG = Algeria; TUN = Tunisia; MAR = Morocco; MRT = Mauritania; LBY = Libya; BRA = Brazil; EU= European Union
(USA=9, 167 $km^2$ CAL 20.5%; CAL=1,879 $km^2$; Pop/km2=30; Pop/$km^2$ CAL=150)

*Source*: UN Statistics.

The region's population has increased from fewer than 30 millions in 1960 to close to 70 millions today. It is expected to rise to 90 millions at the beginning of the twenty-first century. At this rate, in a space of few decades the south coast of the Mediterranean Sea could have a population larger than the EU to the north. Already, there are more children born just in Algeria than in France (more than 900,000 in the former compared with about 700,000 in the latter). This has, of course, implications for training and human resource development.

TABLE 2

HUMAN DEVELOPMENT AND STRUCTURE OF THE ACTIVE POPULATION

|  |  | ALG | TUN | MAR | MRT | LBY | BRA | EU |
|---|---|---|---|---|---|---|---|---|
| Literacy rate (% adults) |  | 57.4 | 65.3 |  | 49.5 | 34 | 63.8 | 81.1 |
| IHD |  | 0.528 | 0.6 | 0.433 | 0.14 | 0.658 | 0.73 |  |
| Rank IHD |  |  | 107 | 93 | 119 | 161 | 87 | 70 |
| Rank IHD-GNP |  | -42 | -5 | -33 | -33 | -47 | -17 |  |
| No. scientists/1000 |  |  | 1.4 |  | 11.6 | 29.5 | 81 |  |
| Higher deg/age group |  |  | 2.2 | 0.9 | 1.1 | 2.5 | 9.4 |  |
| % scientists |  | 42 | 36 | 27 |  |  | 19 | 35 |
| Hab/doctors |  | 2330 | 2160 | 4760 | 11900 | 690 | 1080 | 380 |
| Hab/nurses |  | 330 | 370 | 1050 | 1180 | 350 | 1210 | 150 |
| Actives/tot pop |  | 24 | 30 | 31 | 33 | 24 | 43 | 49 |
| Unemp/actives |  | 24.5 | 16.0 | 15.5 |  |  |  |  |
| Agriculture | 1965 | 57 | 50 | 61 | 89 | 41 | 49 | 22 |
| Industry | 1965 | 17 | 21 | 15 | 3 | 21 | 20 | 36 |
| Service | 1965 | 26 | 29 | 24 | 8 | 38 | 31 | 42 |
| Agriculture | 1991 | 14 | 22 | 46 | 69 | 18 | 28 | 7 |
| Industry | 1991 | 11 | 16 | 25 | 9 | 29 | 25 | 26 |
| Service | 1991 | 75 | 62 | 29 | 22 | 53 | 47 | 67 |

*Source* : UN Statistics.

The performance of the productive systems is difficult to indicate in a comprehensive way using GNP, since GNP statistics fail to capture activities in the informal sector which are, however, important in LDCs. GNP indicators thus give the wrong impression about the general state of productivity in the economy. This is why more interest is placed on the development of certain indicators of human development (HD) and in particular on the discrepancy between the rankings of IHD and GNP. It may be seen from Table 2 that the discrepancies are negative in all cases. The discrepancies are particularly strong for Libya and Algeria, whose GNPs are 'inflated' by petroleum exports and for Mauritania which is dependent on the extraction of iron and minerals for export. The increase in life expectancy is, however, impressive in the region throughout the last 30 years: the countries of the AMU are at present at more or less that level of development the EU countries had achieved in 1960.

The distribution of the active population across the economic sectors varies among the countries in the region. In the region as a whole, the active population in agriculture has decreased throughout the last 25 years in relative terms although with high population growth rate, the agricultural population is, without doubt, bigger now than it was 25 years ago in all the five countries – particularly in Morocco. Only Algeria and, to a lesser extent Libya, have experienced a real 'rural exodus'. In all the countries, we see a

TABLE 3

DEBTS AND PUBLIC EXPENDITURES

|  |  | ALG | TUN | MAR | MRT | LBY | BRA |
|---|---|---|---|---|---|---|---|
| Debt/GNP |  | 53 | 62 | 97 | 227 |  | 25 |
| Debt/hab (US$) |  | 1040 | 863 | 849 |  |  |  |
| Debt services | 1970 | 4.0 | 19.7 | 8.7 | 3.4 |  | 12.5 |
| in % of exports | 1990 | 59.4 | 25.8 | 23.4 | 13.9 |  | 20.8 |
|  | 1994 | 76.0 | 43.5 | 67.6 |  |  |  |
| Pub.exp.educ/GNP |  | 9.1 | 6.0 | 7.0 |  | 9.6 | 3.9 |
| Exp.health/GNP |  | 6.0 | 2.4 | 3.2 | 5.5 |  | 3.9 |
| Exp.mil/GNP |  | 1.5 | 3.2 | 4.5 |  | 8.6 | 1.7 |

*Source*: UN Statistics.

swelling of the tertiary sector, relegating industry to a secondary position.

Unemployment has recently increased in spite of the palliatives offered by the informal sector and has become worrying for the young entering the labour market. Significantly, graduates have been hit hard and the trend is on the increase (particularly in Morocco and Algeria).

## Content and Orientations of Foreign Trade

The following points are at the heart of the concern about R&D in the Maghreb:

- Food self-sufficiency is far from achieved in all five countries, although it is necessary to distinguish Algeria and Libya – which are very dependent on food imports – from Tunisia and Morocco.[2] Food harvests in the region have increased recently since the Gulf War had largely exhausted all the income from tourism.

- If petroleum constitutes the essence of Libyan and Algerian exports, manufactured products dominate exports from Tunisia and Morocco. Among the exported manufactured products of Tunisia and Morocco, textiles occupy a dominant place. But Maghrebian exports are subject to competitive threats – actual and perceived. For instance, competitive devaluations may make Maghrebian export prices less and less attractive and protectionist policies adopted by the MICs may limit exports from the Maghreb (there already exist export quotas to the EU).

- With the exception of Libya, the Maghreb countries are in competition with each other to attract foreign investment. Thus Tunisia and Morocco have developed several free zones. Tunisia is striving to create 'technopoles' to attract, under the status of free zones, investments of high technology. Algeria is striving to attract foreign investments by creating free zones and by inviting foreign capital to participate in the privatisation of public firms, although the political situation is compromising the success of these measures.

The EU absorbs 76 per cent of Tunisian exports and provides 72 per cent of its imports, while the figures for Morocco (1992) are respectively 65 per cent and 55 per cent (Sasson 1993: 623). France, for its part, represents 75 per cent of the EU in these exchanges and remains the principal partner of its old colonies. In order to appreciate the relative importance of this pattern of concentration of exchanges, it would be useful to look at it in the light of the experience of other countries at comparable development levels. Blin and Parisot (1992) have shown that, given the EU as a unique partner to the Maghreb, comparable in economic strength to Japan and the USA, it would emerge that the trade link of the Maghreb countries with respect to the EU is much stronger than that of Brazil and Thailand or even Colombia who trade largely with the different branches of the triad (Japan, USA and the EU). The Maghreb countries are even more satellites as a trade partner to the EU than Mexico is to the USA (Blin and Parisot 1992: 90).

These exchange profiles reflect the 'regionalisation' of the world which is progressing much faster than the so-called 'globalisation'. It is not apparent, though, that the Maghreb comes out of this process with net benefits. This is not perhaps surprising considering that the regions on the two sides of the Mediterranean differ significantly in terms of economic status and geographic size. The central Maghreb, including Algeria, Tunisia and Morocco, occupies a marginal position in its association with the EU countries at 1 per cent of the total imports from the EU, including 2.65 per cent of French exports, 2.2 per cent of Spanish exports, 1.5 per cent of Italian exports and only 0.5 per cent of German exports (Blin and Parison 1992: 66).

With respect to the effects of foreign trade on economic dynamism, the case of Algeria is different from the others insofar as this country bears the symptoms of the so-called 'Dutch disease' (Fardmanesh 1991).[3]

## Education and Training of Human Resources

At the time of decolonialisation (1962 for Algeria, the last country in the region to obtain independence), the Maghreb countries had education systems with limited scope and we find traces of the problem in the modest literacy rates for adults. However, they have made large efforts over the years since to remedy this situation. Local universities now offer training for degrees up to master's level.

TABLE 4

MAGHREBIAN STUDENTS IN HIGHER EDUCATION IN THEIR
COUNTRIES AND ABROAD

|                         | ALG     | MAR     | MRT   | LBY   | TUN    | TOTAL   | SHARE |
|-------------------------|---------|---------|-------|-------|--------|---------|-------|
| Home Country            | 289,000 | 230,012 | 6,595 |       | 87,780 | 613,387 |       |
| France                  | 16,308  | 24,036  | 892   | 60    | 6,750  | 48,046  | 67.0% |
| German                  | 271     | 925     | 14    | 40    | 695    | 1,945   | 2.7%  |
| Belgium                 | 602     | 4,737   | 29    | 10    | 432    | 5,810   | 8.1%  |
| Italy                   | na      | 153     | na    | 257   | na     | 410     | 0.6%  |
| UK                      | 263     | 50      | 5     | 324   | 26     | 668     | 0.9%  |
| USSR                    | 784     | 1,018   | 352   | 34    | 414    | 2,60    | 23.6% |
| USA                     | 325     | 1,062   | 43    | 107   | 484    | 2,021   | 2.8%  |
| Other countries         | 1,343   | 4,340   | 1,410 | 918   | 2,609  | 10,620  | 14.8% |
| Total                   | 19,896  | 36,168  | 2,745 | 1,493 | 11,410 | 71,712  | 100%  |
| (50 countries)          |         |         |       |       |        |         |       |

na: not available
*Source*: J. El Alami *et al.* (1992).

The Maghrebian students abroad follow specialised training or undertake doctoral studies. Maghrebian students in France represent a significant share of PhD students abroad (67 per cent) in higher education. The disparities in the standard of living and the underlying political instability, the unequal relationships between the sexes at home push many of these graduates – particularly those from Algeria – to stay in France or to try their luck in Canada, thus stocking up the 'brain drain'.

The strong dependence on France raises several specific problems. French higher education separates neatly the university which is oriented towards the teaching of liberal professions and research from the Grandes Ecoles which are oriented towards production and the management of enterprises. We have not been able to obtain precise data on the distribution of Maghrebian students between the two networks, however; but the conditions of selective access to the Ecoles would mean students of the UMA would be inclined to go to universities instead.

## Systems of Research and Development

Not much work has been done yet exploring the degree of interaction between the activities of the public research centres and that of the R&D of private firms and on the benefit to the Maghrebian economies arising from these. Our preliminary investigation shows the degree of integration between the different research units with the productive sector inside each country to be extremely weak. This situation may broadly be attributed in part to the following:

• The breathtaking increase in the demographic pressure and the increasing teaching loads which many lecturers of higher education have to handle have had the effect of reducing their research effort. The consequences are also reflected in the effectiveness of training, which tends to be remote from the needs of the productive sector. This research/industry split may also be accounted for in part by the brain drain.

• The productive system in the Maghreb is generally characterised by a diffuse structure. For instance, the industrial system in Algeria consists of fewer than 200 public firms covering the essentials of manufacturing activity without which industry/research liaisons appear more developed, save for the energy and the petrochemical sector. In this case, it is the differentiation and subsequent isolation of production activities with respect to suppliers and clients in a very bureaucratic system which has blocked possibilities for R&D spin-offs.

• Other factors include the weakness of industrial structures and the orientation of research projects. In the period 1981–86, 1229 articles were recorded whose authors were Maghrebian writing in collaboration with their foreign counterparts, mainly from France as shown in Table 5.

TABLE 5

COLLABORATIVE ARTICLES (1981–86): MAGHREB/LARGE COUNTRIES IN R&D

|          | USA | France | Others | Total | France/Total |
|----------|-----|--------|--------|-------|--------------|
| Algeria  | 13  | 230    | 51     | 294   | 78.2%        |
| Morocco  | 38  | 241    | 23     | 302   | 79.8%        |
| Tunisia  | 20  | 314    | 18     | 352   | 89.2%        |
| Libya    | 29  | 6      | 46     | 81    | 7.4%         |
| Total    | 100 | 791    | 138    | 1029  | 76.9%        |
| Egypt    | 469 | 102    | 449    | 1020  | 10.0%        |

(Others: UK, Japan, India, Germany, Canada)
*Source*: J. El Alami *et al.* (1992).

TABLE 6

ALLOCATION BY SUBJECT DOMAINS OF THE ARTICLES BY
MAGHREBIAN ARTICLES 1981–86 (ISO)

|          | MAT  | PHY  | CHM   | ENT   | EAS  | BIO   | BIM  | CLI   | Total  |
|----------|------|------|-------|-------|------|-------|------|-------|--------|
| Algeria  | 11   | 69   | 73    | 19    | 15   | 28    | 46   | 101   | 362    |
| Morocco  | 11   | 41   | 105   | 19    | 26   | 47    | 29   | 70    | 348    |
| Tunisia  | 11   | 64   | 155   | 13    | 22   | 31    | 44   | 76    | 416    |
| Libya    | 7    | 12   | 13    | 12    | 10   | 21    | 14   | 14    | 103    |
| Total    | 40   | 186  | 346   | 63    | 73   | 127   | 133  | 261   | 1229   |
| Egypt    | 27   | 132  | 283   | 242   | 59   | 244   | 145  | 378   | 1510   |
| Allocat. | 1.8% | 8.7% | 18.7% | 16.0% | 3.9% | 16.2% | 9.6% | 25.0% | 100.0% |

| MAT | Mathematics             | EAS | Earth and Air Sciences |
|-----|-------------------------|-----|------------------------|
| PHY | Physics                 | BIO | Biology                |
| CHM | Chemistry               | BIM | Biomedical Research    |
| ENT | Engineering + technology | CLI | Clinical Medicine      |

*Source*: J. El Alami *et al.* (1992).

These articles were divided into eight domains. We observe that only 5.1 per cent were concerned with engineering and technology – a poor proportion if we compare it with Egypt, a non-Maghreb country. Thus it seems that the Maghreb performs better when the discipline is more abstract (physics) and appears somewhat inactive with respect to applied disciplines (such as biology or medicine).

## Conclusion

The Maghreb's geographic proximity to the EU could give it a headstart to expand its share of the world market through exposure to increased foreign competition and subsequent improvement in technical and economic efficiency (Trybout 1992). On the other hand, De Bandt (1994) proposes a strategy of development for the Maghreb based on the internal market and mass production akin to the experience of the more industrialised countries (MICs) in the post-war period. This would call for the creation of protected regional markets to absorb the envisaged production. The underlying argument here is that it would be better for the Maghrebian countries to adopt well-tested technologies and leave the MICs to experiment with new technologies. This, however, would diminish the weight of the case for policy concern with research and development in the Maghreb.

The importance of R&D varies considerably according to the forms of entry into the world market and the patterns of sectoral specialisation (OECD 1989).[4] It is clear that the place of the Maghrebian countries in the international division of labour is in those sectors where the intensity of R&D is the weakest, such as textiles and farm produce. The choice of sectors thus largely predetermines the nature of R&D policies; but it is also possible that the direct and indirect effects of choice of one sector on others could make the global balance sheet uncertain for the economy. Consider, for instance, the supply–demand pattern corresponding to skills and qualifications of various categories.

In Algeria the number of scientific and technical graduates in most disciplines is increasing from year to year. This trend is not, however, matched by growth in the effective demand for graduates. The result has been growing unemployment. This also holds for Tunisia and Morocco. It is thus apparent from the prevailing trend that the increase in qualifications does not necessarily improve the possibilities for the development of local capabilities. Rather it is more likely to enhance the propensity to emigrate. The Maghrebian countries have a more highly qualified labour force than those of the developed countries when they were in the 'Fordism' phase, but the Maghreb experience shows the limitations of the late Fordist system to readily absorb qualified members of the labour force.

FIGURE 2

THE MOROCCAN NATIONAL INNOVATION SYSTEM (NIS)

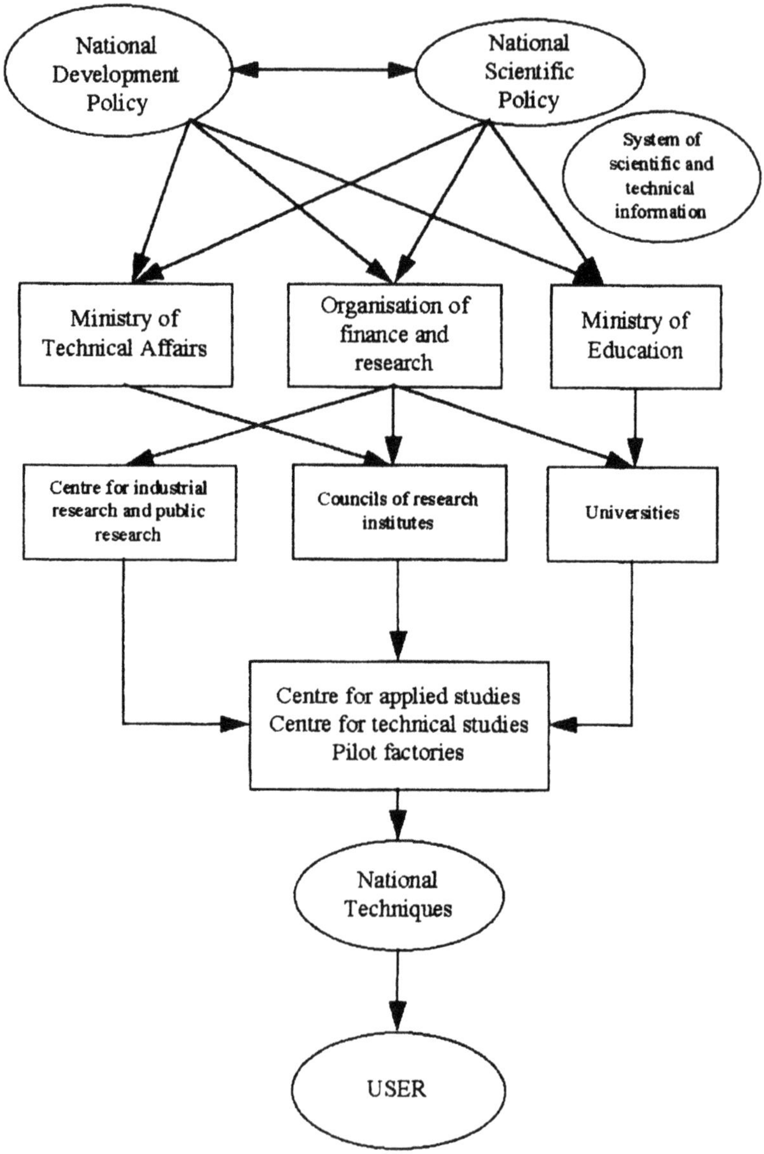

Source: A. Zekri, *Problématique de la Recherche Développement dans les PVD: le Cas du Maroc*, PhD thesis, Lyon 2.

Increase in income without increase in productivity would reduce the competitive edge of exports of labour-intensive industries. Already these industries are dependent on imported inputs, and financing imports often poses problems calling for policy intervention in the form of the provision of subsidies or protection in the context of individual national economies, Maghreb-wide regional integration or an EU/AMU co-operation (Metcalfe 1994).

A characteristic feature of industry in the Maghreb is the absence of large firms except in Algeria. The dominance of industry by small firms is not, however, necessarily a cause of technological backwardness and weak productivity since the scale effect on innovation could be overcome by the provision of appropriate policies that are largely supportive of innovation. Experience in the Scandinavian countries, in Germany and especially in Japan shows that state support in terms of the provision of information services and training and decentralised laboratories to which these tasks can be devolved is crucial for R&D enterprises to take root and bear fruit (OECD 1982).

The French model has shown innovation to be associated with large firms (public and private). To date, R&D has been the preserve of public sector agencies and often of multinational enterprises (MNEs) and national innovation systems have been dominated by interaction between public research centres and large scale firms. The future of R&D in the Maghreb is thus largely contingent on the character of the evolving industrial structures in the region and, more particularly, on the role of MNEs and the extent to which the state would be keen to adjust economic policy with the view to promoting innovation and technological progress in the region.

## NOTES

1. A. Sasson (1993) indicates that the agricultural land covers approximately 21 million hectares for central Maghreb.
2. Morocco harvested 8.5 million tons of cereals in 1991 but only 2.5 million in 1992 (Sasson 1993, p.621).
3. The 'Dutch disease' – so called after the experience of the Netherlands in the 1960s (Corden 1982, Neary and Van Wijnbergen 1986) – is associated with the structural effects of a resource export boom as in the case of oil. The output of the boom sector expands at the expense of the other sectors, particularly the traded goods sectors. The boom would contract the non-oil traded (manufactured and agricultural) goods sectors and expand the non-traded goods sector – or contract it if the resource movement effect is dominant. The boom stimulates demand for non-traded goods and precipitates increases in the relative prices of such goods. The spending effect of the boom thus expands the non-traded sector. Variations of the core model of Dutch disease have sought to explain the expansion of manufactured traded goods sector and the contraction of agricultural traded goods sector in most oil-producing developing countries following the boom of the 1970s. Fardmanesh (1991) argues

that the collapse of oil price as in the 1980s would in due time lead to the expansion of agricultural activities and the contraction of manufacturing and, possibly, non-traded goods sectors.

4.  In order to approach the strategies that could be implemented in the countries of the AMU, in particular in the domain of R&D, we may refer to the studies inspired by the new growth theories and the reformulation retained for the production function (Boyer and Amable 1992): $Y = A * e^{\lambda i} * K^{\alpha} * L^{\beta} * R^{\gamma}$, where K represents physical capital; L, labour; R, R&D and Y, GDP. Econometric studies based on this particular form of production function suggest the existence of substitution between capital, labour and scientific and technical knowledge. Unfortunately, there are no robust data that would allow estimation of the coefficients and parameters of this production function for the AMU. It is, however, possible to conjecture that in the AMU as in other LDCs, capital is rather scarce like R&D, while labour is rather abundant. A well behaved production function assumes choice, but, in practice, choices are made difficult by the non-malleability of physical capital.

## REFERENCES

Abdelmalki, L. and J.L. Besson (1989), *L'Observé Statistique*, PUL, Lyon et Toubkal, Casablanca.

Amable, B. and R. Boyer (1992), 'The R&D Productivity Relationship in the Context of New Growth Theories', *Papiers CEPREMAP*, No.9211, Jan.

Audretsh, D. and M. Vivarelli. (1994), 'Small Firms and R&D Spillovers : Evidence from Italy', *Revue d'Économie Industrielle*, No.67, 1st trimestre, pp.225–37.

Blin, L. and B. Parisot (1992), 'Les Relations Économiques entre la CEE et les Pays du Maghreb', in *Le Maghreb, l'Europe et la France* (directed by K. Basfao and J.R. Henry), Paris, CNRS.

Corden, W.M. (1982), 'Booming Sector and Dutch Disease Economics: a Survey', *The Australian National University Working Papers*, No.079, Nov.

De Bandt, J. (1994), 'Quelle Industrie, Quelle Insertion dans l'Économie Mondiale pour les Pays du Maghreb?', *Annales d'Economie Marocaine*, No.8, Spring, pp.13–24.

Djeflat, A. (1994), 'Education Scientifique et Technique et Impératifs Technologiques de l'Industrie en Algérie', in *La Problématique des Resources Humaines au Maghreb*, colloque du GERRH, Rabat, Diwan.

El Alami, J. *et al.* (1992), 'International Collaboration in Arab Countries', *Scientometrics*, Vol.23, No.1, pp.249–63.

Fardmanesh, M. (1991), 'Dutch Disease Economics and the Oil Syndrome: an Empirical Study', *World Development*, Vol.19, No.6, pp.711–17.

Freeman, C. (1987), *Technology Policy and Economic Performance*, London, Pinter.

Neary, J.P., and S. Van Wijnberger (eds.) (1986), *Natural Resources and the Macroeconomy*, Cambridge, MIT Press.

Nelson, R. (1988), 'Institutions Supporting Technical Change in the USA', in G. Dosi *et al.* (eds.), *Technical Change and Economic Theory*, London, Pinter.

Metcalfe, J.S. (1994), 'Evolutionary Economics and Technology Policy', *Economic Journal*, July, pp.931–44.

Mowery, D. and N. Rosenberg (1990), *The US National Innovation System*, CRM, Working Paper 90.3, Berkeley.

Niosi, J. *et al.* (1992), 'Les Systèmes Nationaux d'Innovation: à la Recherche d'un Concept Utilisable', *Revue Francaise d'Économie*, Vol.7, No.1, pp.215–50.

Niosi, J. and P. Faucher (1991), 'The State and International Trade: Technology and Competitiveness', in *Technology and National Competitiveness*, Montreal.

OECD, 1982, *L'Innovation dans les Petites et Moyennes Entreprises*, Paris.

Sasson, A. (1993), *Biotechnologies in Developing Countries*, Vol. 1, UNESCO, Paris.

# Performance of the Education System and Profile of Industry Demand for Skills in Morocco

## MEHDI LEHLOU

*The education system has performed poorly in Morocco with the result that the proportion of Moroccan children in full time education is one of the lowest in the world. Ironically enough, the rate of unemployment is observed to be higher among those few with high degrees of qualification than among those who are non-trained and/or with only primary or secondary education. This trend is reinforced by the Structural Adjustment Programme (SAP) adopted by Morocco, and if sustained it could undermine prospects for the development of skills that are crucial for technological progress.*

## Introduction

Twelve years after the adoption of the first structural adjustment programme (SAP), the performance of the Moroccan economy remains weak and burdened with debt. GDP has been growing slowly, if not negatively, as was the case, for example, during 1992 and 1993 when the growth rate of real GDP declined from 4.1 to 1.1 per cent. This weakness in the growth rate derives partly from the persistence of weak agricultural productivity, partly from the prevalence of a strong tendency to import in the face of a weak capacity to export and partly from a very weak productivity of labour, capital and physical inputs in the manufacturing sector, or total factor productivity (TFP).

According to a World Bank study (1988), the growth of the modern manufacturing sector in Morocco between 1970 and 1985 derives in large measure from the growth of inputs. The growth of inputs accounted for 93.2 per cent of the expansion of the sector leaving only 6.8 per cent to be explained by improvement of TFP. The contribution of TFP to the

Mehdi Lehlou is Professor of Economics at the University of Mohammed V of Rabat in Morocco. This article is a translated and edited version of the paper entitled 'Systéme Educatif, Enterprises, et Difficultés de la Transition au Maroc', read at the MAGHTECH'94 conference.

expansion of the manufacturing sector is rather low in view of the fact that in modern economic growth TFP contributes, on average, between 20 and 30 per cent to growth performance.

Two factors could be called to account for the sluggishness and the weak productivity and competitiveness of the Moroccan economy since the early 1980s: the poor performance of the education system expressed in terms of low level of training and the growing preference of firms for unskilled workers.

## Performance of the Moroccan Education System

The Moroccan education system is known to have performed poorly both socially and financially. The rate of illiteracy remains one of the highest in the world, at almost 50 per cent of the adult population. The corresponding rate is 40 per cent for Algeria, 31 per cent for Tunisia and 18 per cent for Madagascar (PNUD 1994). The percentage of Moroccan children in full-time education is also one of the lowest in the world. Enrollment during 1986–88 covered 55 per cent of those in the primary school age group and 36 per cent of those in the secondary school age group.

Such high illiteracy and low schooling rates have prevailed in spite of the fact that public and private expenditure on education have often been higher in Morocco than in many of those countries at the same level of development but with higher schooling rates. This means that the performance of the education system in Morocco is sensitive not merely to the amount of resources earmarked for the sector but rather to the economic prudence with which the funds are allocated and managed across the sector. Until the beginning of the 1990s, Morocco devoted on average 7.3 per cent of its GNP to education and achieved an enrollment rate of 40 per cent for the 4- to 23-year-old age group. Other Arab countries which devoted on average 6 per cent of their GNP to education have managed an enrollment rate of about 50 per cent for the same age bracket, and in countries elsewhere in the world with income levels comparable to that of Morocco, an enrollment rate of 50 per cent has been achieved for the age bracket 4-23 with education expenditure at an average rate of 4.5 per cent of GNP. The average duration of full-time schooling is 5.1 years for all levels of education in Morocco, while it is 8.3 years for all other Arab countries and 7.4 per cent on average for countries elsewhere in the world with a GNP per capita similar to that of Morocco. The low rate of enrollment in the face of high expenditure appears to suggest a tendency towards 'education-deepening' with most of the resources allocated for the expansion of tertiary education. This is not, however, the case. Morocco trains only 11 engineers per 1000 inhabitants as against, for example, 77 in Tunisia, 154 in Turkey, 344 in Mexico and 358 in Singapore (World Bank 1993).

TABLE 1

GENERAL ECONOMIC, DEMOGRAPHIC AND SCHOOLING INDICATORS

| | GNP/ head ($) | GNP growth % 1980/89 | Pop. [106] | Pop. Growth % 1990/98 | Ratio expend % | % Urban pop | Educ. as % of GNP | Educ. as % of Budget | % Invest. in Educat. budget | Gross school rate 4-23 years | Average schooling duration |
|---|---|---|---|---|---|---|---|---|---|---|---|
| Morocco | 900 | 1.3 | 25.1 | 2.4 | 73 | 48.5 | 7.3 | 25 | 26.4 | 40 | 5.1 |
| Algeria | 2170 | 0 | 25.4 | 3.1 | 85 | 44.7 | 9..9 | 27 | 26.6 | 53 | 9.1 |
| Tunisia | 1260 | 0.6 | 8.2 | 2.5 | 65 | 54.3 | 6.3 | 14.8 | 10.6 | 54 | 8.2 |
| Libya | n.a. | -9.9 | 4.45 | 4.1 | 89 | 70.2 | 10.1 | 20.9 | 26.4 | n.a. | n.a. |
| Egypt | 630 | n.a. | 54.1 | 2.7 | 74 | 48.8 | 5.2 | 10.1 | 8.1 | 55 | 9.6 |
| Bahrain | n.a. | -4.6 | 0.5 | 4.1 | 50 | 82.9 | 5.7 | n.a. | 5.1 | 67 | 10.5 |
| Iraq | n.a. | n.a. | 18.9 | 3.6 | 91 | 74.2 | 3.8 | 6.4 | 9.4 | 51 | 7.8 |
| Jordan | 1730 | -3 | 4.3 | 3.9 | 95 | 68.1 | 6.9 | 13 | 8.5 | n.a. | 10.4 |
| Kuwait | 16,380 | -2.1 | 2.1 | 4.3 | 65 | 95.6 | 5.5 | 12.1 | 5.2 | 64 | 9.2 |
| Oman | 5220 | 5.3 | 1.5 | 4.1 | 89 | 10.6 | 4 | 14.9 | 19.7 | 50 | 7.3 |
| Qatar | n.a. | -10.5 | 1.4 | 4.8 | 56 | 89.5 | 5.6 | n.a. | 20.5 | 68 | 10.5 |
| Saudi Arabia | 6230 | -5.9 | 14.1 | 4.2 | 87 | 77.3 | 7.5 | 16.2 | 19.2 | 44 | 5.6 |
| Syria | 1020 | -2.1 | 12.5 | 3.6 | 98 | 51.8 | 4.1 | 13.1 | 11.8 | 60 | 9.4 |
| UAE | 18,430 | -8.2 | 1.6 | 4.6 | 46 | 77.8 | 2.4 | 14.2 | 5.1 | 66 | 9.4 |
| Yemen | 640 | n.a. | 8 | 3 | 99 | 43.3 | 6.1 | 23.5 | 13.4 | 42 | n.a. |
| Somalia | 170 | -1.3 | 7.6 | 3.5 | 96 | 36.4 | n.a. | n.a. | 22.6 | 7 | n.a. |
| Sudan | n.a. | -1.8 | 25.2 | 3 | 87 | 22 | n.a. | n.a. | n.a. | 24 | n.a. |
| Mauritania | 490 | -2.2 | 20 | 2.7 | 85 | 42.1 | 4.9 | 22.7 | n.a. | 23 | 3.9 |
| Sub-total* | 1190 | -2.2 | 17.9 | 3.2 | 86 | 56 | 6.6 | 17.1 | 16 | 51 | 8.4 |
| Total | 4250 | -3 | 102 | 3.4 | 78 | 59 | 6 | 13 | 14.9 | 50 | 8.3 |

* Morocco, Algeria, Tunisia, Libya , Egypt, Iraq, Jordan and Yemen.

Source: UNESCO 1991.

TABLE 2

ENROLLMENT RATES (%)

| | MOROCCO | ARAB STATES[1] | REFERENCE COUNTRIES[2] |
|---|---|---|---|
| Primary | 57 | 90 | 87 |
| Secondary | 34 | 55 | 51 |
| Higher | 10 | 13 | 14 |
| | 50 | 57 | 77 |

Source: World Bank 1994.

Notes: 1. Algeria, Tunisia, Libya, Egypt, Iraq, Jordan, Syria and Yemen.
2. Countries of intermediate and low income bracket of which GNP per capita was in range of 650 to 2500 dollars in 1992.

The fact that Morocco spends a lot for a relatively modest result reflects the economic inefficiency of the manner in which the education system is organised and managed. Structural problems abound constraining the expansion of enrollment. Yet there has been little or no policy effort to date to resolve these problems.

For instance, the education system stands without a common language. Failure to decide on the principal language of instruction for training and apprenticeship, especially in the scientific disciplines, has made the education system weak and incoherent. The educational process has become a bilingual mishmash with its products failing neither to gain proficiency in scientific and technological disciplines, nor mastery of Arabic or French. At present, the arrangement is that the main subjects are taught in Arabic until the baccalaureate level. From there on, the medium of instruction is French. This arrangement has, however, been a cause for educational crisis.

A second aspect of the structural problem underlying the Moroccan education system is its fragmentation which makes the effective application of policy difficult. The gap is significant between both the public and the private sector, between the urban environment and the countryside, and within the urban environment itself, between the schools in the poor and peripheral districts and those in the centre and suburban residential districts.

A third aspect of the structural problem facing the educational system is the instability of its programmes, its curricula, instruments and modes of control. This has resulted in a situation where the rate of repeating has increased at different levels, indicating a decline in the rate of learning. It is estimated that close to 15 per cent of those registered in primary schools and 17 per cent in secondary schools are repeating years. About 35 per cent of those enrolled in the primary schools in general are said to withdraw before completion, often discouraged by the prospect of unemployment after completion of their courses and with degrees and school certificates.

### Recruitment Pattern of Moroccan firms and Degree of R&D Orientation

The illiteracy and enrollment rates indicated above are suggestive of a low level of training of the population in the active age group. This is apparent from Table 3 below which indicates, for example, that about two-thirds of the working age population do not have training that would qualify them for 'good use'.

Ironically enough, the rate of unemployment is observed to be higher among those few with high levels of qualification than among those with primary and secondary education, as shown in Table 4.

Thus the unemployment rate among the non-graduates fell in ten years

TABLE 3

ACTIVE AGE POPULATION (URBAN) ACCORDING TO QUALIFICATION

| Diploma | Percentage |
|---|---|
| Without diploma | 63.4 |
| Primary studies certificate | 14.7 |
| Secondary studies certificate | 9.6 |
| Baccalaureate and equivalent diplomas | 3.1 |
| Higher degrees | 3.5 |
| Diploma of junior executive | 1.6 |
| Diploma and certificates of ability or of professional qualification | 4.1 |

*Source*: Ministry of Planning, *Population Active Urbaine*, Statistics Department, 1988.

TABLE 4

RATE OF UNEMPLOYMENT BY LEVEL OF QUALIFICATION IN URBAN
AREAS BETWEEN 1984 AND 1993 (%)

| | 1984 | 1985 | 1987 | 1990 | 1991 | 1992 | 1993 |
|---|---|---|---|---|---|---|---|
| Without diploma | 17.6 | 12 | 11.8 | 11.2 | 11.3 | 11 | 10.7 |
| CEP (Primary Certificate) | 25.2 | 19.1 | 18.9 | 20.8 | 22.7 | 21.4 | 21.5 |
| CES (Secondary Certificate) | 21.3 | 22 | 25.8 | 29.3 | 30.1 | 27.1 | 24.8 |
| Baccalaureate | 14.6 | 17.8 | 27.6 | 36 | 38.8 | 28.6 | 31.2 |
| Higher degree | 3.5 | 4.8 | 6.2 | 8.9 | 10.9 | 10.4 | 13.4 |
| Professional degree | 27.6 | 25.1 | 27.4 | 32 | 33.5 | 33.5 | 32.5 |
| Altogether | n.a. | 8.3 | 12.8 | 15. | 16 | 15.9 | 15.9 |

*Source*: Ministry of Planning, *Enquetes sur l'Emploi Urbaine*, Statistics Department 1993.

by almost 7 per cent, going down from 17.6 per cent in 1984 to 10.7 in 1993, and almost tripled among the graduates going up from 14.6 per cent in 1984 to 38.8 in 1991 before falling to 31.2 in 1993. A similar pattern is observed for those with higher degrees. Unemployment among holders of degrees and technicians with professional training in 1991 was three times more than in 1984. It is important to observe here that the global data mask the difference between the graduates with university education (except medicine and engineering), for whom the unemployment rate increased from 6.5 per cent in 1984 to 23.3 in 1990, and the graduates with non-university education (schools, medicine, normal training, etc.) for whom unemployment remained stable for the period at around 11 per cent. The situation of the holders of degrees of professional training, already very bad in 1984 (with an unemployment rate of 27.6 per cent), deteriorated further with the proportion of the unemployed among this active age category reaching 33.5 per cent in 1991 and 32.5 in 1993.

It appears that in Morocco, the increase in the level of education does not go hand in hand with the decrease in the unemployment rate. On the other hand, the chances of employment appear – ironically enough – to increase with illiteracy. This may sound absurd, but there are several reasons for this state of affairs to have occurred. A major factor in this regard is the preponderance of employers, in particular those in the informal sector who prefer a labour force without qualification in order to minimise cost. For them the training acquired in schools and other centres is of no use in the workshops, and training for the best of the recruits could be provided in-house. Such employers would often prefer to take on labour without any qualification, particularly if it would accept their conditions, including their organisational or disciplinary norms. Recruits with few or no qualifications are likely to accept the work they are offered without any condition regarding either salary or the duration of work. On the other hand, those with a higher level of education would tend to be anxious about remuneration and the status of their jobs; but this would make them unpopular among employers.

The competitiveness of the technologies which Moroccan firms adopt and their commitment to research and development leave a lot to be desired. According to the World Bank (1993), the level of investment devoted to the development, acquisition and diffusion of technology by firms in Moroccan manufacturing industry is rather low. Not surprisingly, firms are generally weak and scarcely competitive in the world market. In 1990, Morocco's expenditure on technology was around 350 million dollars, about 1.4 per cent of GDP, and less than 2 per cent of gross returns from the manufacturing sector. This relates to the acquisition of foreign technology, including equipment, goods and consultancy services. Expenditure concerning the diffusion of technology, in terms of technical assistance between Moroccan enterprises is negligible. Expenditure on R&D only increased to around 50 million dollars (0.2 per cent of GDP in 1990), a proportion which falls short of the ones achieved by, say, India (0.9 per cent in 1987), Korea (2 per cent in 1987), Brazil (0.6 per cent in 1986) and Mexico (0.6 per cent in 1986). Industrialised countries invest on average between 2 and 3 per cent of their GDP in R&D (World Bank 1993).

At the level of the firm, as at the national economic level, training aimed at human resources development and investment in R&D are crucial for enhancing competitiveness. At the level of the firm, new needs, linked to the growing complexity of production processes, would call for more communication, better circulation of information, and a better trained and qualified human resource factor. Competitiveness at international level will thus require the firm to be specialised and professionalised with emphasis on R&D activities.

At the global level, the competitive drive has led to a reduction in manufacturing goods and services. This implies the growing significance of research and design tasks.

Interdependence between economies and the growth of international trade create conditions for greater competitiveness where those with the best qualified human resources can call the tune because they possess the most scientific and technological mastery, skills and know-how. For instance, Korea annually trains almost 300,000 graduates of higher education (276,500 in 1989), among whom almost 41,000 are engineers, for a country of 43 million people, while Morocco, with 26 million inhabitants, trains about 16,000 – that is a ratio of 8 to 100 graduates between the two countries – a ratio which by itself explains the difference in income, productivity and growth between the two economies (UNESCO 1991).

## Conclusion

From the discussion above, the following points emerge by way of conclusion:

- The prevailing economic and social system in Morocco is largely conditioned by policy priorities aimed at a 'balanced budget'. This has led to reduced public expenditures and has involved retrenchment, including compression of salaries and limitation of administrative employment; cuts in public health and education have been particularly sensitive to the application of this contractionist policy.

- Structural adjustment appears to have led Morocco to move more and more towards a 'bazaar economy' rather than a modern market economy. A market economy implies the availability of a large number of investors, producers, sellers, buyers and consumers, acting as free agents in their own rights, while a bazaar economy is characterised by the presence of only traders and consumers and the absence of investors and producers of wealth and employment.

- There is a real 'primarisation' of the Moroccan economy. Even the traditionally skill-driven aspect of the tertiary sector is now dominated by activities that are being increasingly deskilled as evidenced, for example, by the increase in the share of family employment in total employment.

All this indicates the contradiction between the liberalisation and internationalisation objectives through structural adjustment programmes and the means adopted to attain these.

REFERENCES

Ministry of Planning (1994), *Enquetes sur l'Emploi Urbain*, Department of Statistics, Rabat.
Ministry of Planning (1988), *Population Active Urbanie*, Department of Statistics, Rabat.

PNUD (1994), *World Report on Human Development*.
UNESCO (1991), *World Education Report*, Paris.
World Bank (1988), *The Impact of Liberalisation on Market and Industrial Adjustment*, Washington, DC.
World Bank (1993a), *Development de l'Industrie Privè en Maroc* Vol.1. Washington, DC.
World Bank (1993b), *Rapport sur le Renforcement du Secteur Privè en Maroc*, Washington, DC.
World Bank (1994), *Population et Resources Humaines*, Washington, DC.

# Tertiary Education and Technological Progress in Transitional Economies: Whither Demand Pull?

## GIRMA ZAWDIE

*This article probes why investment in education in general and in the tertiary sector in particular has failed to translate into technological progress in developing countries with reference to the case of the Maghreb. Universities in such countries produce graduates a significant proportion of whom often fail to be absorbed into productive employment. Structural adjustment programmes which seek to curtail expansion of tertiary education on account of broadening opportunities for primary and secondary education, however sound, beg the question that long run growth feeds on the capability to absorb and adopt technologies and introduce innovative systems of production and management. Reformed and reoriented, the tertiary system in the Maghreb could provide the basis for promoting need-based research and development which could impact on the production function of the economy of the region. The problem of tertiary education is not so much that it has received too much emphasis as that it has been wrongly oriented, promoting 'supply push' rather than responding to perceived and actual technology needs.*

## Introduction

Policy concern with educational expansion in developing countries stems from the presumption that investment in education is crucial for technological progress and economic growth. But in many developing countries poor economic performance is observed in the face of marked educational expansion, and 'graduate' unemployment and underemployment prevail in spite of a growing demand for skills. This has led many to ask whether continued investment in tertiary education would be justifiable

Girma Zawdie is Lecturer in Development Studies and Director of Studies in the David Livingstone Institute of Overseas Development Studies (DLIODS) at the University of Strathclyde, Glasgow, UK.

at all in the light of prevailing socio-economic circumstances in developing countries. Emphasis on tertiary education, it is argued, would mean high opportunity costs for developing economies. It diverts resources from primary and secondary sectors and generates skill profiles that are scarcely compatible with the skill demand profiles in such economies. If the growing number of university and college graduates in developing countries often find themselves 'overqualified' in relation to the prevailing skill demand profile, the question then is what is the relevance of tertiary education to the objective of economic growth?

The scepticism expressed against investment in tertiary education is not without reason. It does not, however, deny tertiary education an important role in the making of economic progress. Rather it confirms that the link between education and growth is not as straightforward as is often assumed, and suggests the need to explore the factors behind the lack of correspondence between educational expansion and economic growth.

Studies in economic growth have evolved significantly over the last four decades (Solow 1956, Denison 1967, Mansfield 1968, Leonards 1971, Williams 1973, Griliches 1984, Easterlin 1981, Roemer 1990, Barro and Sala-i-Martin 1995). Thus, what started as a simple neo-classical model in the 1950s, explaining growth in terms of accumulation of capital and labour, given technology and subject to the law of diminishing returns, has in recent years sought to achieve empirical and theoretical adequacy by focusing on technological change – previously imputed as a 'residual' component – as a point of departure in explaining long-run growth. This would give pride of place to the role of education, including research and development; but, despite the growing body of empirical work on this line, the manner in which the 'education factor' translates into economic growth remains unclear. The link between the two is often complex. Amsden (1989) resorts to the broad brush to explain the paradox emerging from the link: there is no educational equivalent to Say's Law, she argues, whereby merely to produce educated people would *ipso facto* generate demand for their skills. This would imply that education provides a necessary but not a sufficient condition for economic growth. But to conclude from this that developing countries, particularly those in Africa, have already had too much education and that they should shift the policy emphasis to factors other than education would be to misunderstand the nature of the problem in these countries. The issue at hand is not so much the unemployability of the output of tertiary education in developing countries – a point nonetheless borne out by evidence – as it is about the broad policy regimes within which the apparently counterproductive character of tertiary education has evolved.

In this article we argue that the limited scope for technological change and the collapse of economic growth in many parts of the developing world, including the Maghreb region, stems largely from the failure of policy to match education with the prevailing social, economic and technological circumstances. Education in these countries has predominantly been of the 'supply push' type in the sense that its provision has been 'state engineered' to suit the post-independence political aspirations of the ruling elite. Education policy was consequently geared primarily to the manning of sprawling public sector bureaucracies and to meeting the administrative, technical and research skill requirements of the largely foreign-aid supported import substitution projects operating imported technologies within heavily protected markets. Skill was thus provided, given the technology, but for lack of absorptive capacity in the economy, the imported technologies seldom succeeded in deepening and widening the stock of skills and in promoting indigenous technological progress.

In principle, education is expected to impact on economic growth through its effect on technological progress. Educational and technological progress interact most fruitfully when general economic policy and education policy are congruent, and when the magnitude, character and content of education are consistent with the technical possibilities in an economy at any given point in time. Educational priorities – and hence education policy – should, of course, change as an economy moves through different levels of development. Growth will be large or small depending on the magnitude of technical progress; and technical progress will be little or great as the educational system is or is not geared to its promotion. Generally speaking, at lower levels of development, investment in primary and secondary education is considered to be more relevant to the objective of capacity building and long-run technological progress than the expansion of tertiary education. However robust the evidence in support of this, the significance of the role that tertiary education plays in the process of growth and development cannot be overlooked. Developments in managerial and science and technology-based skills arising from the tertiary sector are crucial for the effective utilisation of the human and material resources available to developing economies and hence for the development in such economies of 'social capability', which constitutes the basis for technological progress and long-term economic growth (Abramovitz 1986).

The remainder of this article will first address the conceptual basis of the link between investment in tertiary education, the process of economic growth and the growing trend in the unemployment and underemployment of the educated. Based on this, the article will explore strategies for translating investment in tertiary education into technological progress and sustainable economic growth in developing countries with reference to experience in the Maghreb.

## Conceptual Framework

The expansion of productive employment in a not yet fully developed economy would depend, in large measure, on the extent to which the restrictive effect of structural bottlenecks on growth can be mitigated by policy measures. Measures targeted at the quantity and quality supply of factor inputs and the level of technological know-how would necessarily call for investment in education at all levels, if in a priority order. But while the effective absorption of crude labour depends much upon the rate of output growth within the confines of the production possibility curve, the productive employment of skilled manpower deriving from the secondary and the tertiary sector would turn on the rate at which technological improvements take place in the economy, creating opportunities for the substitution of imported factor inputs by local ones. The development of indigenous technological capability thus improves prospects for the absorption of high level technical manpower and also provides for the expansion of the economy, enabling it to absorb more and more of the vast reserve of unskilled and semiskilled labour without, however, compromising productivity growth.

In developing countries, industrialisation objectives have been pursued with the optimistic assumption that technologies appropriate to their respective circumstances would be readily available from the 'world technology shelf' (Stewart 1978, Huq and Zawdie 1988). The extent to which imported technologies prompt and support the development of indigenous technological capability would, however, depend, *inter alia,* on the orientation of the educational strategy and the extent of its integration with the production function of the economy. Properly oriented, the generation of high level professional skills, far from marginalising unskilled and semi-skilled labour, can provide the necessary condition for the effective absorption of such labour. The converse is, however, what is observed in many countries where inappropriate policies have led to the pursuit of perverse educational priorities and job markets operating on the implicit assumption of substitutability between high and low level skills. This we shall see below. But let us first consider the implication for technological progress, productive employment and sustainable economic growth of the supply of high level skills deriving from tertiary education.

The link between the provision of high level skills and the prospects of technological progress may be illustrated by using the simple production function scheme relating GDP on the Y-axis and the quantum of skilled, semi-skilled and unskilled labour in productive employment on the X-axis. At the initial stage of the growth process, where developing countries in general find themselves, aggregate production function may be represented by OA. For a given level of technology, defining the skill-mix requirement per unit of output and the absorption capacity of the economy, aggregate employment has its limit at Oa. The supply of highly skilled manpower in excess of what is warranted by the absorption capacity of the economy becomes effectively redundant, and would often find itself a convenient outlet either by competing with semi-skilled and unskilled labour for available employment opportunities or by emigrating to skill-deficit economies. Removing constraints on the absorption capacity of the economy would require, *inter alia,* development of a science and technology capability and the provision of managerial and organisation skills across the spectrum of economic activities.

In seeking to explain the mechanism which links education to productivity of labour in employment, contemporary economic thought has downgraded the value of cognitive learning – previously seen as the main contribution of education to economic growth (Parnes 1962, Tinbergen and Bos 1965, Bennett 1967) – and emphasised instead the 'screening role' of educational institutions. This performs a useful role for employers in certifying that job applicants have the personality traits they seek. In the lower reaches of the economy, the traits sought include punctuality, persistence and discipline. Further up the scale the qualities required include self-esteem, self-reliance, versatility and capacity for leadership. On this view, employers hire people not for what they know but for what they are. The specific skills needed for work in particular activities, it is argued, are acquired on the job rather than through formal education. The persistence of higher returns to higher rather than lower educational qualifications is explained by the existence of internal labour markets (Blaug 1972a, 1972b, 1985).

FIGURE 1

SKILL DRIVEN GROWTH TRENDS

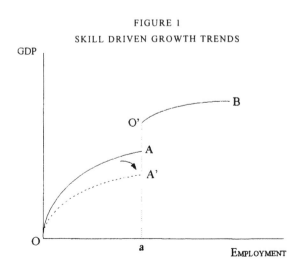

The problem with this view is that when it comes to policy, it tends to be nihilistic. If general and not specific skills are what matter most, it is not clear as to what is to determine the scale, structure and content of the educational system. Moreover, recent studies appear to have restored some of the earlier faith in human investment and growth accounting by linking wage-measured productivity gains to cognitive skills (Knight and Sabot 1991), and by widening the definition of investment and focusing on the rate of growth of investment (Anderson 1990).

Higher degrees of education may serve as a basis for labour market screening. But policy overemphasis on the screening role of education, deriving from a static view of the economy with fixed job opportunities and with no scope for technological progress, could deprive education of a sense of dynamic purpose. Consequently, competition for limited jobs often results in the pursuit of impressive, if irrelevant, educational qualifications. This approach to education is hardly capacity building, and indeed maybe counterproductive (Dore 1976, 1980). Higher education, in particular, should be sought for its dynamic contribution to technological progress and economic growth, rather than as a means of displacing unskilled labour in activities where the use of such labour would, in fact, be more economic. This, however, calls for a reorientation of educational policy in the light of prevailing socio-economic conditions and future opportunities, and also for the provision of the effective management of resources available to the economy.

The shift from OA to O'B and beyond represents improvements in indigenous capability in production, investment and innovation, attributable in large measure to the integrated management of education, technology and economic policies. At successively higher levels of growth, activities become increasingly diversified and skill-intensive, and the economy achieves higher degrees of competitiveness with real wages rising. This has been the experience of newly industrialising countries such as Korea. It is not, however, observed in many developing economies where the experience has been one of being locked into low technology equilibrium in the face of increased investment in education. In most of these countries education policy is not matched with economic policy; nor economic policy with resource endowment. Consequently, the influence of the education function on the production function of the economy – and hence on its absorption capacity – has been marginal; and this has left the economy fragile and potentially vulnerable to demographic pressures and other external shocks. Hence possibilities for 'growth reversals' as shown in the diagram by the shift of the aggregate production function from OA to OA'. Growth reversal is associated with chronic balance of payments difficulties, the persistence of government deficits, indebtedness, massive unemployment and political instability.

A number of African countries are known to have experienced negative growth during the 1970s. This contrasts sharply with the experience during the 1960s when post-colonial national economies grew relatively rapidly. The growth achieved during the 1960s did not, however, derive from capability development. It resulted partly from windfalls obtained from favourable export markets and partly from liberal foreign capital inflows which contributed more to the entrenchment of highly protected and inefficient import substituting capital intensive projects with marginal learning effects than to the enhancement of the absorption capacity of the national economies. Thus, in effect, a good part of the investments during the 1960s represented wasted capital, so that the initial growth effect of investment could not be sustained in later years when the supply of foreign capital was to become tight and export markets for traditional commodities unfavourable. Indeed, by the 1970s debt servicing on account of the capital borrowed during earlier years had become a serious burden on African economies, as these economies had not grown enough to pay off borrowed capital. Moreover, following the oil crisis of the 1970s and the recession which seized the world economy during the 1980s, traditional export markets were no longer buoyant and favourable enough to provide a robust export earning base for debt servicing as well as growth. The upshot of all this for African economies was growth reversal.

The commitment of African governments for increased expenditure in the provision of education, far from providing the solution to the problem of growth reversal, was part of the problem itself. This was because education policy in contemporary Africa has for the most part been based on the Emersonian tenet that 'if one made a better mousetrap the whole world would beat a path to one's doorstep'. This approach to education policy cannot, however, be productive of technological progress and sustainable growth to the extent that it begs the question as to what makes the mousetrap better. Supply does not create its own demand.

Concern with the problem of growth reversals has in recent years led to policy prescriptions in the form of structural adjustment. However, structural adjustment policies recommended by the World Bank and the IMF have largely been short-termist in orientation, focusing on retrenchment of public expenditure, control of money supply and liberalisation policies aimed at correcting price distortions in the factor and product markets. Structural adjustment of economies vulnerable to growth reversals would, however, be incomplete if the package of policies stopped short of addressing the supply side problems which account for the stunting of growth. This has led to a major revision of the structural adjustment policy package to accommodate the long-term view of the economy through involvement of the state in capacity building programmes aimed at enhancing production, investment and innovation capabilities. The role of education is absolutely crucial in this. But for education to be effective in its capacity enhancing mission, it is important that it be matched with economic policy, so that educational programmes may cater for the prevailing skill demand of the economy as well as providing the technology basis for its future growth.

### 'Supply Push' versus 'Technology Infusion'

Historically, technological progress in the now mature industrialised economies started with the gradual development of 'home grown' technology. This involved continuous, if painstaking, attempts at invention and innovation through the empirical process of trial and error. The professionalisation of research and development at a later stage in their development accelerated the rate of technological progress by providing a scientific approach to the development of indigenous capability in invention and innovation and hence for the accumulation of 'knowledge capital'. Contemporary technological progress in these economies derives from a balanced contribution of 'science push' forces at the upstream reach (involving basic research) and 'demand pull' forces at the downstream reach (involving applied research and development).

In the newly industrialising countries (NICs) such as Korea, Taiwan, Singapore, Malaysia, India, Brazil and Mexico, the secret for technological progress rests on their ability to adapt, adopt and emulate imported technologies through the critical learning of the state of the art provided by the 'world technology shelf'. Education – and particularly higher education – has been a major facilitating factor in this exercise. But, as mentioned above, the effectiveness of education as a basis for technological progress would very much depend on the nature of economic policy and prevailing socio-economic circumstances. This is apparent from the Korean experience. Until 1960 educational expansion in Korea led to educated unemployment. Since a policy change in 1960, however, educational expansion has been associated with rapid growth and there has been a virtuous circle: as education expands, it makes purposeful transfer of technology quicker and more efficient than otherwise. GDP expands making it easier to expand education and providing jobs for the educated as well as for the unskilled and the semi-skilled. This in turn enhances prospects for technological progress through learning by doing, learning by adapting, learning by design and learning by innovation (Krauss 1989).

In many African countries, investment in tertiary education has not produced a research and development capability, or where it has, as in the case of the middle income Maghreb countries, R&D initiatives have for the most part remained remote from industrial practice (Oukil 1989). Much of this is due to lack of need assessment and policy targeting of expenditure in education, and the absence of a network of interactive links between institutions of higher education and industry. Like the technology function, the education function in developing countries in general has been supply-dominated. Both functions have been complementary, one providing the basis for the other; and in their interactive relationship the two together have created and consolidated a monopolistic structure of production relations, thus effectively narrowing the scope for competition, for innovative capacity building and hence for the sustainable expansion of the economy. Consequently, while policy favoured 'supply push' technology and the education function, targeted at the modern sector of the economy, remained subservient to the prevailing technology function, the scope for indigenous innovation has been limited to learning by tinkering in the so-called 'informal sector' (Matthews 1973). But to the extent that the informal sector is disorganised and irregular, it cannot be expected to provide a robust basis for exploiting to the full the indigenous innovative potential.

The 'supply push' phenomenon was created by the absence of any interactive link between those developing technologies and those targeted to be users of these technologies. This phenomenon thrived on the assumptions that availability of technology was the principal constraint on growth and that demand for technologies was given, if supply can be guaranteed, demand can be cultivated through diffusion. The 'supply push' trend was consequently reinforced by the policy bias in favour of central planning and import substituting industrialisation. 'Supply push' thus often led to the adoption of inappropriate technologies in developing countries, technologies which have had little or no learning effect. As such, it represented missed opportunities by alienating demand. It has consequently been growth restrictive. This calls for a major revision of policy in favour of decentralisation and competition so as to allow the effective expression of need profiles across the economic spectrum and to enable the education and technology functions in the economy to cater for these needs. The transition from a centralised to a decentralised system of economic management cannot, however, be expected to be instantaneous. Nor does it occur as a smooth process. Entrenched policy preconceptions deriving from the culture of central planning have to be revamped, and vested interests created and sustained by state-induced monopoly culture have to be dislodged to give way for the institution of a competitive culture. This process of 'creative destruction' would take time, which could be long or short, depending on how actively and judiciously the state applies itself in providing the capacity that would allow the efficient interaction between the supply and the demand functions of the economy.

The provision of education in the framework of a university–industry interactive system is crucial for capacity building. The question is one of drawing a balance between the skill development objective and the 'knowledge accumulation' objective of education (Roemer 1990). The former addresses the prevailing demand profile of the economy, and the latter provides the basis for technological progress. The two functions of education are not unrelated, but what is important is that the balance between them is bound to vary at different stages of economic growth. Thus, for example, in a predominantly peasant economy, the dominant function of education would be to equip farmers with skills that would help them raise their productivity. Tertiary education aimed at the accumulation of 'knowledge capital' would, in the circumstances, remain of marginal significance until the economy developed a sufficiently diversified structure. Activities at a higher level of development would call for high level skills and R&D support in order to be competitive and efficient. The role of education in the process of growth and development is thus not simply to enhance the diffusion of given technologies, perpetuating the 'supply push' syndrome, but to provide the broad basis – what Abramovitz calls 'social capability' – for the development indigenous technology through learning by production, learning by adaptation and learning by innovation (Dahlman, Ross-Larson and Westphal 1987). It is this process of 'technology infusion', rather than technology transfer and diffusion, as in the conventional sense, which would enhance transition of economies from low income to middle income and then to high income status. The transition from supply push technology transfer and diffusion to need-oriented strategy of technology development is demonstrated in Figure 2.

FIGURE 2

UNIVERSITY–INDUSTRY LINK BASED ON NEED-DRIVEN SYSTEM OF
TECHNOLOGY DEVELOPMENT

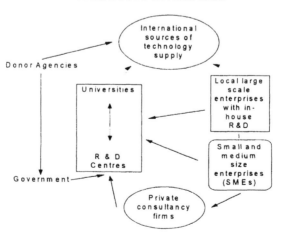

## Education and the Economy in the Maghreb

The three core Maghreb countries fall in the category of 'low middle income' economies. In 1993, per capita income was $1,040 for Morocco, $1,720 for Tunisia and $1,780 for Algeria. In all three countries, the share of services in GDP is preponderant (51 per cent in Tunisia, 53 per cent in Morocco and 43 per cent in Algeria in 1993), followed by industry (32 per cent in Tunisia, 31 per cent in Morocco and 43 per cent in Algeria). In all the three countries, too, the share of industry in GDP has increased between 1970 and 1993: from 24 to 31 per cent in Tunisia, from 27 to 32 per cent in Morocco, and from 41 to 43 per cent in Algeria. But during the same period the share of manufacturing GDP increased for Tunisia (from 10 to 19 per cent) and for Morocco (from 16 to 18 per cent), while it declined for Algeria (from 15 to 11 per cent). Meanwhile, the share of agriculture declined for Tunisia (from 20 to 18 per cent) and for Morocco (from 20 to 14 per cent), while it increased for Algeria (from 11 to 13 per cent) (World Bank 1994).

Prospects for moving to higher levels of economic status for these countries would largely depend on their ability to internalise the innovative products of science and technology and to become innovative and competitive. The three countries have followed different paths of economic development since independence in the late 1950s and early 1960s. Industrialisation by import substitution and international sub-contracting have been some of the approaches used. All three have had a good measure of technological and scientific experience over the last three decades, with science and technology policies and programmes constituting an integral component of their development strategies.

The Maghreb economies are significantly better off by the average African standard, where average per capita income is $520 (1993). But as in most of the African economies, growth in the Maghreb has been deteriorating in recent years. For instance, for the periods 1970–80 and 1980–90, the average annual growth rates of GDP per capita were respectively 1.5 and zero per cent for Algeria; 3.2 and 1.6 per cent for Morocco; and 4.1 and 1.3 per cent for Tunisia (World Bank 1994). One possible explanation for the deteriorating trend of economic growth in these countries is that science and technology policy has done little to prompt the development of innovative capability.

This is apparent from the Table 1 showing incremental capital output ratios (ICORs) for the three countries, which are not only unfavourable but also show a deteriorating trend.

The ICOR data for the three countries offer no evidence of innovation of any significance, with the ICORs having doubled in each case. Indeed, the occurrences of innovation in all three cases have been few and far between,

TABLE 1
INCREMENTAL CAPITAL OUTPUT RATIOS (ICORs) FOR
THE MAGHREB COUNTRIES

| Country | 1970–1980 | 1980–1993 |
|---------|-----------|-----------|
| Morocco | 3.2       | 6.2       |
| Tunisia | 3.1       | 7.8       |
| Algeria | 7.8       | 13.8      |

Source: Based on data from World Bank (1994).

while dependence on the import of foreign technologies has remained unabated over the years. For instance, of the total patents registered in each of the Maghreb countries, the proportion deriving from foreign sources has invariably been more than 85 per cent. For the early 1980s, the corresponding proportion was 92 per cent for Morocco, 89 per cent for Tunisia, and 99 per cent for Algeria (Akeb, 1984). All three are now facing the problem of technological obsolescence, and would need to renew their technology stocks, but find themselves under severe economic constraint to do so either through the mechanism of international technology transfer or through the development of indigenous innovative capability.

One study on Algeria (Oukil 1989) shows that the development of innovative capability indicated by registered patents has been rather sluggish (see Table 3 below). This trend would raise questions as to the efficacy of the science and technology policy which Algeria has pursued assiduously since its independence in 1962 to make the research and skill development role of tertiary education purpose-oriented. According to the same study, research and development activities propped by government funding have remained remote from industrial practice. Most of the observed incremental innovations derived from the informal R&D effort of industrial establishments with hardly any back up from universities and R&D institutions. Moreover, shortfalls in industrial skill supply have been in evidence, suggesting that activities in the tertiary education sector have generally remained poorly linked to the needs of industry, despite the preoccupation with science and technology policy.

In Morocco, 30 to 35 per cent of university graduates are said to be vulnerable to explicit unemployment. A strong tendency is also observed for industrial firms in Morocco to recruit those with little or no education and to spend little, if any, on research and technology (Lehlou 1994). Not surprisingly, the percentage of Moroccan school age children in full-time education is known to be the lowest in the region as may be seen from Table 2.

TABLE 2

ENROLLMENT IN PRIMARY, SECONDARY AND TERTIARY EDUCATION

| | Primary | | Secondary | | Tertiary | |
|---|---|---|---|---|---|---|
| Country | 1970 | 1992 | 1970 | 1992 | 1980 | 1992 |
| Morocco | 52 | 69 | 13 | 28 | 6 | 10 |
| Tunisia | 100 | 117 | 23 | 43 | 5 | 11 |
| Algeria | 76 | 99 | 11 | 60 | 6 | 12 |

*Source*: World Bank (1994).

TABLE 3

PATENTS REGISTERED IN ALGERIA: 1966–86

| Year | Total Patents Registered | National (per cent) | Foreign (per cent) |
|---|---|---|---|
| 1966 | 244 | 1.64 | 98.36 |
| 1967 | 415 | 0.72 | 99.23 |
| 1968 | 382 | 2.09 | 97.90 |
| 1969 | 387 | 3.62 | 96.38 |
| 1970 | 390 | 3.59 | 96.41 |
| 1971 | 377 | 2.92 | 97.08 |
| 1972 | 327 | 3.03 | 96.94 |
| 1973 | 350 | 1.43 | 98.57 |
| 1974 | 464 | 2.37 | 97.62 |
| 1975 | 586 | 1.02 | 98.97 |
| 1976 | 466 | 1.72 | 98.28 |
| 1977 | 433 | 2.78 | 97.22 |
| 1978 | 462 | 1.52 | 98.48 |
| 1979 | 423 | 1.18 | 98.81 |
| 1980 | 354 | 1.13 | 98.87 |
| 1981 | 353 | 3.12 | 96.88 |
| 1982 | 327 | 2.14 | 97.85 |
| 1983 | 293 | 5.12 | 94.88 |
| 1984 | 345 | 8.69 | 91.30 |
| 1985 | 277 | 6.86 | 93.14 |
| 1986 | 257 | 12.84 | 87.15 |

*Source*: Oukil (1989), based on data from INAPI (1979 and 1988).

This makes Morocco a low wage economy attractive to investors but without a sound skill and technology base for sustainable growth. The application of structural adjustment programmes appears to have reinforced the deskilling trend in the economy. Technology transfer practices provided capacity for the employment of unskilled or semi-skilled labour but did little to promote the development of organisational and managerial capability. With expatriate technology suppliers being also responsible for the design, construction and commissioning of projects as well as for provision of technical, organisational and managerial skills, little room is left for the development of local skills in project management. A similar pattern is also observed in Algeria where project operation, co-ordination, monitoring and organisation of production is for the most part covered by expatriate expertise. Saad (1994) notes that technology transfer arrangements have not, in any significant way, sought to promote the development of local skills to 'adapt and modify imported technology according to local requirements'.

It is thus apparent from the Maghreb experience that technology transfer hardly helped directly or indirectly to enhance learning, and hence the accumulation of knowledge and technological progress. Nor is there any significant evidence that tertiary education helped to meet industry's needs through the production of relevant skills and the provision of R&D support. The products of tertiary education, far from creating capacity through the management and development of technology, have found themselves landed on the margins of the local labour markets, alienated, dissatisfied and inclined to emigrate. At this rate, tertiary education in the Maghreb has still a long way to go before it can make an impact on the production functions of the national economies in the region.

## Conclusion

In the Maghreb countries, transition from low middle to high middle income status would require the application of a science and technology policy that is capable of stimulating the development of indigenous innovation at all levels of industrial production and reducing dependence on the import of technology from abroad, particularly if this does not translate into the development of a local capability. This could be achieved by adopting a science and technology policy that would bring the activities of universities and research centres closer to the needs of industry. This means that universities will have to be reorganised and research and training programmes defined in the light of the prevailing needs in the economy. The economy will also need to be liberalised, enabling micro-enterprises to articulate their needs and thus providing the demand basis for the development of a research and consultancy capacity and hence for the expansion of tertiary education.

The link between institutions of tertiary education and R&D centres on the one hand, and industry on the other, could be direct where universities and R&D centres take industrial research and consultancy contracts; or it could be indirect where universities and R&D centres serve a back-up role aimed at enhancing the research and consultancy efforts of private firms engaged in the skill-intensive task of monitoring the specific needs of small and medium size industries and providing for them. This approach, learning from given technologies to be able to improvise for periodically emerging industrial needs, would enhance prospects for the development of indigenous technological capability by reducing the scale of dependence on technology transfer from abroad. It helps industry to be competitive and efficient and tertiary education to be a dynamic vehicle of economic growth.

From this discussion the conclusion emerges that for developing countries to achieve technological progress, it would be crucial for education policy to be matched with economic policy. It has been shown that education – and particularly tertiary education – has failed to translate into technological progress mainly because the policy context within which it evolved has been at fault. Reform and the reorientation of tertiary education and the liberalisation of the economy would be the relevant starting point for rectifying the policy failures of the past and for rehabilitating the role of science and technology as a basis for sustainable economic growth in the Maghreb.

## REFERENCES

Abramovitz, M. (1986), 'Catching Up, Forging Ahead and Falling Behind' *Journal of Economic History,* June.

Akeb, F. (1984), 'Inventeurs s'Abstenir,' in *Algerie Actualites,* No.976, 28/06-4/07.

Amsden, A. (1989), *Asia's Next Giant: South Korea and Late Industrialisation,* London: Oxford University Press.

Anderson, D. (1990), 'Investment and Economic Growth', *World Development,* Vol.18, No.8.

Barro, R. and X. Sala-i-Martin (1995), *Economic Growth,* New York: McGraw Hill.

Bennett, W.S. (1967), 'Educational Change and Economic Development', *Sociology and Education,* Vol.40, No.2.

Blaug, M. ((1972a), 'Economics of Educational Planning in Developing Countries', *Prospects,* Vol.2, No.4, pp.431–41.

Blaug, M. (1972b), 'The Correlation Between Education and Earnings: What Does It Signify?', *Higher Education,* Vol.1, No.1, pp.53–76.

Blaug, M. (1985), 'Where Are We Now in the Economics of Education?', *Economics of Education Review,* Vol. 4, No.1, pp.17–28.

Dahlman, C., B. Ross-Larson and L.E. Westphal (1987), 'Managing Technological Development: Lessons from the Newly Industrialising Countries', *World Development,* Vol.15, No.6, pp.759–75.

Denison, E.F. (1967), *Why Growth Rates Differ: Post War Experience in Nine Western Countries,* Washington, DC: Brookings Institute.

Dore, R. (1976), *The Diploma Disease: Education, Qualification and Development,* London: Allen & Unwin.

Dore, R. (1980), 'The Diploma Disease Revisited', in *Selection for Employment versus Education,* Sussex, IDS, Vol.11, No.2, pp.55–61.

Easterlin, R. (1981), 'Why Isn't the Whole World Developed?', *Journal of Economic History,* Mar., pp.1–17.

Griliches, Z. (1984), *R&D, Patents and Productivity,* Chicago: University of Chicago Press.

Huq, M.M. and G. Zawdie (1988), 'Investment in Research and Development: an Economic View Point', *Science, Technology and Development,* Vol.6, No.2.

Knight, J.B. and R.H. Sabot (1991), *Education, Productivity and Inequality,* Oxford University Press.

Krause, L.B. (1989), *Issues of Macro Adjustment Affecting Human Resource Development in Malaysia* (mimeo).

Lehlou, M. (1994), 'Systéme Educatif, Enterprises et Difficultés de la Transition au Maroc', MAGHTECH'94, Sfax, 7–9 Dec.

Leonard, W.N., (1971), 'R and D in Industrial Growth', *Journal of Political Economy*, Vol.79, pp.232–56.

Mansfield, E. (1968), *Industrial Research and Technical Innovation*, New York: Norton.

Matthews, R.C.O. (1973), 'The Contribution of Science and Technology to Economic Development', in Williams, B.R. (1973).

Oukil, M.S. (1989), *The Function and System of Industrial Research and Development in Algeria*, Glasgow, PhD thesis, University of Strathclyde.

Parnes, H.S. (1962), *Forecasting Educational Needs for Economic Development*, Paris: OECD.

Roemer, P. (1990), 'Endogenous Technological Change', *Journal of Political Econom.y*, Vol.98, No.5, pp.71–102.

Saad, M. (1994) 'Transfer and Use of Advanced Technology in LDCs and Impact an Organisational Change and Learning: Evidence from Algeria' MAGHTECH '94.

Solow, R. (1957), 'Technical Change and Aggregate Production Function', *Review of Economics and Statistics*, Vol.39 , pp.312–20.

Stewart, F. (1978), *Technology and Underdevelopment*, London: Macmillan.

Williams, B.R. (ed.) (1973), *Science and Technology in Economic Growth*, London: Macmillan.

World Bank, (1994), *World Development Report: 1994*, Washington, DC: Oxford University Press.

# Science, Technology and Society: What Makes the Culture of Innovation?

## RIADH ZGHAL

*The article is an attempt to explain the evolving culture of innovation in the Maghreb in terms of social and cultural development and against the historical background of colonial occupation. Colonialism brought societies under attack and imposed dominant cultures disrupting the balance of indigenous social forces, marginalising the existing cultural system and instilling the culture of dependence. Decolonisation sought to provide the basis for cultural revival and the conditions for the choice and adoption of foreign technologies and ideas that would promote indigenous innovative effort. The emergence of an active research community is crucial for the advancement of science and technology, but the removal of social barriers is a necessary condition for the culture of innovation to thrive in post-colonial societies.*

## Introduction

A ninth century Arab philosopher, Abou Hayan Attawhidi, wrote, 'Science is made for action and action for life'. Contemporary society now owes its position in large measure to developments in science and technology over the years. In terms of Kuhnian paradigm (Kuhn 1970) science is destined to provide answers to questions and to resolve problems faced in daily life. Science and its application – that is technology – evolve parallel to social demands. This makes science a social product, a cause and consequence of civilisations in history.

As implementation of knowledge and know-how, technology may be defined as a concrete expression of human behaviour obtained through the trial and error procedure of generating innovations. Innovations come in two forms: those concerning the material and technical systems (hardware), and those placed in the category of infra-technology or know-how involving abilities, skills and organisation in the workplace (software). The emergence

Professor Riadh Zghal is Dean of the Faculty of Economics and Management of the University of Sfax, Tunisia. This paper is a translated and edited version of the paper presented at the MAGHTECH'94 conference.

of innovations and their diffusion and application across the socio-economic spectrum have to a great extent been conditioned by prevailing modes of organisational structures and management styles.

In the Maghreb, as in many other less developed regions, there is a wide gulf between science and its application, so that the bulk of the technology that is needed to meet demand has often had to be imported. Moreover, social problems prevail in these countries creating a barrier which frustrates the translation of scientific knowledge into innovative capability and the optimal use of imported technology. This does not, however, mean that developing countries are incapable of innovation and technological progress. For them to be able to exploit their innovative potential they would need to remove the barriers inhibiting technological progress through the application of appropriate policy measures. The object of this article is to highlight the social/cultural obstacles which constrain the emergence of active scientific research communities in countries such as those in the Maghreb. To this end, the remainder of the article is organised in three parts, discussing seriatim the relationship of society to its culture, the perception of science by the research community and the state of research and development from the vantage point of the firm.

## Relationship of Society to its Culture

The cultural system of a society undergoes an evolutionary process, driven by dynamic forces deriving from three fundamental orientations:

- social transformation deriving from 'action of the society on itself' (Touraine 1974), or social dynamism;

- cultural exchange between societies, one society being attracted by other cultures, or cultural transfer and diffusion provoked by 'model cultures' prevailing in dominant societies; and

- the initiative and ability of a cultural system to assimilate created or borrowed models.

These three tendencies influence the evolution of the scientific and innovative culture of society and the relationship between social, economic and technological trends and cultural parameters (Zghal 1994). The evolving pattern of development would depend on whether a society chooses to resolve problems confronting it in the context of its own culture, or whether it would rather opt for borrowed cultures.

In the context of colonial influence, societies find themselves subject to domination. This means adoption perforce of cultural parameters, which, being alien to them, restrict their creative capacity. Societies under

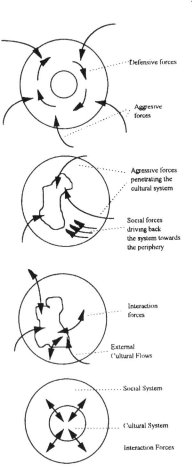

**Figure 1. Societies under attack**

The interaction forces between
social systems transform themselves
in defensive forces against the
attack. The cultural system hardens
and freezes

Defensive forces

Aggresive
forces

**Figure 2. Dominated Societies**

The cultural system is weakened
by the attacks of dominating
cultures. It is driven back to the
social periphery

Aggressive forces
penetrating the
cultural system

Social forces
driving back
the system towards
the periphery

**Figure 3. Autonomous
Dynamic Societies**

The cultural system transformed slides
progressively towards the centre of the
social life. Its contours are more supple. and
the external cultural influences penetrate it
without weakening it. Some positive interactions
between the social system and the cultural system
on the one hand, and between the latter and the
extra-social environment on the other hand, are
developing. The external forces which try to
prevent the 'cultural recovery' are neutralised.

Interaction
forces

External
Cultural Flows

**Figure 4. Autonomous Societies**

The cultural system is at the centre
of the social life.
The interaction between the two systems.
cultural and social, is complete.

Social System

Cultural System

Interaction Forces

*Source:* R. Zghal, La culture de la dignité et le flou de l'organisation, CERP Tunis 1994
pp.85–92.

aggression build systems of defence against 'aggression' or, failing this,
would submit, if grudgingly, to the forces of alien culture. Colonial regimes
thus posed serious political constraints on social creativity and innovation.
On the other hand, decolonisation has sought to provide the basis for
cultural revival in a way which, while asserting the independence of society
from domination by external influence, also promises the choice and
adoption of new value systems that help to create and strengthen the science
and technology basis for cultural development. On the basis of their
historical experience, societies may be categorised as: autonomous (pre-
colonial) societies; societies under attack, dominated societies, autonomous
and dynamic (post-colonial) societies.

In the Maghreb countries, the disrupting influencing of colonialism deprived society of the opportunity of independent development and sought instead to entrench a culture of 'inferiority complex' and dependence. Negative self-evaluation has subsequently resulted in the emergence of a mentality of fatalism. This, in turn, has had the effect of slowing down the development of innovative tendencies, thus depriving society of the ability to resolve problems through the mastery of technologies. The purchase of technologies from abroad consolidated the structure of dependence. In a society dominated by alien culture, there was no basis for the question of the suitability of technology to local circumstances to be taken on board. Even if innovating individuals or institutions existed, there were few social forces to capture, develop and diffuse whatever innovations were already in supply.

### The Perception of Science and the Research Community

The richer countries are, the more they invest an important part of their GDP in research, and hence the more diffused research activities are throughout economic organisations and social institutions in such countries. The converse is usually the case in the LDCs. This means, other things remaining equal, the gulf between the LDCs and rich countries is rapidly widening, making the possibility of 'catching up' a daunting proposition. In the circumstances, it is not surprising that the bulk of science remains the privilege of rich countries.

On the other hand, developing countries often invest in education and training that give credentials rather than expertise to enhance their mastery of technology. This has much to do with the way societies in the LDCs value education – education for certificates and certificates for employment. There is little or no incentive for economic and scientific actors, for instance, to engage in research and development committed to delivering innovation. Education and training are thus innovation-neutral and economic activities turn on technologies supplied from traditional sources in advanced countries. Thus cultural value systems underlying the behaviour of post-colonial compradore states operate as a constraint on the development of the culture of innovation. Consequently, the transition from imitation to innovation would appear virtually unthinkable without radical changes in social and cultural orientation.

Innovation and technological progress would in turn promote transformation of the social and cultural landscape. The development of a research culture is thus absolutely paramount in developing countries. A number of factors, however, militate against this. For instance, in the absence of the culture of documentation, resulting in a weak information capability, decision makers in developing countries have no basis to challenge the suitability of technologies originating from developed countries. Consequently, they are placed in a position that would make them vulnerable to being either hoodwinked by salesmen who approach them with 'sweeteners' in the form of kickbacks and/or manipulated through political arm-twisting. Decisions thus made are often at variance with the principle of rational investment choice based on the real profitability objectives of the firm.

The absence of any protection of intellectual property contributes equally to diminish the status of the researcher and thus constitutes an unfavourable condition for the promotion of research and development enterprises and the flow of innovation in LDCs.

Another important factor unfavourable to the rapid development of research and innovation is the absence of a network of links between universities, research institutions and industrial firms. This absence is the corollary of the break between the spheres of social life and science on the one hand, and of the technological dependence reflex which impregnates the behaviour of economic actors. The firm recruits few people and invests little or not at all in research and development. The university generally makes do with standard lessons and would publish its research in international journals. Universities in the LDCs are generally interested in issues of international order, that is, issues which interest entrepreneurs, politicians and intellectuals of the advanced countries. Generally, the researcher acquires honour and pride in having works published in international journals and uses this to echo professional contributions to those responsible for academic recruitment or promotion. We understand, then, how much the development effect of the existing national research effort is minimal where users show little attention to it and where the strategy of research involves developing and reinforcing relations with the international scientific community as a matter of priority.

Also unfavourable for research-driven innovation in the LDCs is the structure of the community of researchers and their behaviour. We do not even know if we can call it a community because researchers in the LDCs are dispersed in the absence of associations and efficient networks for projecting debates, for the development of research, and for the mobilisation of synergies. Researchers in the LDCs often operate individually rather than in concert. The scope for co-operation and synergy is pre-empted by a conflict of individual interests. This arrangement is, however, unsatisfactory in view of the complexity of contemporary research problems which call more and more for consortium initiatives to identify innovative solutions in a multidisciplinary context.

The prevailing economic conditions in LDCs and the undervalued status of science education together reinforce the unfavourable behaviour and attitudes of society toward scientific research and innovation. Badly paid in the face of the difficulties of daily life, the researcher or the teacher would rather venture to moonlighting to make ends meet. Thus the scope for an innovative and original scientific research is narrowed in proportion.

## The Firm, Research and Development

Obstacles to the emergence of technological innovations relate either to the extra-organisational environment or to the intra-organisational environment of the firm.

### Extra-organisational Environment

At the extra-organisational level, the most important obstacle is the breakdown in the activity of R&D. This breakdown derives from the low level of investment in R&D; the absence of R&D at the level of industries; and the absence of a social environment providing for the mobilisation of skills for the mastery and development of science and technology. Salomon (1986: 216) notes that 'under-development creates no pressure on the social setting to provide conducive circumstances for scientific and technological research'. In modern industrial societies, on the other hand, research and development activities are well established: and the assimilation and mastery of technology are hardly infrastructure and skill constrained.

The extra-organisational environment is also constrained by the absence of mechanisms for integrating the scientific and technical systems. This deprives the production system of synergies and of training effects: absence of inter-sectoral integration, absence of integration between research and development activities, absence of links between the industrial productive system and the university training system, and absence of integration between scientific research and industrial research. Dispersion instead of integration has multiple effects, including:

• the absence of prospects for scientific research and therefore its marginalisation;

• the absence of a capability to master the technological changes which occur in a sectors consequent upon the shortage of qualified labour in the economy. (The textile and the tourist sector in Tunisia are major exporting sectors in the economy but suffer from shortages of qualified labour. The shortage is felt more in the textile sector which is exposed to important technological transformation and to the effects of the liberalisation of international trade); and

- the absence of links between the scientific system and the productive system of the economy reduces the chances of training of engineers and industrial researchers who could apply their creativity and innovative abilities to industrial use. The absence of strong engineering activity reinforces dependence on and preference for imported technologies and distaste for all that is produced locally.

The absence of this engineering structure is responsible for reducing the chances of assimilation and the mastery of imported technologies and therefore of exploiting the full extent of the benefits deriving from the transfer of technology. As Salomon (1986: 218) notes, 'When no endogenous capacity exists to control the application of a technical system, there is *transport* and not *transfer* of technology.'

*Intra-organisational Environment*

The weaknesses of the extra-organisational environment find their counterpart in the intra-organisational environment. Two major handicaps characterise the intra-organisational environment: sub-standard training and the style of the authoritarian and hierarchical command system.

The operation of firms without an orientation to research and development will in the long run deprive them of the capability for providing the innovation base for attaining competitive performance.

Hierarchical structures and the associated communication networks set obstacles limiting the scope of synergies between the scientific knowledge of managers and the technical know-how of operators. Actually the centralisation of power and decision making and the existence of many hierarchical screening procedures blocking and/or deforming ascending information reduce the positive interaction between those who conceive ideas and those who put them into practice. Furthermore, they discourage initiative and innovation. In our research on the Tunisian firm, we have shown that quite often innovation at the level of the operators was either ignored, sanctioned or else appropriated by management (Zghal 1994, 1989). On the other hand, when the structure is flexible, the barriers between management and the operators are reduced substantially; there is technological mastery resulting in innovations which are adapted to the circumstances of industrial activity (Denieuil 1992). If this synergy between managers and operators is necessary, it is that technology is multi-dimensional whose implementation demands the congruence between its different components.

Actually effective application of technology cannot be attained without the accumulation of know-how. If science is at the basis of the production of technology, know-how is at the basis of its operation.

The implementation of imported technologies requires multiple adjustments and transformations, which demand the exercise of creativity and innovation at the level of the managers, often comparable with those who conceive ideas, as well as at the level of the operators.

The distinction between those who conceive ideas and those who carry them out is crucial for the mastery and appropriateness of technology. The former, in principle holders of a scientific knowledge, are called to exercise creativity in order to improve the operational performance of the equipment. The latter, on the other hand, have to contend with the operational constraints of equipment. Creativity is exercised, for instance, through an ordering of instruments, the installation of machinery and equipment, the organisation and management of maintenance, sequencing of operations, co-operation, and mechanisms and flows of information. There are a multitude of particulars which do not appear in the instruction manuals of instruments and the installations of equipment. This makes assimilation of technological mastery and the continual exercise of creativity difficult. The implementation of this 'mental process' is a tribute to social organisation within the firm insofar as it promotes the flow of information, motivation, co-operation, creativity and synergies between actors, in contrast to the rigidity of authoritarian structures and their derivatives in terms of loss of information, discouragement of initiative, waste of material and human resources, and the absence of creativity.

## Conclusion

The question about the process of the integration of science and technology in development may be diagnosed at two levels of analysis: at the level of the firm or organisation and at the level of society. Each of these levels would involve a need for the understanding of the production technology applied and its appropriateness. Both at the level of society and the firm, there are obstacles which constrain the realisation of production and mastery objectives.

At the level of society, social organisation is characterised by numerous disconnections between sectors, institutions and activities. These result in waste and prevent the mobilisation of synergies – including absence of functional links between university scientific research and industrial production, between training and production sectors, and between sectors of activity.

At the level of the firm, the organisational structure inspired by Taylorism and by the bureaucratic hierarchy multiplies the barriers between the different categories of personnel, created by splits preventing the free flow of information, initiative and the systematic use of innovations. One of the serious consequences of this absence of integration and of synergies is the absence of a research and development activity aimed at translating inventions into innovations and innovations into social demand.

The product of science and the mastery of technological innovation are socially and culturally determined. Innovations in turn demand the elaboration of new types of social structure and relationships involving new attitudes and value systems compatible with and complimentary to new science and technology.

## REFERENCES

Denieuil, P.N. (1992), Les Entrepreneurs du Développement, l'Ethno-Industrialisation en Tunisie, Research from Sfax, L'harmattan.

Hajji, N. (1991), 'Système Scientifique et Technologie et Développement', in Technologies Nouvelles et Enjeux Socio-Economique, M.A. Roque (ed.), ICEM-Publisud.

Kardiner, A. and R. Linton (1969), L'Individu dans sa Societé, Gallimard.

Kuhn, T. (1970), The Structure of Scientific Revolutions, Chicago, Chicago University Press, 2nd edn.

Malnowski, B. (1958), The Dynamics of Culture Change, New Haven, Yale University Press.

Salmon, J.J. (1986), Science, Technologie et Développement: le Problème des Priorités, Revue Tiers Monde, Vol. 37, No.105.

Touraine, A. (1974), Pour la Sociologie, Du Seuil.

Zghal, R. (1989), Hiérarchie et Processus de Pouvoir dans les Organisations, Elites et Pouvoir dans le Monde Arabe, Du CERES.

Zghal, R. (1994), La Culture de la Dignité et le flou de l'Organisation, CRP.

# Irrigation, Agricultural Development and Economic Growth in the Maghreb

NIGEL R. MANSFIELD and NICOLA S. RIDDELL

*The article examines the significance of irrigation for agricultural development and economic growth in the Maghreb. Diffusion of agricultural practices has the effect, inter alia, of stimulating a chain of need-related technological innovations. Much, however, depends on the extent of activities in the agricultural sector. The agricultural sector in the Maghreb and its reform in the late 1980s are reviewed. The article probes factors that influence the efficiency and sustainability of irrigation schemes in the light of experience in other developing countries.*

## Introduction

The importance of irrigation for regions where rainfall is erratic and deficient has been recognised by a number of authors including Barrow (1987), Hillel (1987) and Stern (1989), among others. The drive for self-sufficiency in food production has been particularly important for the adoption of irrigation projects in developing countries.

Irrigation schemes are implemented to make up for rainfall deficiency and to satisfy the water requirements of crops. With irrigation, farmers have a better chance to diversify their crops than without it. Employment and income will increase, and so also will the number of days in a year worked per hectare (Chambers 1988). Diffusion of irrigation practice can also contribute towards the development of indigenous technological capability by providing opportunities for exploiting the derived demand for irrigation-related and other agricultural machinery and equipment.

Irrigation-induced technological development is in evidence in countries such as Pakistan, and particularly in the Punjab region where the local capital goods sector emerged on the back of the 'green revolution' (Aftab and Rahim 1987).

Dr Nigel Mansfield is Director of Postgraduate Courses and Senior Lecturer in the Department of Civil Engineering, University of Strathclyde. Nicola Riddell is Faculty Research Scholar in the David Livingstone Institute of Overseas Development Studies, Department of Civil Engineering, University of Strathclyde, Glasgow, UK.

There is also some evidence of an agricultural-led indigenous capital goods sector in the Maghreb. For example, there exists in Algeria an indigenous agricultural machinery enterprise which carries out, in its several plants, research and development, production, distribution, maintenance and the import and export of farm equipment and agricultural machinery. The machinery this firm manufactures (using up to 50 per cent of local components), includes tractors, engines (for tractors, lorries, combine-harvesters and mechanical appliances), farm machinery such as ploughs, and sowing machinery. After about ten years of operational experience, the firm has managed to attain its designed volume of output; but there is still some idle capacity.

The significance of such spin-offs would, however, depend on the extent of agricultural development in the first place and on the extent of the growth of effective demand arising from agricultural expansion. The immediate concern would thus be to see that favourable conditions are created for agriculture to grow on a sustainable basis. In this respect, the design and management of irrigation schemes are critical. In the remainder of this article, the significance of irrigation will be explored as regards agricultural development in the Maghreb countries.

## Agriculture in the Maghreb

The agricultural sector has always played an important role in the Maghreb economies. In 1990, agriculture accounted for 13 per cent of GDP in Algeria, and 16 per cent in Tunisia, and in Morocco (World Bank 1992). Of the total population in Algeria, 24 per cent is in agriculture. The corresponding figure for Tunisia is 24 per cent and for Morocco 35 per cent (FAO 1992b). Agricultural exports are low and agricultural imports high. Moreover, the growth of cereal production in all three countries is unable to keep up with the high population growth. In Tunisia and Algeria cereal imports are greater than production as may be seen from Table 1 below.

TABLE 1

THE STATE OF IRRIGATION AND FOOD PRODUCTION IN THE MAGHREB AND
THE INDIAN SUB-CONTINENT

| Country | Pop. Growth 1980–90 (%) [1989–2000] | Production of cereals, growth 1965–89 (%) | Production of cereals, tons (000) 1989 | Cereal imports tons (000) 1990 | Irrigated land as % of arable land 1991* |
|---|---|---|---|---|---|
| Bangladesh | 2.3 [1.8] | 2.3 | 28,796 | 1,726 | 34.0 |
| India | 2.3 [2.1] | 3.2 | 199,816 | 447 | 27.5 |
| Pakistan | 3.1 [3.1] | 4.0 | 21,018 | 2,048 | 82.2 |
| Algeria | 3.0 [2.8] | 0.3 | 1,698 | 5,185 | 5.5 |
| Morocco | 2.6 [2.4] | 1.9 | 7,429 | 1,578 | 14.5 |
| Tunisia | 2.3 [1.9] | 0.2 | 635 | 1,439 | 8.0 |

*Note:* * taken from FAO (1992a)
*Source:* World Bank (1992).

Agriculture in the Maghreb is largely rain-fed, and the low and erratic rainfall since the 1970s appears to have made it increasingly fragile. Irrigated cultivation in Tunisia and Algeria holds only a minor role in the agricultural sector. About 5.5 per cent of arable land was irrigated in Algeria in 1991; and in Tunisia, the corresponding figure was 8 per cent (FAO 1992b). Public investment in agriculture in Tunisia concentrated on irrigation, but still food production has remained low.

Morocco has been more agriculture-oriented than Algeria and Tunisia. Government policy in Morocco has for the most part sought to promote earnings from agricultural exports and to decrease dependence on imports such as sugar. The 1973–77 National Plan aimed to invest heavily in the construction of large dams to increase irrigated land. By 1990, approximately 500,000 ha of irrigated land was developed with 80 per cent covering large-scale schemes. This compares with just 60,000 ha in 1956. Moreover, there are plans to build 40 dams, which will allow another 800,000 ha (500,000 ha for small- and medium-scale schemes) to be used for irrigated agriculture (Jouve and Belghazi 1993: 24). In 1991, 14.5 per cent of arable land in Morocco was irrigated (FAO 1992b).

In Algeria, on the other hand, the emphasis was on industrialisation. Agricultural production here is poorly managed and organised. An inventory of soils in 1986 estimated that 1.083 million ha could be irrigated by 2010, but this figure is considered to be a little too optimistic in view of the present rate of irrigation development, which is less than 4000 ha per year (Bedrani 1993).

A common problem facing agriculture in all three countries is the scarcity of water, as evidenced in the drought of 1988 and 1989 (van Tuijl 1993; Findlay 1994). As well as the inefficient use of water, population growth, urbanisation and expansion of the industrial/manufacturing sector in these countries have diverted water from agricultural use (see Table 2). For 1980–90, average annual population growth in Algeria was 3.0 per cent; in Tunisia, 2.3 per cent; and in Morocco 2.6 per cent (World Bank 1992). There is, thus, a need to optimise the application of water in the Maghreb. This can be achieved by, among other things, the provision of more and better irrigation facilities.

TABLE 2

WATER WITHDRAWAL AND USE IN THE MAGHREB

|  | Water withdrawal as per cent of available water | Per cent of water used for M&I | Agriculture |
|---|---|---|---|
| Algeria | 16 | 26 | 74 |
| Morocco | 37 | 9 | 91 |
| Tunisia | 61 | 10 | 90 |

*Note*: M&I = municipal and industry
*Source*: van Tuijl (1993)

Countries in the Indian sub-Continent such as Pakistan and India have achieved food self-sufficiency with the application of irrigation to their agriculture. Irrigation has, however, played a minor role in food production in the Maghreb.

## Agricultural Reform and Transition in the Maghreb

As of the 1980s, all three Maghreb countries have pursued strategies that were broadly market-oriented. They all adopted structural adjustment programmes (SAPs) in order to create more diversified and resilient economies. Policies in all three countries have been geared towards liberalising their marketing, pricing and trade regimes. Algeria's policy shift was, however, more radical than that of the other two, as Algeria was a 'centrally planned, socialist economy' (FAO 1991).

TABLE 3

GROWTH OF PRODUCTION

Average Annual Growth Rate (per cent)

|  | GDP | | Agriculture | | Industry | | Manufacturing | | Services | |
|---|---|---|---|---|---|---|---|---|---|---|
|  | 1965–80 | 1980–88 | 1965–80 | 1980–88 | 1965–80 | 1980–88 | 1965–80 | 1980–88 | 1965–80 | 1980–88 |
| Bangladesh | 2.4 | 2.7 | 1.5 | 2.1 | 3.8 | 4.9 | 6.8 | 2.4 | 3.4 | 5.2 |
| India | 3.6 | 5.2 | 2.5 | 2.3 | 4.2 | 7.6 | 4.5 | 8.3 | 4.4 | 6.1 |
| Pakistan | 5.1 | 6.5 | 3.3 | 4.3 | 6.4 | 7.2 | 5.7 | 8.1 | 5.9 | 7.4 |
| Algeria | 6.8 | 3.5 | 5.7 | 5.6 | 7.1 | 3.8 | 9.5 | 6.1 | 6.7 | 2.7 |
| Morocco | 5.6 | 4.2 | 2.4 | 6.6 | 6.1 | 2.8 | .. | 4.2 | 6.8 | 4.2 |
| Tunisia | 6.6 | 3.4 | 4.5 | 2.4 | 5.7 | 5.1 | 6.4 | 2.9 | 6.4 | 2.7 |

*Source*: World Bank (1990)

Structural adjustment for agriculture in the Maghreb concentrated on making the market work to enhance efficiency in agricultural production, reduce dependency on imports and promote exports (FAO 1991). In 1986–87, all three countries encountered a process of agricultural reform for different reasons. In Algeria, the pressure for reform in favour of market-oriented agriculture was induced when oil prices fell in 1986, and subsequent deteriorations in current accounts and debt service costs were experienced. The reform was induced in Tunisia by the widening macro-economic imbalances experienced in the early 1980s.

In Algeria, agriculture before the reform consisted of large-scale, capital-intensive or state farms and small private farms, with the former, however, receiving priority in the distribution of equipment, inputs and credit. During 1973–86 cereal yields stagnated in the large-scale socialist farms, while they increased in the private farms (FAO 1991: 64). During the 1980s there were many attempts to reform socialist farming systems, but these were unsuccessful and it was consequently decided that the socialist farms should be dismantled. In 1987–88 these farms were divided into smaller units of private farms, and farmers were given more autonomy with a view to improving agricultural performance, reducing dependence on food imports, and curbing rural–urban migration.

In Tunisia the main objectives of agricultural reform, which took place from 1986 onwards, were to increase the role of the private sector in agriculture, improve the conservation and management of scarce water, and increase irrigated agriculture; hence public investment in agriculture (although decreasing from 21 per cent of total investment in 1960–61 to 16 per cent in 1977–84) concentrated on irrigation, taking 43 per cent of total agricultural investment in 1985–86 (Radwin et al. 1991: 40). The reform in Tunisia has taken place with the assistance of World Bank loans in the form of agricultural adjustment programmes, with particular attention being paid to land tenure systems, soil conservation and the halting of desertification, water resource conservation, and development of the fisheries sector.

Agricultural performance in Morocco during the 1980s was generally favourable, with cereal, pulse and oil crop production almost doubling between 1979–81 and 1989 (FAO 1991: 67). The 1988–92 Five-Year Development Plan of Morocco involved reform of the public sector by privatising many state companies and adopting liberalisation policies to encourage private sector investment. Privatisation and liberalisation policies have also been pursued in Algeria and Tunisia. The main objectives of Morocco's agricultural reform were to 'enhance agricultural production and self-sufficiency through the expansion of modern, irrigated agricultural production; and to develop the export potential of agro-industries.' (FAO 1991: 67).

## Irrigation Performance in the Maghreb

*Tunisia*

In Tunisia, only 5 per cent of the cultivated land is irrigated. A major aspect of agricultural policy in recent years has been to promote investment in irrigation schemes. But on most of the installed schemes they appear to be poorly managed and underutilised. In 1991, the area effectively irrigated was only 68.6 per cent (i.e., 394,000 ha out of a potential 574,000 ha). The utilisation rate of land under irrigation now varies from region to region, generally ranging between 70 and 95 per cent, depending on climatic conditions.

About 63 per cent of irrigation in Tunisia is privately operated on small-scale farms. But most of these farms had access to only small amounts of fertilisers, thus accounting for poor agricultural performance in spite of the investment in irrigation schemes in recent years.

*Morocco*

Since 1965, Morocco has given priority to its agricultural sector in its development policies with a view to promoting agricultural exports to finance imports, achieving food security and providing raw materials and surplus for industrialisation. Agricultural development was supported by the development of hydro-agricultural schemes. The share of agricultural investment in general, which was 42 per cent from 1962 to 1972, has decreased since, but appears to have stabilised at around 20 per cent.

Investment in irrigation, particularly in the construction of large hydro-agricultural schemes, has always been a top priority for the Moroccan government, whose objective it is to develop one million ha by 2000.

The development of irrigation in Morocco, based on water from regulatory dams and/or groundwater extraction, has been considerable. Modern irrigation increased more than eight-fold, from 60,000 ha in 1965 to 500,000 ha in 1990 (80 per cent of these being large-scale schemes). Moreover, there has been the construction of 34 dams, with six also in progress or planned. Together, these 40 dams are intended to allow Morocco to irrigate 800,000 ha., which, however, is only about 15 per cent of all cultivable land. There has been a recent increase in cultivated land due to an increase in population pressure on land, mechanisation and more favourable climatic conditions.

*Algeria*

Agriculture in Algeria plays a less significant role in the economy than in the other two Maghreb countries. It constitutes only 15.2 per cent of total value added and 13 per cent of GDP. Moreover, agricultural growth has remained weak and negative. During 1970–80, for example, agriculture in Algeria grew at the average annual rate of -3.1 per cent (Bedrani 1993). There has been irregularity of agricultural production, particularly of cereals, which indicates a weak mastery of natural conditions by farmers, who actually do not have enough resources to fight against poor climatic conditions.

Yields in Algeria have stagnated for all crops and are weak in comparison with Morocco and Tunisia which have similar climates.

TABLE 4
COMPARISON OF CEREAL YIELDS IN THE MAGHREB
(AVERAGE 1982–86; kg/ha)

|  | Algeria | Tunisia | Morocco |
|---|---|---|---|
| Hard wheat | 676 | 826 | 1227 |
| Soft wheat | 704 | 1284 | 1319 |
| Barley | 714 | 566 | 860* |

* for 1982–1985
Source: Bedrani (1993), p.10

In addition to poor yields, Algeria has been experiencing a weak growth of cultivated land and irrigated land as shown in Table 5.

TABLE 5
DEVELOPMENT OF CULTIVATED AND IRRIGATED LAND (000 ha)

|  | 1939 | 1949 | 1954 | 1960 | 1966 | 1970 | 1975 | 1980 | 1985 | 1990 |
|---|---|---|---|---|---|---|---|---|---|---|
| Cultivated land | 6541 | 5887 | 6910 | 6983 | 6779 | 6821 | 7167 | 7510 | 7509 | 7661 |
| - of which irrigated |  |  |  | 242 |  | 270 |  | 341 |  | 364 |

Source: Bedrani (1993: 14). (Based on data from different annual statistics for Algerian agriculture)

There has been some extension of land, but this has been where fertility is poor and rainfall low. Moreover, agricultural land in Algeria has suffered from erosion, salinisation, deforestation and over-grazing. Thus land productivity is very weak. Climatic conditions have also been unfavourable in Algeria since the beginning of the 1970s, which also explains, at least in part, the low efficiency of the use of fertilisers. There has been a significant increase in the quantity of fertilisers used, but yields have remained stagnant for cereals and increased only modestly for other crops.

Faced with a weak performance of the economy in general and agriculture in particular, with the oil crisis in 1986, and with poor prices of hydrocarbons, Algeria has been trying since the late 1980s to improve economic performance through implementation of structural adjustment programmes.

A soil inventory in 1986 estimated that 1.083 million ha could be irrigated by 2010. However, this objective appears too optimistic when compared with past annual implementation rates of irrigation schemes. Also, it is not clear as to how these works and the development of land for irrigation are going to be financed. Given that crop yields in Algeria are poor, increasing yields will certainly be a principal source of agricultural growth, as will also be investment in irrigation, according to a recent World Bank report (1988). (See Table 6.)

TABLE 6
PERCENTAGE CONTRIBUTIONS TO GROWTH OF
AGRICULTURAL PRODUCTION

| Action | 1988–1995 | 1996–2010 |
|---|---|---|
| 1. Increase in yields | 56 | 27 |
| 2. Investment in irrigation | 35 | 55 |
| 3. Reduction of fallow | 9 | 5 |
| 4. Development of the South | – | 13 |

Source: Bedrani (1993: 43).

The efficiency of irrigation schemes in the Maghreb will obviously be hampered by the severe shortage of water there (there is also an increasing demand for water from the municipal and the industrial sector). However, in spite of this, a review of the irrigation schemes in the Maghreb appears to show the main problems of irrigation to be:

• high investment and operation costs: North Africa and the Middle East, compared with other regions, have the highest costs in the world (FAO 1986: 40);

• a low level of technological and management capability. Morocco trains only 16,000 engineers, compared with 41,000 in Korea. Moreover, in 1989, the percentage of the relevant age group enrolled in tertiary education in Morocco was only 11 per cent, in Algeria 11 per cent and in Tunisia only 8 per cent (World Bank 1992);

• poor maintenance, as was the case in the irrigation projects in Morocco (e.g., the Doukkala Irrigation Projects) and Tunisia that used modern technologies;

• poor project implementation;

• poor provision of extension services;

• low level of local manufacturing for agricultural machinery.

## Conclusion

The Maghreb countries have been experiencing transition since the late 1980s. Over time, traditional agriculture in the region has been replaced by more capital-intensive schemes, but this has caused urban unemployment to increase. Food prices were, however, set at levels too low to stimulate farmers to produce more than what they would need.

Structural reform in the Maghreb has strengthened encouragement for the public sector, with responsibility being placed on the private sector to absorb public sector activities or for these to become self-regulating. Privatisation policies in Morocco and Tunisia have provided a place for private capital in the economy, but free market activities have taken longer to evolve in Algeria. Not until the 1991 disruptions did the large-scale public industrial ventures start to move towards autonomy.

Although these structural adjustment measures had provided positive results by the 1990s, domestic growth rates were still more influenced by the productivity of the agricultural sector than by improving the commercial and the agricultural sector. For example, good harvests in 1991 led to high growth rates in Morocco and Tunisia, while crop failures in 1992 led to a decline (Spencer 1993: 38). Moreover, except for tax breaks provided to Moroccan farmers until 2000, little attention has been paid to the vital question of land reform and increasing domestic food production. These can be improved by increased investment in irrigation.

One method of improving irrigation efficiency and performance would be to adopt methods that would allow water to be used efficiently, or to use less water per unit of output.

To increase the efficiency of on-farm water use and to save water, two methods may be considered: first, one could improve existing surface irrigation techniques; and secondly, one could introduce new irrigation technologies, such as sprinkler or micro-irrigation. It has been calculated that micro-irrigation can save up to 30 to 50 per cent of water compared with surface irrigation, and that it significantly increases yields (van Tuijl 1993).

One of the main differences in irrigation between the Maghreb and the three Middle Eastern Mediterranean countries covered in Table 7 is that the latter have managed to successfully apply modern on-farm irrigation technologies and water saving techniques, which reflects their superior irrigation performance and efficiency. Table 7 further illustrates the difference in use of modern irrigation technologies between the two groups of countries.

TABLE 7

MODERN IRRIGATION TECHNOLOGIES IN THE MAGHREB AND THREE MIDDLE EAST COUNTRIES

| Country | Total irrigated (000 ha) | Sprinkler and/or micro irrigation (000 ha) | Per cent |
|---------|--------------------------|--------------------------------------------|----------|
| Algeria | 400 | Na[a] | NA |
| Morocco | 853 | 135[b] | 16 |
| Tunisia | 394 | 45 | 11 |
| Cyprus | 55 | 27 | 49 |
| Israel | 213 | 213 | 100 |
| Jordan | 50 | 43 | 86 |

Notes: a. Not available.          b. Out of which 15,000 ha are under micro-irrigation
Source: van Tuijl (1993)

However, micro-irrigation is costly and requires application of a high level of skill. Moreover, for it to be efficient, it requires a reliable and continuous water supply at the farm location, which could prove to be difficult in Maghreb irrigation. An upgrading of the existing irrigation infrastructure would also be required. The investment cost implications of all this cannot be underestimated, although it is also important to determine in each case the minimum scale beyond which increasing investment in micro-irrigation would add more to cost than to benefit. Meanwhile, agricultural policy in the Maghreb countries should be directed towards removing the structural constraints on the diffusion of efficient irrigation practices. This will call for the provision of training services, infrastructure and appropriate technology hardware.

It is important that these constraints on the performance of irrigation projects are removed, so that such projects can, upon successful implementation, be made to contribute towards agricultural expansion and economic and technological development in the region.

## REFERENCES

Aftab, K. and E. Rahim (1986), 'The Emergence of a Small-Scale Engineering Sector: The Case of Tubewell Production in the Pakistan Punjab', *Journal of Development Studies*, Vol.23, No.1 (Oct.).

Barrow, C. (1987), *Water Resources an Agricultural Development in the Tropics*, Longman, London.

Bedrani, S. (1993), *Le Secteur Agricole et ses Perspectives à l'Horizon 2000: Algerie*, Final Report (June), European Community Commission.

Chambers, R. (1988), *Managing Canal Irrigation: Practical Analysis from South Asia*, Cambridge University Press, London.

Findlay, A.M. (1994), *The Arab World*, Routledge, London.

Food and Agriculture Organisation (1986), *Irrigation in Africa South of the Sahara*, FAO Investment Centre Technical Paper No.5, Rome.

Food and Agriculture Organisation (1991), *The State of Food and Agriculture 1991*, Rome.

Food and Agriculture Organisation (1992a), *Production Yearbook*, Rome.

Food and Agriculture Organisation (1922b), *The State of Food and Agriculture 1992*, Rome.

Fransman, F and K. King (1984), *Technological Capability in the Third World*, Macmillan, London.

Hillel, D. (1987), *The Efficient Use of Water in Irrigation: Principles and Practices for Improving Irrigation in Arid and Semiarid Regions*, World Bank Technical Paper No.4, Washington, DC.

Jouve, A.M. and S. Belghazi (1993), *Le Secteur Agricole et ses Perspectives à l'Horizon 2000: Maroc*, Final Report (Sep.), European Community Commission.

OECD (1988), *The Sahel Facing the Future*, Paris.

Radwin, S., V. Jamal and A. Ghose (1991), *Tunisia: Rural Labour and Structural Transformation*, Routledge, London.

Spencer, C. (1993), *The Maghreb in the 1990s*, IISS, Adelphi Papers, London

Stern, P.H. (1989), *Small Scale Irrigation*. Intermediate Technology Publications, London.

Thabet, B. and M. Allaya (1993), *Le Secteur Agricole et ses Perspectives à l'Horizon 2000:*

*Tunisie*, Final Report (July), European Community Commission.

Van Tuijl, W. (1993), *Improving Water Use in Agriculture : Experience in the Middle East and North Africa*, World Bank Technical Paper No. 201, IBRD, Washington, DC.

World Bank (1990), *World Development Report 1990*, Oxford University Press, Oxford.

World Bank (1992), *World Development Report 1992*, Oxford University Press, Oxford.

# Sustainable Energy For Development

## JOHN TWIDELL

*Sustainable development depends greatly upon the capacity to increase the supplies of renewable energy. Many new renewable energy technologies now provide regular commercial energy supplies, especially for niche opportunities or where unwanted emissions have to be minimised. Of the many possibilities for harnessing the continuing energy flows in the natural and the human environment, hydro-electricity, wind turbines, photovoltaics, solar heat, biomass and waste treatment are the main industries. During the last 15 years there has been growing experience world-wide with equipment and installations, and increased appreciation of the institutional factors involved in the implementation of renewables as clean technology. Today it is an advanced subject, much dependent on modern materials, micro-electronic control and new methods such as electric power load management. This article summarises common lessons learned, especially from Europe, to formulate a strategy for sustainable development.*

## Introduction

Renewable energy may be defined as 'energy obtained from the continuous and repetitive currents of energy occurring in the environment' (Twidell and Weir 1986, 1987). Recently, energy arising from the otherwise natural decomposition of waste from industry, commerce and urban complexes, such as landfill gas, has been included as 'renewable'. Moreover, with a world-wide interest in 'sustainability', renewable energy is included as an essential component of sustainable development alongside the recycling of materials and life-cycle economic assessment.

The significance of renewables as serious components of modern energy supply has been growing inexorably over the last 20 years. This relates to a wide range of factors (Burtland 1987) that include: OPEC oil price increases, the Three Mile Island nuclear power accident, acid rain, famines

Professor John Twidell is Director of the Anthony Marmont Sustainable Energy Technology Centre at De Montfort University, Leicester, UK. This article was read at the MAGHTECH'94 conference.

and droughts in sub-Saharan Africa, the Chernobyl nuclear accident, environmental impact, carbon dioxide protocols, the Gulf War, polluter-pays policies, external costs of pollution in eastern Europe, leukemia clusters and enhanced radiation protection. It is the international and environmental scale of these happenings that is significant. In each case a strategic and significant move to renewables would have lessened the impacts and abated the causes of the events.

The development of new renewable energy technology has advanced steadily over the last 20 years, so that most basic research has been completed and commercial implementation is established (Twidell 1990, British Energy Association 1991). The majority of renewable energy systems and devices are technically proven, with the requirement now to reduce costs, improve reliability and establish commercial viability. The major handicaps are now institutional, with a general lack of strong or steady markets and a need for acceptable environmental impact (Twidell and Brice 1992). This article addresses these problems. The growth of modern renewable energy plant in both demonstration projects and in commercial business is significant now in Europe and world-wide. Examples of a growth in trade of about 30 per cent per annum over several years, as in Danish wind power (Danish Energy Agency 1990), are known (Johansson, Kelly, Reddy and Williams 1993); and so too are rapid spurts in activity, such as the recent 500 per cent per annum growth of wind power in England and Wales (Stevenson and Pershagen 1993, Klein and Schmid 1992).

However, despite its growth, the absolute amount of new renewable plant remains low in comparison with established energy supplies. Fossil fuels have a dominant role in all countries, and nuclear power is a significant component in the electrical power supply of most industrialised countries. Yet, despite the success of the conventional fossil and nuclear energy supplies, these are now clearly constrained by their polluting emissions and total life-cycle and external costs (Hohmeyer 1988, Ottinger 1988). Moreover, nuclear power is only for centralised steam-turbine electricity systems and is linked to weapons proliferation. Therefore fossil and nuclear fuels have limitations, even though modern economies are almost totally dependent on them. Renewables provide sustainable, clean, secure and diversified energy, yet their 'capture area' is large, equipment is capital intensive and the source of the power in the environment, although free, is not ultimately controllable. Taking all these varied factors into account, including institutional factors, the general picture is that the front-runners in renewables are not only environmentally efficient but also price competitive with fossil and nuclear supplies.

The remainder of this article discusses the categories of renewable energy technologies including accepted renewables, new renewables, clean-up renewables and integrated renewables.

## Accepted Renewables

These include large hydro, biomass consumption (including firewood for cooking) and geothermal, all of which have been in use for many years, and at present contribute to 25 per cent of world primary energy use.

### Biomass Combustion

Firewood and wastes from agriculture and timber have always been prime energy supplies. According to official statistics these now represent 15 per cent of world primary energy – an average of 40 per cent in developing countries and at least 3 per cent in industrialised countries (Johansson *et al.* 1993, Hall 1991). Pulp, timber, cane sugar and oil palm industries use waste biomass as essential energy sources for factory production, usually in combined heat and power systems. There is a general realisation that far more energy could be harnessed from crop waste.

Biomass combustion for steam-turbine electricity generation is well established, especially in the sugar cane industry and with agricultural wastes. The efficiency of electricity generation is generally low; but combined heat and power generation is the norm, with heat used locally in the industrial process.

Biomass combustion, especially for household cooking and heating, is largely unrecorded and not fully recognised as a resource in central government statistics. This is a difficulty with most 'autonomous' energy systems, including solar energy for heat. Consequently, attention is shifted unwittingly to centralised energy supplies and grid electricity generation.

### Large Hydroelectricity Generation

Public electricity supply is 100 years old and hydro turbines have always been utilised as prime movers. Generation is extremely efficient with no thermal waste or noxious emissions. Today, 15 per cent of world electricity is from hydro power, and there is the technical potential that this can be increased by a factor of four, mostly in developing countries including the former Soviet Union. Large hydro schemes have usually required special government capital funding programmes, but after about 15 years of operation with no fuel costs, the electricity becomes cheap. Very large projects, however, attract much criticism for environmental and social disruption.

### Geothermal

In many parts of the world, hydrothermal energy is an obvious resource, frequently tapped for domestic and commercial heat, and for steam-turbine electricity generation. The world total geothermal electricity capacity is now 6,000 MW, increasing at about 10 per cent per annum. Research continues slowly in tapping subterranean heat from granite 'hot dry rocks' (Shock 1984) and, indeed, from the magma. However, it is realised that the present geothermal energy potential is localised.

*Interpretation*

These three forms of energy supply have proven technology, but can only be developed as cost effective sources in places of peak potential. In practice, these potentials are regional in scale; distances as short as 50 km may separate a forest area from grassland, mountains from plain, and hot aquifer outlets from normal water tables. Renewable energy is best developed from local-scale practical implementation where working experience is gained, financial commitments limited and 'hot spots' of supply and demand optimised. Moreover, despite universal knowledge of the technologies, institutional and cultural factors frequently determine whether or not resources are developed. From these experiences, it is clear that the ultimate potential of renewable energy is not limited by technology, but by environmental, financial and institutional constraints.

Therefore it is not sensible to make single planning decisions concerning any new form of renewable energy over large scales of distance. The correct decisions should be 'local' where there are 'niche opportunities' that are economic and acceptable to the local planning authorities (Department of the Environment 1991). Most countries are at least 1000 km in scale, and so centralised national planning decisions for single forms of renewable energy cannot be justified. The UK government fell into this trap with the original grand scheme for 2000 MW of ocean wave power off north-west Scotland for electricity transferred via undersea cable and a super grid to the English Midlands (ETSU 1991). This project has now ceased, with the current emphasis on the local development of small-scale wave power in near-shore positions (Whittaker, Long, Thompson and McIlwaine 1991).

## New Renewables

These include wind, passive and active solar (active for water heating and passive for buildings), biofuels, small hydro, wave, tidal, photovoltaic and photochemical. Most of these technologies, except photovoltaic power and photochemical fuels, had been developed and used before the 1950s, when cheap oil discouraged further commercial interest. However, renewed motivation came as a reaction to the OPEC oil price increases of the 1970s. What is not fully appreciated is that in the intervening 20 years, great advances were made in modern materials, particularly plastics and composites, and electronics. It is these advances that have made the recent developments in renewable energy so different from the earlier systems. One view of events is that the use of cheap oil enabled a surge in scientific and manufacturing knowledge that can now be utilised for clean technology. Fossil fuels have been a fortunate gift to mankind, but their benefits are being overtaken by environmental harm (Houghton, Jenkins and Ephraums 1990).

However, the dominance of fossil fuel and nuclear power systems has created hierarchies and vested interests that have great difficulty in changing to more modern technology, especially to the demands of clean and sustainable technology. Therefore some of the most negative institutional factors for renewables are entrenched in conservative engineering: an example is the reaction against the use of electricity grids for the import and export of power between many relatively small and varying power generating nodes. Such power sharing is technically possible, especially by remote switching, but is discouraged by tariff structures and connection charges. A further difficulty for renewables, as experienced also by nuclear power, is that the systems are capital intensive – there being no fuel charge. Fossil fuel systems, which have relatively low capital but high on-going costs, have encouraged accounting criteria for rapid pay-back times and low capital costs. Recent interest in gas-turbine electricity generation is an extreme of this policy. In contrast, renewable energy projects, as with nuclear power, usually require special capital investment programmes allowing pay-back over, say, ten years rather than two. The ultimate benefit accrues if the equipment is well built and lasts for over 20 years, in which case the profit appears in later years rather than earlier.

*Wind Power*

The generation of electricity from modern wind turbines is now established technology, yet with many developments to come. World-wide, there are about 20,000 turbines, with the most cost effective option for grid integration being of about 400 kW capacity and 40 m in rotor diameter (Klein and Schmid 1992). A typical capacity factor on a good site (>6m/s wind speed average) is 25 to 30 per cent. Such turbines may be expected to supply 20 to 40 per cent of total annual energy into a local grid. The remaining 60 to 80 per cent can be integrated from other more predictable renewable or fossil sources. Turbine installed costs have decreased steadily to a minimum of about $US 750 per rated kW. Price per unit of electricity depends crucially on financial rates of return and period of loans. Over a ten-year period, at 6 per cent return, the generating cost is about $US0.07/kWh, which is competitive against the total generation, pollution and external costs of fossil or nuclear generated electricity.

The wind power programme in Denmark (Danish Energy Agency 1990) is a good example of a successful policy that could be applied to other forms of renewable energy. Success has given great confidence to the industry, which has sold machines world-wide over the last ten years to total export earnings of 500 MECU and the employment of 3,500 man-years. The gradual progression of the state support from small individual plant to utility machines has been established, so the Danish programme has now advanced to the establishment of the world's first offshore wind farm in a situation typical of large future potential.

*Solar Heat*

Initially, most R&D interest was in 'active' solar water heating. While important developments still occur, the main solar developments now relate to the 'passive' heating and cooling of buildings. Buildings consume about 30 to 40 per cent of the prime energy of most nations, and so they are essential targets for local renewable sources and energy efficiency. At higher latitudes, where heating is a main demand, there are now many examples of passive solar buildings with virtually no conventional heating plant (Twidell and Johnstone 1995). The temperature is maintained by a combination of insulation, solar gain through and on to the sun-facing facades, heat recovery from air ventilation and liquid wastes, metabolic heat and casual gains from electricity services.

One of the important aspects of passive solar building design is the extent to which the principles are becoming known to architects: it is now likely that individually designed buildings in Europe will be modelled in advance for energy efficiency and will include passive solar features. Despite this success, however, there has been little change in the mass building market which can probably only be influenced by changes in the building regulations.

*Biofuels*

There are many ways that biological plant material may be treated to provide immediate or secondary fuels (Hall 1991). Direct combustion is well established, but other processes include gasification, fermentation, anaerobic or aerobic microbiological digestion, extraction of oils, and chemical transformation into refined products. All biofuels are carbon based and produce carbon dioxide when utilised. However, this does not add to the threat of global climate change since the raw material would have decomposed to the same state in any case, with the carbon recycled globally in photosynthesis. In general, biomass utilisation is far less polluting than fossil fuels, which add to the carbon dioxide in the atmosphere and produce harmful particulates and sulphur and nitrogen oxides. It should be stressed that biomass sources are natural chemical stores of energy, in contrast to the 'mechanical' sources of renewable energy in water and the wind. Therefore biofuels are the main contenders for alternative transport fuels. For instance, rape seed oil is increasingly converted to rape methyl ester (RME) to produce a clean alternative liquid fuel to conventional diesel oil (Devitt *et al*. 1995). The RME is used in conventional and adapted engines.

*Small Hydro Turbines*

There have been advances in the installation and operation of small hydro power stations of a capacity around 1 MW to as small as a 5-kW micro-hydro (Harvey 1993). At the lower range, the systems may interface with the grid, usually using induction generators, or may be autonomous. In the latter case, an automatic load management system may operate to present a 'positive feed forward' controllable load for frequency regulation, so eliminating the need for relatively expensive, negative-feedback mechanical control. There have been advances also in the use of composite and organic materials for turbine construction. Small and micro-hydro installations usually seem trivial for power utilities, but looked at from another point of view, they can provide important income for individual operators. However, such individuals usually meet hostile institutional difficulties and only the most persistent achieve success. It is an area of development where government has to make favourable legislation to lessen the power of vested interests and monopolies.

*Wave Power*

The potential from harnessing power in the waves is large for seaboard countries, especially when a prevailing wind arrives across a long ocean fetch as on the Atlantic coasts of Ireland, the UK and Norway. However, despite a major government-funded programme in the UK, there is no proven ocean-going device (ESTO 1991). Attention has turned sensibly to nearshore and on-shore devices of relatively small scale and where long weak grids need power reinforcement. Such a system now operates in Scotland (Whittaker *et al*.1991). When such 'hot spots' or 'niche opportunities' are successful, the technology may grow to large-scale systems. Sadly, this natural progression from proven and economic small scale to larger scale was not followed in the immediate post-OPEC activities of many governments.

*Tidal Power*

Where marine geophysical formations support large tidal ranges of at least 10 m it is reasonable to consider a barrage and low-head hydro plant for electricity generation. Several countries have possible sites for major installations, as in the Severn Estuary where 15 per cent of England's electricity could in principle be generated (Baker 1991). However, governments balk at the large capital costs of such projects, despite the 100-year and longer lifetimes with no fuel costs. The mistake is not to realise that tidal power, as with wave power, can be installed as marginal developments to new harbour walls, barrages for roads and flood relief, and at other such sites.

*Photovoltaic Power*

'Clean electricity with no moving parts' is the powerful concept of photovoltaic solar-cell power together with long-lifetime, modular construction and installation, minimum maintenance, and easy and low-environmental impact operation. Energy transformation efficiency from sunlight to electricity per unit area is about 15 per cent in commercial modules and up to 28 per cent in research cells. Manufacture world-wide is now 55 MW per annum peak power capacity, worth $US 0.8 billion with growth at about 10 per cent per year. The major difficulty is the large, but reducing, capital cost of about $US 8 per peak watt, producing electricity now at $US 0.30/kWh today and at $US 0.15/kWh by 2000. Present commercial markets are mainly for maintenance-free autonomous installations for communications, rural and urban services, and small, remote power, usually for lighting. While these special markets are now assured and growing, the latest R&D is for grid-linked power on buildings and alongside motorways, for instance, where the balance of systems costs may be minimised and where the power provides peak electricity for commerce or air conditioning. Research support is producing improvements on all fronts, including several recent developments from organic and photo-chemistry which promise cheap mass production of basic cells. There is little doubt that photon-generated electricity from sunlight will be a major component of power in the future.

*Photochemical*

A significant breakthrough for solar energy utilisation will be the direct transformation of sunlight into chemical energy for fuels such as hydrogen. Such processes mimic the principle of photosynthesis and several methods are known from laboratory experiments.

## Clean-up Renewables

Not only do renewables reduce pollution of the environment, but a number of the technologies may also be used to reduce pollution from other sources, e.g., wastes. The anaerobic digestion of sewage and organic wastes is perhaps the most established technique. The biogas formed is about 50 per cent methane and 50 per cent carbon dioxide and may be used as a relatively low grade fuel for heating and electricity production. CHP from such gas is becoming standard in sewage works, with the electricity used on site and often exported. Alternatively, the carbon dioxide may be dissolved out in water, leaving concentrated methane to be exported to natural gas mains or used as a high grade fuel.

Landfill sites for urban waste will naturally produce biogas, usually called landfill gas. 'Landfill gas sites' are constructed to collect the gas by pumping and to control the leachant from entering the water table. The gas may then be used in internal combustion engines for electricity production and sale to the grid. The benefits are not only the energy production, but also the conversion of methane to carbon dioxide. Per molecule, methane is about 60 times more effective than carbon dioxide in causing global warming, so the gas should not be released direct.

The Non-Fossil Fuel Obligation in the UK (Twidell and Brice 1992, HMSO 1992) has led to several innovative methods of electricity production, including the use of chicken litter as a combustion additive or for anaerobic digestion for biogas to fuel internal combustion engines. The combustion of urban waste for steam turbine electricity production qualifies in the UK as a renewable non-fossil fuel. However, using urban waste without attempting to recycle most of the components is controversial.

**Integrated Renewables**

Renewable energy harnessed from the natural environment is never a steady and controllable supply. Some sources such as tides are highly predictable, and some such as wind are very variable. This seeming lack of 'firmness' is frequently used as a criticism of renewables. However, most electricity network loads are not 'firm' either, yet the electricity supply system adapts. Fortunately, modern control systems allow many methods for controlling both supply and demand, especially on electricity networks. In addition, there are opportunities for storing energy, especially in chemical form.

One example will be given to show how modern control methods and lateral thinking may utilise renewable energy fully and produce firm supply. The island of Foula in the Shetland Islands to the north of Scotland has an innovative electricity system under computer control for its 40 inhabitants in 25 buildings (Sommerville 1984, 1991). The system has the following characteristics:

- a 60-kW, 17-m rotor diameter, wind turbine, with generator speed controlled by the electrical load between 48 and 53 Hz;

- about 50 lighting, power and heating loads switched in at one-tenth Hz intervals as the frequency increases due to strengthening wind speed, thus presenting an increasing total load to prevent overspeed of the turbine. As the wind speed decreases, the heaters drop out every one-tenth Hz, so leaving power for the most essential loads;

- a 20-kW hydro plant that starts generating in no-wind conditions, and can reverse to pump water for storage at periods of very high wind power;

- a 25-kW diesel generator that comes on in no-wind and no-hydro conditions; and

- a pricing mechanism and in-house information displays that encourage consumers to understand the system and reduce load as the diesel-only condition of high price electricity approaches.

The system was installed by the Windharvester Company of the UK to replace the previous diesel-only electrical system and household fossil fuel heating. The wind and hydro turbines together supply the electrical power which also provides hot water and building heat. There has been about 90 per cent substitution of fossil fuel, with increased heat for the previously damp and cold houses. This system on Foula is 'embryonic' of systems on similar principles for 'positive feed forward' control methods that could integrate renewable energy supplies of several kinds into national energy supply systems. There are ample methods available from demand-side electricity management to enable renewable energy generation to be matched to loads in a network.

### Conclusion

Many types of renewable energy supply are now firmly established with successful demonstrations and much commercial experience. In general, the basic technology is proven and the need is to provide steady and growing markets. Further R&D is, of course, needed. However, this should be supported by governments and from growing commercial activities.

Some renewable energy technologies such as wave power and photochemical systems do not yet have sufficient successful demonstration in commercial conditions, and for all the technologies there are always further research improvements to be made. Therefore, government and industrial support is always needed in long-term programmes. The aim of these developments should be to provide energy for niche opportunities in the first instance and to allow markets to grow from the most favourable situations.

A major advantage of renewable energy over fossil fuels and nuclear power is the lack of harmful emissions, including carbon, sulphur and nitrogen oxides and radioactive products. In this way, renewables do not have the high external and social costs of their competitors. As a major form of clean technology, renewables have to be supported for a sustainable world future.

## REFERENCES

Baker, C. (1991), 'Tidal Power', *Energy Policy*, Vol.19, No.8, pp.792–97.
Bruntland G.H. (ed). (1987), *Our Common Future*, World Commission on Environment and Development, Oxford University Press, Oxford.
Danish Energy Agency (1990), *Wind Energy in Denmark*, Ministry of Energy, Copenhagen.
Department of the Environment (1991), *Draft Planning Policy Guidance Note: Renewable Energy*, London.
Devitt, M., D. Drysdale, I. MacGillvray, R. Thompson and J.W. Twidell (1993), 'Biofuel for Transport – an Investigation into the Viability of Rape Methyl Ester as an Alternative to Diesel Fuel', *International Journal of Ambient Energy*, Vol.14, Oct., pp.195–218.
ETSU (1991), *Wave Energy Review*, ETSU R60, AEA, Harwell, Oxon.
Hall, D.O. (1991), *Biomass Energy, Energy Policy*, Vol.19, No.8, pp.711–37.
Harvey, A. (1993), *Micro-Hydro Design Annual*, Intermediate Technology Publications, London.
Her Majesty's Stationery Office (1992), *Renewable Energy*, Energy Committee 4th Report, London.
Hohmeyer, O. (1988), *The Social Costs of Energy Consumption*, Springer-Verlag, Berlin.
Houghton, J.T., G.J. Jenkins and J.J. Ephraums (1990), *Climate Change*, Cambridge University Press, Cambridge.
Johansson, T.B., H. Kelly, A.K.N. Reddy and R.H. Williams (1993), *Renewable Energy Sources for Fuels and Electricity*, Earthscan, London/ Island Press, Washington, DC.
Klein, H.P. and J. Schmid (1992), *Eurowin: the European Wind Turbine Data Base*, Annual Reports from 1990 and 1991, EC DG XII, Brussels.
Ottinger, R.L. (1990), *Environmental Costs of Electricity*, Oceana Publications, Washington, DC.
Shock, R.A.W. (1984), *An Economic Assessment of Hot Dry Rocks as an Energy Source for the UK*, ETSU R34, ETSU, AEA, Harwell, Oxon.
Sommerville, M. (1984), *Optimal Use of Wind and Diesel Generation on a Remote Scottish Island*, Proc European Wind Energy Association, Hamburg, pp.681–84.
Sommerville, M. (1991), *The Foula Wind/Hydro/Pumped Storage Electricity System*, Proc.6th Conference on Energy for Rural and Island Communities, Energy Studies Unit, University of Strathclyde, Glasgow.
Stevenson, W.G. and B. Pershagen (1993), *IEA Wind Energy Report 1992*, NUTEK, Stockholm.
Twidell, J.W. (1991), 'Changing Directions to Renewable Energy', *British Annual Energy Review 1990*, pp.63–72, British Energy Association, London, June.
Twidell, J.W. and R. Brice 'Strategies for Implementing Renewable Energy', *Energy Policy*, Vol.20, pp.464–79, May.
Twidell, J.W. and C.M. Johnstone (1994), 'Strathclyde University's Passive Solar, Low-energy Residences with Transparent Insulation', *International Journal of Solar Energy*, Vol.52, pp.85–109.
Twidell J.W. and A.D. Weir (1987), *Renewable Energy Resources*, Spon, London.
Whittaker, T.J., A.E. Long, A.E. Thompson and S.J. McIlwaine (1991), *Islay, Gully Shoreline Wave Energy Device*, ETSU WV 1680, ETSU, AEA, Harwell, Oxon.

# PART III
# LESSONS OF EXPERIENCE
# FOR THE MAGHREB

# The Dynamics in Technical Change: A Comparison between the Maghreb and Mexico and the Significance of the Maquiladora Experience

## DENIS REQUIER-DESJARDINS

*In the North–South integration process, Europe is to the Maghreb as the United States is to Mexico. The openness of markets in the North to products from the South could provide the South with benefits of increasing returns, thus broadening the scope for technological change and enhancing the 'catching up' process. The similarities and differences between the positions of the Maghreb and Mexico are discussed and questions are raised as to whether the positive features of the Mexican experience in technology development could be replicated in the Maghreb. The article concludes that the Maghrebian economies could learn from the Mexican maquiladora experience in their effort to integrate with the European Union with respect to transnational commodity chains.*

## Introduction

The last two decades have seen a rapid expansion in the network of global firms and their activities. This has had far-reaching implications for the pattern and growth of international trade, investment flows, diffusion of technology and technological progress in the context of North–South economic links. A unique feature of this globalisation trend is its association with the growing significance of area, country and region specificities, on the one hand, and the emergence of distinct, but broad, economic areas centred around Japan, the United States and the European Union, on the other. Among countries in the South, the ones that are most likely to benefit from association with the emerging centres of economic activities, (in terms of trade and investment flows and technology transfer), are those that are

Denis Requier-Desjardins is Professor of Economics at the Université de Versailles Saint-Quentin-en Yvelines Orinte, France. This article is a translated and edited version of the paper presented in French at the MAGHTECH'94 conference.

geographically – and possibly culturally and historically – close to these centres, such as Mexico (in the case of the USA) and the Mediterranean zone countries (in the case of the European Union). Much, however, would depend on how these countries in the South conduct their trade with their partners in the North.

Recent developments in the theory of international trade and regional integration have focused on externalities and increasing returns to explain the advantages of interventionist trade policies, such as the building up of commercial and economic blocks which mainstream trade theory would, however, rule out as being generally non-optimal in Paretian terms. In particular, increasing returns may stem from intra-industry trade in specific intermediate products and production rationalisation prompted by preferential relations between the firms of the area.

A major source of increasing returns is technical change and innovation. The process is enhanced by the efficiency of national innovation systems. In a trade area some technical spillovers may occur based on the development of trade relationship and capital flows from one country to another. The stability of the trade relationships within the area is also a strong incentive for forging partnership between firms of different countries.

This is particularly of interest to developing countries which become part of an integrated trade area, the leadership of which is performed by one or several industrialised countries. Developing countries could envisage new opportunities of 'catching up' through the effects of technological externalities stemming from partnership with firms of their developed counterparts in their particular areas. Trade blocks could in this respect become integrated production zones (Requier-Desjardins 1993).

Of course, the extent of the benefits to be derived from participation in an integrated trade area rests heavily on the framework of technological and innovative partnership between firms in the area. However, such partnerships and the technological benefits derived from them have so far been observed to apply to firms based in developed countries, as in the case of the OECD. There have so far been few opportunities for firms of the Third World or even of the newly industrialised countries to enjoy the benefits of technological spillover effects arising from partnership with firms in developed countries (Freeman and Hagedoorn 1994). It should be noted, however, that the occurrence of technological spillovers does not necessarily mean 'catching up' in every case, even when the mechanisms for the diffusion of innovations concerning mature technologies are in place (Lucke 1993).

The aim of this article is to examine the technological spillover effects arising from the Mexican and Maghrebian partnerships with the United States and Europe, respectively.

These cases display two examples of the North–South integration process. Of course, given the differences between the levels of development, the likely spillover effects are bound to be directed from the North to the South: the openness of the market in the North for products from the South, in the context of some kind of partnership between the firms of the two sides, could enhance opportunities for increasing returns. This brand of integration could provide firms in the South with a stimulus to be competitive through technological change, thus entailing a catching-up effect. In this diffusion process, integration within border-crossing commodity chains would be of paramount importance.

In the remainder of this article, the relevant features of the two sets of partnerships will be compared, with particular reference to the *maquiladora* experience of economic integration across transnational commodity chains and the technological and organisational spillover gains from it. Based on this, the article will assess the extent to which the *maquiladora* experience in Mexico may be replicated successfully in the Maghrebian countries. In comparing the two cases, the article draws on some recent literature, such as the contributions of Bensidoun and Chevallier (1994) and Chevallier (1994).

## Maghreb and Mexico: Parallels and Differences

The average annual value of the Euro–Mediterranean trade flows amounts roughly to $70 billion, approximately equal to the level of the Mexico–North-American trade. During the last two decades, the Maghreb–Europe and the Mexico–North American annual trade flow have slightly grown by roughly 7 to 8 per cent. The bilateral trade link between Mexico and North America has developed over time, while the one between the Mediterranean zone and Europe has weakened.

However, it has to be pointed out that the relationship between the Mediterranean zone and Europe is more complex than its counterpart across the Atlantic, insofar as it involves more than one county on both sides of the trade partnership. The Euro–Mediterranean trade link has two distinct components – one between Germany and the eastern Mediterranean (Turkey) and the other between the Maghreb region and southern Europe (France, Spain and Italy). Geographical proximity is of paramount importance in the latter case, as is shown by the intensity of the relationship between Morocco and Spain and Tunisia and Italy.

Let us concentrate on the relationship between the Maghreb and Europe. The annual trade flows are on average slightly less than $30 billion, which is less than the half of the Mexico–North America flows. By contrast with Europe's trade relations with other developing zones, Euro–Maghreb trade has been consistent. Over the last 20 years, the Maghreb region has increased the percentage of manufactured goods within its exports to Europe, from 6.5 to 28.4 – a feature it shares with Mexican exports to North America. Algerian exports concentrate mainly on oil and energy products. One the other hand, the increase in the proportion of the manufactured exports of Morocco (from 8.9 to 60.4 per cent) and Tunisia (from 18.8 to 70.6 per cent) is particularly striking. These export proportions are comparable to that of Mexico, which stands at roughly 70 per cent. But whereas Algeria's exports to Europe exceed its imports from Europe, Morocco and Tunisia have had a trade deficit with Europe, contrasting with Mexico's slightly favourable trade position with North America.

The Mexico–North America and the Maghreb–Europe links have broadly similar underlying features:

• The intensity of trade relations takes place within a long-lasting framework of complex and ambivalent relations, characterised by historical episodes of indirect or direct political domination by the northern partners. The legacy of colonial domination is reflected in the existence of a huge population of immigrants from the southern partners and/or by the diffusion of cultural values and the widespread use of the language of the North. The impact of North–South geographical proximity is also significant in both cases.

• This intensity of the North–South relationship is reinforced by specific trade agreements, such as association schemes between the European Union and Maghrebian countries and the tariff exemptions for the Mexican *maquiladoras*. These agreements are in the process of being superseded either by free-trade discussions between Europe and the Maghreb or by the implementation of NAFTA.

• The concentration is mainly on intra-branch trade, underlining the existence of integrated production relations within some commodity chains – the Mexican and Maghrebian firms operating as sub-contractors of American and European firms, respectively.

However, some differences between the two situations do exist. For instance, trade negotiations are developing along different lines. NAFTA opens the American market to Mexican products and the Mexican market to American products. On the other hand, the European market is fairly open to tradable Maghrebian products, but the Maghrebian market is not freely open to European products yet. However, one has to take into account the small share of the Maghreb in European trade, compared with that of Mexico in North American trade.

## Mexico: the *Maquiladora* Experience

NAFTA was launched at the beginning of 1994. But Mexico had at that time a long experience of integrated industrial production with foreign firms through sub-contracting arrangements. Its industrial strategy was mainly based on import-substitution until the 1980s.

The *maquiladora* regulation was set up in 1965 when the Bracero Programme, allowing the temporary entry to the United States of Mexican farm workers, was cancelled. It provided for foreign investors, mainly American companies at the beginning, to take advantage of the regulations of the American tariff book allowing duty-free access to the US market of products being assembled in Mexico and based on American parts or intermediates. Duties were levied only on the value added in Mexico, i.e., mainly cheap labour. The Mexican state promoted this kind of investment in the border areas by removing import duties on parts to be assembled and re-exported and by relaxing its tough regulations concerning the ownership of Mexican firms by foreigners. Thus the maximum share of foreign capital for investment in this region was set at 49 per cent. This was subsequently increased to 100 per cent.

Over 30 years of operation, the *maquiladoras* have contributed significantly to employment expansion (around 500,000 today), mainly in the border cities such as Tijuana, Mexicali, Ciudad Juarez and Matamoros, where up to 40 per cent of total employment rests on *maquiladora* industry. It has obviously accelerated the growth of these cities, and, according to some, contributed to a slow down in the predicted growth of Mexico City. However, for years the low technological level of the *maquiladora* activities has been a major factor behind the low level of qualifications of the workforce.

The *maquiladoras* enjoyed a first period of rapid growth in numbers from a total of 74 in 1967 to 620 in 1980. The 1982 debt crisis entailed a lowering of the total number, but, even then, the number had increased to 1125 in 1987 and to around 2000 in 1992 (Zepeda 1994). But the path followed during the 1980s and early 1990s shows some new features compared with the previous period.

First, the steady growth of the *maquiladora* industry occurred during a period of economic trouble at the national level. The growth of the *maquiladora* industry thus contrasted sharply with the slackening, and, indeed the regression, of import-substitution industries which accounted for the bulk of Mexican industry.

Second, the *maquiladora* industry evolved from assembly plants based on a low-paid, poorly-qualified workforce to high-level industrial activities. This amounts to a sectoral shift in the composition of its output and labour force. The share of the textile and clothing industry has diminished while the share of the car industry and electronics has grown. This shift has had some impact on the general technological level of the *maquiladora* industry. According to Hualde, Mercado and Zepeda (1994), in cities such as Tijuana, Juarez or Monterey, two-thirds of the *maquiladoras* could be classified as medium or high technology activities. This trend is particularly apparent in the car industry. Here the *maquiladoras* are no longer assembly units drawing on the comparative advantage of a cheap workforce, but rather production units integrated into transnational sub-contracting networks built by global firms aiming to internalise network externalities. As a result, Castel (1994) stresses that Tijuana has the strongest concentration of high-tech companies in Mexico. This evolution is likely to have some impact on the qualification and skills of the workforce.

Third, one may witness the growth of non-American direct investment inflows in the *maquiladora* industry – mainly Japanese and Korean. These flows are attracted by strategic goals different from cheap labour costs, which were the major point of attraction for American investors during the previous period. In 1992, there were some 70 Japanese-owned *maquiladoras*, 55 per cent of which were operating in electronics; and Korean-owned *maquiladoras* in Tijuana created job opportunities for 1200 (Kenney *et al.* 1994).

The emergence of a new generation of *maquiladoras* has put Mexico at the crossroads of a new export-led development process characterised by an upward shift along the commodity chains and the building up of the technological complexity of industry in general. The process of upgrading of the technological level and complexity of the *maquiladora* industry and of exploiting the backward and forward linkages it entails could be enhanced by three mechanisms:

- the upgrading of the skills of the workforce employed in the *maquiladora* industry;

- the technological or organisational spillover effects likely to affect the *maquiladora* suppliers; and

- the building up of *maquiladora* 'industrial districts' in border towns, thereby reinforcing the *maquiladora* spillover effects by creating proximity externalities.

*Upgrading the Skills of the Workforce*

Some trends in work organisation and technical change within the *maquiladora* industry are apparent, particularly among the Asian-owned *maquiladoras* (Kenney *et al.* 1994), where the principles of 'just-in-time' and 'total quality' as well as flexible production technologies, including computerised equipment are applied. These technologies are likely to improve workforce skills.

Employment is still characterised by the preponderant share of a poorly-qualified workforce involving youth and female workers for the most part. Growth of qualified employment has been noticed recently, particularly in high-tech *maquiladoras;* but this has been marginal. Labour turnover is high, thus limiting returns on investments in training. On the other hand, mobility could boost the diffusion of skills between *maquiladoras.* Wages are relatively low. Consequently, the income multiplier effect on the border zones and the X-efficiency type externalities are low.

### Spillover Effects

The backward linkage effect of the *maquiladoras* is poor (Zepeda 1994), as the share of local industrial inputs is low. The trends are, however, ambiguous: in the electrical equipment industry, for instance, the share of local inputs is growing, while it is diminishing in electronics.

In some cases, sub-contractors' networks do build up to supply the *maquiladora* industry, especially subsidiaries of the American car industry producing spare parts, or electronic components for the telecommunications industry. But there is a limited impact on suppliers of factors or on the emergence of a local market of qualified workers which could enhance productive systems along the border. Yet some spillover effects can be seen, such as the diffusion of the 'just-in-time' principle across the *maquiladora* suppliers in Tijuana and Juarez (Hualde, Mercado and Zepeda 1994).

### Maquiladora Industrial Districts

The concentration of the *maquiladora* industry in some cities, mainly on the border, involves dynamics which may be explained in the context of the 'industrial district' hypothesis. There exist local institutions connected to the *maquiladora* industry. These include mainly business associations, but such links have not until now led to a set of specific interactions with training institutions or innovation centres. Consequently, the local innovation system has been far from robust (Hualde, Mercado and Zepeda 1994).

However, the situation varies elsewhere. Cities in the interior, such as Guadalajara with a high-level educational and research infrastructure, or Monterey, one of the historical birthplaces of Mexican industrialisation which has been granted the opportunity of welcoming *maquiladoras* by a 1983 decree, show more of an interrelationship between *maquiladora* and 'traditional' industries and a concentration of local, positive, externalities stemming from this linkage.

Local negative externalities are also much in evidence (Tamayo and Tamayo 1994). These occur in the form of environmental pollution stemming from the lack of proper infrastructure for industrial effluent treatment; poor environmental monitoring and control; and a high rate of urbanisation fuelled by the mass arrival of migrants from the interior lured by perceived job opportunities.

Summing up, the evidence on the *maquiladora* contribution to Mexican industrial development is not unambiguous. Nor may the *maquiladora* initiative be written off as having been of no value. What is clear is that the *maquiladora* experience to date scarcely matches the East Asian experience of export-led industrial growth. The *maquiladora* experience in Mexico is, however, an evolving one, so that one cannot preclude the scope for some local, positive benefits stemming from the transfer of technology and skills generated from the activities of the *maquiladora* industry.

The implementation of NAFTA, thoroughly restructuring the framework of the Mexico–United States trade relationship, introduces some uncertainty about the future of the *maquiladoras* (Zepeda 1994). Some contend that the impact of NAFTA will be marginal. It will, however, make the *maquiladora* regulations redundant and will promote direct investment flows. Others argue that the northern border could lose its specific competitive advantage as *maquiladora*-like production units spread throughout the country, thus entailing the '*maquiladorisation*' of the Mexican economy.

The *maquiladora* is beginning to lose its juridical specificity with the revision of the regulations enabling the *maquiladora* to have a share of the local market and with the *maquiladora* industry exporting under regulations other than the original terms of the American customs provision.

The implementation of NAFTA is likely to weaken the specific export advantages of the border *maquiladoras* towards the United States and the likely positive effects of the concentration on this location. However, the flow of direct investment to Mexico may increase and this would make the *maquiladoras* a model of positive externalities for cities in the interior.

## Can the *Maquiladora* Experience be Replicated in the Maghreb?

The *maquiladoras* are in many ways unique to Mexico. Direct replication of these in the Maghreb environment is therefore out of the question. There are, however, useful lessons that the Maghrebian countries may learn from the evolution of the *maquiladoras*. Success for initiatives analogous to the *maquiladoras* would rest on the evolution in the Maghreb of industrial export specialisation and on the results deriving from direct investment strategies of firms in the industrialised countries – in this case, the European Union.

### *Industrial Export Specialisation*

The export specialisation of Morocco and Tunisia, the two countries most concerned with this issue, is characterised by the predominant share of textiles and confectionery. These together represent 42 and 53 per cent of the total exports of Morocco and Tunisia, respectively, to the EU in 1993. Textile production for export is also quite developed in the *maquiladora* industry, but is on a steady decline in terms of relative significance, unlike in the Maghrebian countries where it is still on the increase.

Generally speaking, the textile industry is not a sector given to the generation of far-reaching technological spillover effects. But the industry in Morocco and Tunisia enjoys a fairly good share of the French market. It thus shows a fair level of integration with the French textile industry, which could enhance technological transfer from abroad.

The electrical equipment industry comes second in the industrial exports of Morocco and Tunisia. Electronic exports, which represented 6 and 7 per cent of the total exports of Morocco and Tunisia, respectively, in 1993 have shown rapid expansion in recent years. In this kind of industry, the scope for technological spillover effects is broad. Already, there exist in Tunisia some export-oriented production units of electronic components. The contribution to industrial value added of these units is, however, marginal and there is no evidence to suggest that the scope for their expansion is at all apparent (Ben Yahia 1990). They embody a potential for technological spillover in high-tech industry, nonetheless.

On the other hand, compared with its importance in the *maquiladora* industry in Mexico, the car industry in the Maghreb constitutes a small share of industrial activity, indicating that investment flows into this sector have been weak. The production of mass-consumption, high-tech goods could set in train a great deal of technological spillover. In this respect, Ould Aoudia (1994) refers to the Japanese investments in mass-consumption, high-tech manufacturing in south-east Asia which have since been used as export platforms to third countries. Moreover, this model more or less conforms with the Mexican strategy of integration into NAFTA.

## The Trend of Direct Investment

Kebabjian (1994) points out that Maghrebian countries would benefit from a free-trade area with Europe if this brought capital inflows, particularly direct investment, to them. This would clearly be a precondition for the unleashing of technological and organisational externalities as witnessed in the *maquiladora* case.

Capital flows to the Maghreb have so far concentrated on the two countries exporting manufactured goods to Europe – Tunisia and Morocco. A good part of this capital is of public origin – bilateral or multilateral. Private capital flows are also growing and a good share of these flows is made up of direct investment. In Morocco, they accounted for 10 per cent of the total inflow in 1992, as against a mere 2 per cent at the beginning of the 1980s. Tunisia shows a roughly equivalent figure for private capital inflow (9.6 per cent in 1992), but with a more moderate growth despite the fact that it has been open to foreign capital for a longer time than Morocco.

Yet the distribution of these investments is not very favourable to the generation of massive technological spillover effects. In Morocco, the recent wave of investment is affecting mainly the banking industry. In Tunisia, the relevant sectors are oil, tourism and, within the manufacturing sector, the textile industry. Foreign investment in Tunisia accounts for 60 per cent of total textile exports under a 'special investment zone' regime, akin to the *maquiladora* regulation. In the textile industry, however, production is delocalised to take advantage of low wage costs of production. Investment in machinery and equipment has been weak latterly in this sector, following the weakening of the traditional comparative advantage bestowed by low wage cost. This has resulted in the closing of some plants in the textile industry.

However, the Moroccan and the Tunisian textile industry are integrated into the European industry – Morocco, for example, imports French fabrics and exports clothes to France. This industry is becoming more and more conscious of the necessity for the diversification of products and for upgrading the skills of the workforce in order to develop the capability of the whole industry. This attitude is reflected by the widespread adoption of 'just-in-time' procedures in the management of production. This could be considered as an element of organisational spillover, but it is not a massive move, and the issue of the low technological level of the industry, particularly in the lower links of the commodity chain, such as clothing – typical of the links transferred to Maghreb – remains.

This integration trend has some unfavourable aspects. Foreign investment partnership agreements with Maghrebian countries involve mainly European – typically French – firms, and French industry has lost a rather large share of the high-tech, mass-consumption goods markets. This is at odds with the *maquiladora* experience in which such goods have featured prominently in terms of technological spillover effects. So the preferential link with French industry could not be seen as an advantage for the Maghreb in the light of the *maquiladora* experience.

Moreover, the Maghreb has yet to compete with the southern countries of the EU for upgraded integrated supply activities. For example, the Spanish automotive spare-part industry is reportedly the most efficient in the world, according to a report in *The Economist* in November 1994, thanks to the pervasive diffusion of 'just-in-time'.

The move of Asian investors in the *maquiladora* industry is not likely to be replicated in the Maghreb either as no new flow of non-European investment has been reported in the Maghreb in recent years. The Japanese used some countries of the EU as a hub for getting into the European market, especially in the high-tech, mass-consumption manufacturing sectors. For example, they chose to invest in electronics and the auto industry in the Barcelona region and in the electronic components in the Madrid region at the end of the 1980s after Spain joined the EU. Today the Maghrebian countries are challenged, as possible hubs for penetrating European markets, by eastern European countries. However, the Maghreb's comparative advantage over eastern Europe as a source of cheap labour remains, and on that, among other factors, will revolve the prospect of the Maghreb/Europe process of integration.

## Conclusion

What conclusions can we draw from this comparison of the Maghreb with the *maquiladora* experience in Mexico?

The Mexican experience shows the impact of the transfer of some labour-intensive links of the commodity chains controlled by global firms of industrialised countries on the development of technological capability in developing countries. The Mexican experience can be invoked by the Maghrebian countries as a tentative guide as to how they would need to conduct the process of their trade integration with the EU. The comparison also allows us to draw lessons for industrial policy which the Maghrebian countries could put to good use. One such lesson is the necessity to develop sub-contracting mainly in the sectors most favourable to technological and organisational spillovers, namely the high-tech, mass-consumption product manufacturing.

REFERENCES

Bensidoun, I., and A. Chevallier (1994), 'Les Echanges Commerciaux Euro-Méditerranéens', *Economie Internationale*, No 58, 2ème trimestre.
Ben Yahia, D. (1990), *Analyse des Facteurs de Blocage et Perspectives de Développement de l'Activité Electronique Tunisienne*, mémoire de DEA, Université Lumière Lyon II.
Castel, O. (1994), 'Les Milieux Entrepreneuriaux dans l'Industrialisation Mexicaine: Une Chronique Séculaire', in *Entrepreneurs du Tiers-Monde* (Beraud, Perrault dir.), Maisonneuve et Larose et les Editions de l'Orient.
Chevallier, A. (1994), 'Les Echanges CEE–Maghreb en Rétrospective : Repères Statistiques', in *Vers une Zone de Libre-Echange Europe-Maghreb*, Cahier du GEMDEV No.2, October.
Freeman, C. and J. Hagedoorn (1994), 'Catching up or Falling behind: Patterns in International Interfirm Technology Partnering', *World Development*, Vol.22, No.5, May, pp.771–80.
Hualde, A., A. Mercado and E. Zepeda. (1994). 'Industrialización y Caambio Tecnológico en la Maquiladora Fronteriza', Communication au Séminaire international organisé par le COLEF (Colegio de la Frontera Norte) et l'Organisation Internationale du Travail sur le thème *'Les*

*Maquiladoras au Mexique: Présent et Futur du Développement Industriel*' au COLEF (Tijuana, Mexico), 23–25 May.

Kenney, M., J. Romero and D. Won Choi (1994), 'Japanese and Korean Investment in the Maquiladoras: What Role in Global Commodity Chains?', Communication au Séminaire International Organisé par le COLEF (Colegio de la Frontera Norte) et l'Organisation Internationale du Travail sur le thème '*Les Maquiladoras au Mexique: Présent et Futur du Développement Industriel*' au COLEF (Tijuana, Mexico), 23–25 May.

Kebabdjian, G. (1994), 'Les Pays du Maghreb ont-ils intérêt à une Zone de Libre-Echange avec l'Union Européenne', in *Vers une Zone de Libre-Echange au Maghreb*, Cahier du GEMDEV No.22.

Krugman, P (1991), 'The Move towards Free Trade Zones', *Economic Review*, Dec. (repris dans *Problèmes Economiques*, No.2289 du 2 September 1992).

Lucke, M. (1993), 'The Diffusion of Process Innovations in Industrialised and Developing Countries: a Case Study of the World Textile and Steel Industry', *World Development*, Vol.21, No.7, July, pp.1225–38.

Ould, Aoudia, J. (1994), 'L'Europe et sa Proximité: Le Cercle Vertueux des Délocalisations', in *Vers une Zone de Libre-Echange Europe–Maghreb*, Cahier du GEMDEV No.22, October.

Requier-Desjardins, D. (1993), 'Commerce Mondial et Systèmes Productifs: Une Réappréciation des Rapports Nord–Sud', in *Technologie et Développement Humain* (Abdelmalki, dir.), Lyon, L'interdisciplinaire.

Tamayo, J. and L. Tamayo (1994). 'Industrialización en la Periferia : Maquila y Urbanización Marginal en Matamoros', communication au séminaire international organisé par le COLEF (Colegio de la Frontera Norte) et l'Organisation Internationale du Travail sur le thème '*Les Maquiladoras au Mexique: Présent et Futur du Développement Industriel*' au COLEF (Tijuana, Mexico), 23–25 May.

Zepeda, Miramontes, E. (1994), 'EL TLC y la Industrialización en la Frontera norte de México', communication au séminaire international organisé par le COLEF (Colegio de la Frontera Norte) et l'Organisation Internationale du Travail sur le thème '*Les Maquiladoras au Mexique: Présent et Futur du Développement Industriel*' au COLEF (Tijuana, Mexico), 23–25 May.

# The Maghreb Road to Transition: The Appeal of the Chinese Experience

*Based on a cursory review of science and technology trends in China, the article argues that there is much of relevance in the Chinese experience for the Maghreb countries to emulate. China has used science to emerge strong, confident and capable of withstanding external pressures that would have otherwise seen it swing from one end of the ideological spectrum to the other. On the other hand, the Maghreb economies have not been as robust and confident and had to swallow wholesale the structural adjustment programme as prescribed by the World Bank, putting prospects of long-run growth at risk. The paper indicates areas for future Sino–Maghreb co-operation, and, at variance with SAPs, emphasises the role of the state in the promotion of science and technology for the development of the region.*

## Introduction

Among low-income countries, China is one of the few that have made impressive strides in the development of scientific and technological capability.[1] China is now on the threshold of the 'third revolution'.[2] China's experience might in many ways be a *suis generis* case, so that it would be naive at best, and meaningless at worst, for countries in the Maghreb to seek a model in China for wholesale adoption. On the other hand, the Chinese experience can be emulated under different circumstances. But then, the following questions are bound to arise. First, what are the requisite conditions that the Maghrebian countries would need to meet to transform the scientific and technological landscape in the region? Second, how can the Chinese experience influence the Maghrebian countries to be in the mainstream of global scientific and technological development?

In this paper, it is maintained that the problem of transition in developing countries relates not merely to the making of ideological shifts but instead to the condition of the national science and technology system. The latter has a

Farid Benyoucef is Researcher and Lecturer in Economics at the University of Algiers, Algeria.

major influence on the long-run growth process. The substance of transition is thus different from the political fad of 'instant conversion' to 'capitalism' and the 'market economy' which has apparently carried the day in many developing countries since the collapse of the Communist system in the 1980s. The application of structural adjustment programmes (SAPs) in the countries of the Maghreb, however, appears to have pandered to ideological fad rather than to the provision of sound scientific and technological bases for sustainable development. Indeed, the neglect by the SAPs of the mechanisms for science and technology (S&T) development in the Maghreb has been conspicuous. The claim that SAPs would provide the basis for a transition to a market economy by cutting down the role of the state has, however, been challenged on many occasions. Rolling back the state has in many cases, including in the Maghreb, led to a contraction of government expenditures, leaving, *inter alia*, the fate of science and technology education and research and development (R&D) activities hostage to fortune. History also shows that the development of the market economy would be difficult, if not impossible, in the absence of well informed agents of supply and demand in large number, capital, entrepreneurs and institutions providing for civil and political freedom. While these requisites are absolutely indispensable for the market economy to have a firm foothold and evolve and for S&T and R&D capabilities to develop, they are, however in scarce supply in many developing countries including those in the Maghreb.

Transition to a market economy is pursued as a policy objective in developing countries because it is thought to be the best way forward for contemporary trends in technological progress.

Some developing countries – China among others – have a great deal of accumulated experience in R&D. This provides a base on which to build. If China is striving almost successfully on the way towards achieving scientific and technological progress, it may be surmised, can the Maghreb countries be far behind? A cursory review of China's experience in this respect would be instructive for the Maghreb countries.

## China's Scientific and Technological Scheme

The history of China is closely intertwined with the history of science and scientific breakthroughs. The world indeed owes a great deal to China for its numerous and useful scientific discoveries throughout history. The Mao period was, however, generally anomalous insofar as the political upheavals that modern China had to go through during the cultural revolution in particular were anathema to scientific and technological development. The post-Mao regime was, on the other hand, an attempt to restore China to the traditional path of S&T by removing the political constraint imposed by the institution of Communism.

Science and technology have helped modern China to manage, with a certain degree of success, its most pressing problems ranging from epidemics to overpopulation and from desertification to land development and flood control.

During the period of the Communist regime, however, S&T were used mainly for the development of a military–industrial complex. China was bent on developing a nuclear capability, mainly for political reasons. Moreover, the government sponsored research in space science and telecommunications, biotechnology and laser projects with the view to enhancing the military capability of the state. The politicisation of science and technology had thus clearly limited the scope for innovation. Since the introduction of the economic reforms in 1978 under Deng Xiaping, S&T have been placed top on the reform agenda. Consequently, universities and scientific research centres related to corporations or to the Chinese Academy of Sciences have experienced a profound change in orientation and have developed the R&D capability that would make them the power house of innovation and development. China is now open to influence and to be influenced by global economic, scientific and technological trends. Moreover, a brand new relationship is being forged between military-related research and civilian research, as numerous military-based initiatives are being gradually transformed to serve civilian objectives.

## Research and Development

The reform of R&D activities in China started with the reform of the Chinese Academy of Sciences' research and management policy. Even before its founding in 1949, the Chinese Academy of Sciences (CAS) had played the role of the national comprehensive research centre which set the pace and the standard for the other national and local research institutions. Under the Mao regime, the CAS's main research tasks concentrated, for obvious reasons, on defence, heavy industry and to a certain extent on agriculture. In particular, space, electronics, automation and telecommunications received growing shares of manpower, material and finance from the state. Having thus contributed to the early development of China's A-bomb, H-bomb and satellites, the CAS has become, especially since 1978, more of a training centre that is transferring researchers and research results to a growing number of civilian sectors.

The conception of the the CAS's research policy has also been reviewed since 1978. The former top-down conduct of the CAS's scientific management has been modified; and since the Seventh Five-Year Plan, the CAS has been free to set research priorities in response to a predefined comprehensive research strategy set by the central authorities. Starting within this comprehensive and mandatory set of national key projects, the CAS freely sketches out its research work plan; defines its timetable; supplies human and financial means and conceptualises the research projects.

For instance, during the Five-Year Plan 1991–95, as a major research institution, the Academy was put in charge of new national key projects such as bioengineering and remote-sensing techniques and 11 related sub-projects. This is over and above its involvement in 47 major projects, 140 sub-projects and 529 special activities. More than 110 research units comprising up to 7,000 scientific and technical personnel participate in the Academy's workload.

In line with the reform of the economic structure and the S&T management system, the Academy, like the universities, is seeking through its activities to project a positive rapport with the outside world, building strong lateral ties with production departments, enterprises and local authorities, and entering into new forms of scientific and technological co-operation such as contract research, technology transfer, technical consulting, personnel training and the setting-up of allied entities of scientific research and production.

In order to strengthen R&D activities, several types of new technology development firm have been set up by the Academy. Since 1985 the total number of firms that have been created by the Academy exceeds 400. Among these are 12 Academy-run firms, five Academy and local government-run firms and 23 joint venture enterprises. Research activities have resulted in innovations which have been successfully commercialised by joint ventures. For instance, the Oriental Scientific Instruments Import and Export Corporation, operating under the aegis of the Academy, is engaged in trade partnership with firms in more than 20 countries. This has helped the Academy's scientists to upgrade their laboratory facilities and databases and has also enhanced the Academy's position in the international technology market.

The 1978 reforms had allowed the Academy to engage in scientific co-operation with foreign institutions. The Academy has since sponsored 5,888 people to study abroad: 4,165 as visiting scholars and 1,723 as postgraduate students. Besides, the Academy and its institutes have signed co-operation agreements with their foreign counterparts and universities of more than 50 countries, as well as with international organisations. The Academy has also joined the World Laboratory as one of its founders. In the long run, the reforms aim to make the Academy develop into a comprehensive research centre composed of national laboratories (research institutes), national science and engineering centres, R&D centres for resources and environment, joint open laboratories and R&D institutes affiliated to high technology enterprises.

## Higher and Professional Education

The 1978 reforms were also intended to tackle the numerous problems that crippled the educational system during the Mao period. A greater decentralisation has been introduced in higher education in order to allow universities to adapt their teaching programmes and management procedures to the provinces' prevailing needs. Universities are today free to hire faculty staff and to select students. University boards enjoy a greater freedom in financial and human resources management. For instance, out of roughly 1,100 universities, high schools and professional centres of excellence, almost two-thirds (700) are under the provinces' direct control.

In addition to the 16,000 professional and technical training centres that welcome high school leavers and turn them into skilled technicians and professionals much needed by a growing economy, a total of 114 universities have been set up since 1986. These have a combined enrollment capacity of 23,000 students each year. The universities train students who want to acquire practical knowledge designed to make them readily employable. The specialities offered by these universities are generally discussed and approved by joint committees in which university managers and active professionals regularly meet to adjust the academic courses in line with the economy's requirements. The duration of studies does not exceed three years. Outstanding students are offered the opportunity to pursue graduate studies in renowned universities to prepare them for high-level professional jobs.

China's new industrial policy has, since 1978, set in motion programmes for a comprehensive modernisation of the country's educational and research institutions. This is pursued as part of China's strategy to emerge as a centre of technological and economic dynamism. The signs are already there suggesting that this objective is not far out of reach. One such sign is the role played by the Chinese overseas who bring to their homeland financial resources but, most importantly, technical, entrepreneurial and commercial state-of-the-art skills and expertise.[3]

## The Maghreb Experience in S&T

### Background and Constraints

As Djeflat (1993) points out, 'The scientific and technical option in education is theoretically linked in all countries to the technological policy pursued in production' and 'the evolution of scientific and technical training in education should reflect the technological change occurring in production.' To what extent does this statement hold for the Maghrebian countries?

Historically, industrialisation in the Maghreb involved the processing of raw materials based on the use of a large supply of labour. Each process was often undertaken on the basis of turn-key principles. Technicians and professionals who were to operate the established industries were often recruited and specially trained for the project itself with no spin-off for the educational system. The education system, on the other hand, was least oriented to serving the economy's real needs. Indeed, education and production looked like two separate spheres with almost no intersection and with each training its necessary personnel for itself. One sphere's supply of skills rarely met the other's demand to the point that no sizeable market for skills emerged. Wages were determined administratively and were not linked to actual or potential productivity. As production kept on using imported 'ready-to-use' technology and with wages unrelated to productivity, there was almost no drive for innovation and thus for technological accumulation.

This problem which militated against the accumulation process was aggravated by a number of factors, including shortfalls in the supply of capital for investment in the promotion of the S&T and R&D effort of the Maghrebian countries; the underlying inefficiency of the market mechanism in these countries; the preponderance of rent-seeking behaviour and the culture of bureaucracy; and the heavy hand of governments, often at the cost of freedom of thought.

## Prospects for Technology Development in the Maghreb

New technologies are central to the capitalist mode of production and its reproduction. As costs related to manpower and raw materials tend to equalise globally in a number of new technology-using industries, innovation, inventions, scientific research and technology development appear to be the only sustainable path towards cost cutting and profitability. It is a natural tendency of capitalism to develop technically in a manner aimed at shortening the socially-necessary labour time and increase surplus value. Profit thus drives technical progress and, in return, the search for more technical progress tends to enhance profitability. However, scientific research and technology development represent costly and time-consuming activities. In financial terms, the ratio of scientific research to technology development is considered by specialists to be 1 to 100, so that for every dollar spent on research it takes a hundred dollars to come up with a new and competitive technological product. It would, therefore, appear quite impossible for the countries in the Maghreb to engage individually in technology development ventures. They would instead need to pool resources in well-defined, common, scientific projects and also engage in joint ventures with foreign partners, such as China. This common endeavor is vital if the Maghrebian countries are to catch up in some technologies, given the constraints on their R&D effort posed by shortages in the supply of capital and skills. Pooling these scarce resources and organising a bigger regional market for technology products may help some new technologies to thrive through economies of scale and higher levels of factor productivity.

Redefining a new regional industrial policy by singling out some sectors and specialising in them would require each of the Maghrebian countries to seek technological niches while providing the framework for economic agents in each country to seek synergies with their counterparts in the other countries. A good example of this relates to the pipeline transporting gas from Algeria to Italy through Tunisia, or the proposed pipeline to link Algeria and Spain through Morocco. Such projects would call for the involvement of non-Maghrebian partners to provide the technology and investment resources. The involvement of foreign partners would also ensure the survival of the projects even in the face of political disputes among the Maghrebian countries.

The Europeans have already shown the way by creating common undertakings such as Eureka, Airbus or Aerospatiale because of the need to cut costs and sustain the competitive pressure of new technologies. The Maghrebian countries can emulate this experience to build on some sectors in which they have individually capitalised some experience. As areas where new technologies can be applied, electronics, telecommunications, energy, among others, may be singled out as priority sectors in which capital – local and foreign – skilled labour and institutional reforms could be concentrated.

In electronics, the Maghrebian countries have built some plants using mostly conventional technologies. In Tunisia and Morocco, assembly lines operate using completely knocked-down kits; and in Algeria electronic plants operate as both assembly and manufacturing lines. The regional production of electronic goods is limited to the first generation of goods such as radio receivers, recorders and television sets. In Algeria the government sought to develop the manufacturing of electronic goods by producing most of the components locally. However, the growing demand for more modern electronic consumer products, such as colour and remotely-controlled television sets, satellite dishes and hi-fi image and sound systems, has forced the industry to switch rapidly to the importation of technologically updated components which are not yet produced locally.

The electronics industry may represent one major field where scarce capital and skilled labour in the Maghreb can work marvels for a larger regional market craving for electronic goods. Indeed, it may even induce the necessary reform in electronics teaching and research programmes that would allow Maghrebians to master new electronics technology and participate in the reduction of costs for a diversified and high value- added industry.

Telecommunications are another promising field as far as new technologies are concerned. The telecommunications-related new technologies such as fibre optics, digital technology and multimedia are challenging activities for Maghreb businessmen, public decision-makers and scientists. Telecommunications coupled with electronics and software constitute high growth industries globally. The projected earnings for 2000 approach 200 billion dollars, of which more than a quarter would accrue from applied software (Finkelstein 1992). The progressive rejection of the conventional electromechanical technology world-wide on behalf of digital technology has fostered a gigantic shift in the industry's structure. As integrated circuits, microprocessors and software make a forceful entry into the telecommunications industry, large international groups are converting their capital and especially their skilled resources into those fields.[4]

As with electronics, the telecommunications industry is mostly concentrated in Tunisia and Morocco in assembly plants often operated by foreign corporations. The production scale remains modest. In Algeria the industry is relatively more developed. Telephone sets are, for example, produced in large numbers while nine of the ten needed components are manufactured locally, although the technology used is conventional. This is, however, an advantage as any strategic shift towards the new digital technology would require proficiency in the handling of conventional technologies. Unable to opt for the costly satellite telecommunications technology, Algeria has chosen to go digital by planning to wire the whole country by using fibre-optic cables (1,100 km had already been laid in 1991).[5]

The building of such fibre-optic networks will induce the growth of new technologies in electronics, such as components and microprocessors and in computers, such as software development. Software is one of the fastest growing branch of computer sciences. It is a high value-added activity and it may be a sector worth investing in and developing for the Maghrebian countries, provided that higher education teaching programmes are reformed and modernised as has been done in Bangalore in India and elsewhere.[6]

Carving a niche in this highly competitive industry is at this stage beyond the capabilities of the Maghrebian economies. That is why it is all too vital for the three countries to venture together in this and other areas of investment in collaboration with foreign concerns.

Opting together for this new technology would require the Maghrebian countries to adopt a new industrial strategy, reformulating the programmes of education and training institutes of technology. The aim is to provide the targeted industry with the necessary talents and skills ranging from engineers to operators and maintenance personnel. Another opportunity that could be exploited by the Maghrebian countries relates to the pool of expatriate talent and skills that might, as in the case of China, provide the region with badly needed technical, managerial, commercial, financial and engineering resources.

## Prospects for Sino–Maghreb Co-operation

In the objective of promoting science and technology-based development, the Maghreb countries would benefit from collaboration with each other and with countries beyond the region, and particularly the emerging developing countries such as China. These countries have capitalised long and sound technical experience which could be transferred to the Maghreb without involving heavy cost. The following are some possible areas in which worthwhile Sino–Maghreb co-operation could be explored.

### Remote-sensing Techniques

China's space technology is not only up-to-date but is also price-competitive when compared to what may be obtained from the developed space powers. Chinese satellite capacity may thus be leased by the Maghrebian countries on favourable terms to serve objectives ranging from sensing and probing ground and underground resources (water and minerals), to exploring the yet virgin seabed.

### Techniques for Fighting Desertification

China has for some time now devised a research and technical progamme for controlling desertification. In the Maghreb, the desertification process has resulted in the loss of arable and fertile land. In view of this advancing problem in the Maghreb, scientific co-operation with China is one possible option that could be investigated.

### Irrigation Techniques

China is well known historically for the mastery of irrigation techniques. Hydraulic engineering is part of well-established technical expertise and a comprehensive training programme. Chinese experts in this field have worked marvels so far in some provinces, even though many others have not benefited yet. The vastness of the country and the diversity of climatic conditions have had limiting effect on the diffusion of hydraulic engineering skills. However, the Maghreb could learn from China's experience in dam-building and in small and medium-sized irrigation networks that are often well adapted to specific conditions and are mostly labour-intensive and capital-saving.

*Nuclear Technology*

Chinese nuclear technology is well developed and seem to be secure. The transfer of this technology to the Maghreb for the purpose of generating electrical energy would be costly and inappropriate because the Maghreb is well-endowed with cheaper sources such as oil and particularly gas. This does not, however, preclude the need for any transfer since nuclear applications are numerous. For instance, radioisotope development and production could generate social and financial profit in medicine, agriculture, biotechnology, agro-industrial products preservation and refrigeration techniques. Development based on Algeria's Chinese-made nuclear reactor could benefit from co-operation between China and the Maghreb in the development of common scientific and industrial initiatives.

*Medical Techniques*

Some of the medical techniques used in China are almost as old as the country itself. Specifically, Chinese techniques such as acupuncture, mesotherapy or so-called soft medicine using natural substances are today internationally established and have gained respect in many developed countries. The attractions of these techniques are that they are relatively cheap and labour-intensive and would suit not only the Maghreb's economic structure but also its cultural penchant for the use of natural drugs and herbs.

**Conclusion**

Compared with China, the Maghrebian countries are technologically weak. This would make them potentially vulnerable to political pressures and prompt them to adopt policies that are not necessarily supportive of long-run development effort in the region. Much would, however, depend on what and how they choose to promote growth and development individually and in concert. The short-term option provided by SAPs is, strictly speaking, a non-starter insofar as the application of such programmes marginalises initiatives for the development of a capability in science and technology.

Yet structural adjustment of the economies is necessary. Distortions will need to be rectified and inefficiencies removed. The challenge for policy is to approach the task of adjustment in the context of the long term. This will require the state in the Maghreb to concentrate on resource conservation and human resource development through S&T programmes. The conventional belief that economic growth is contingent upon the exploitation of labour and capital (including natural resources) begs the question of sustaining the growth process itself. A lesson which the Maghrebian countries can learn from the contemporary experience of China is that it is only through the development of their S&T base that they can manage effectively to remove the constraints on the sustainability of growth and development of their individual economies. This route to transition may be arduous, costly and time-consuming but could be rewarding. In the long run, economies thrive on science and technology.

## NOTES

1. But China (like India) constitutes a special case in the low income category as narrowly defined by the level of per capita income.
2. This refers to post-industrial activities involving science and technology-driven research and development. The pattern of development hitherto has been of economies of different countries evolving from agricultural development to industrial development and to the development of skill-based (or science and technology-based) activities across the economic spectrum.
3. Chinese outside mainland China have generally been observed to be more entrepreneurial, innovative and dynamic than their kith and kin on the mainland, suggesting the dominance of a counter-innovative political and ideological influence unleashed by the Communist revolution; but, for all that, the Chinese have not lost the flair for enterprise and innovation. The entrepreneurial behaviour of individuals of Chinese extraction outside mainland China is consistent with Evert Hagen's (1968) minority thesis that when people are pushed to the wall the instinct for survival would often find a convenient outlet in enterprise and innovation.
4 The ten biggest corporations in the sector handle more than 65 per cent of the global market. Five of them appear among the biggest corporations that dominate the electronics industry. Out of these, three are active in computers (Motorola, ATT and NEC). This oligopolistic structure has enabled the corporations to reap economies of scale in each field of activity (telephones, electronics and computers) and sustain the costly R&D effort (6 billion dollars for ATT and 5.4 billion for IBM in 1991).
5 This technology offers many technical and economic advantages including: shorter times needed for installing networks; easier extension possibilities of networks; lower operating and maintenance costs; lower investment costs; economies of space; ease of application in rural areas; and possibilities for exploiting the diverse services arising from the same cable network in the much-heralded multimedia information highway.
6. India has lately become one of the major exporters of software (worth around 2 billion dollars in 1993).

## REFERENCES

Benyoucef, Farid (1980), *A Study of Economic Integration in the Maghreb*. MSc thesis, Denver University.
Coughlin, Peter (1991), *Industrialisation at Bay: African Experiences*. Academy Science Publishers, Nairobi.

Djeflat, Abelkader (1993), *Technologie et Système Educatif en Algérie*. Co-edition UNESCO-CREAD-Médina, Office des Publications Universitaires, Alger.

Finkelstein, Joseph (1992), 'Capitalism and Technology'; in *Dialogue*, No.4.

Hagen, E.E. (1968), *The Economics of Development*, Irwin, London.

Overholt, H. William (1993), *China: the Next Economic Superpower*, Weidenfeld & Nicolson, London.

Yachir, Fayçal (1992), *La Maditérran dans la Revolution Technologique*. Forum du Tiers-Monde. L'Harmattan, Paris

# The Role of the State in Technology Promotion in Developing Countries: An Agenda for the Maghreb

MOZAMMEL HUQ

*The article examines the difficulties of promoting technological capability in developing countries and reviews the role of the state in technology promotion. An attempt is made to test the proposition that, as latecomers, developing countries are fortunate in that they have available a stock of technologies to draw upon. Evidence on technology absorption and promotion (or lack of it) in selected developing countries is presented. It becomes apparent that a dynamic learning process has to be fostered. Market forces cannot be relied upon to comprehend the externalities which are involved in the absorption and diffusion processes. Hence the need for a supportive role of the state in technology promotion in developing countries. The article draws some lessons for the developing countries in general and for the Maghreb countries in particular.*

## Introduction

Since the early 1970s, there has been an upsurge of discussion on technology promotion in developing countries[1] and, by the 1980s, a consensus had emerged that this is far from the simple process of comparing alternative techniques in order to identify the least-cost method of production. Concern merely with static profit maximisation fails to take account of elements such as the costs and benefits of technology learning and the externalities generated. In other words, technology promotion in developing countries involves dynamic elements in the processes of the adoption and diffusion of technology.

For Lall (1987), failure to consider LDC innovation and generation of technology is the missing link in contemporary analysis in Third World

The author is Senior Lecturer, Department of Economics, University of Strathclyde, Glasgow. He is grateful to Roy Greive and Girma Zawdie for their valuable comments on an earlier draft. Research assistance provided by Aklilu Tefera is also acknowledged. The article is based on the author's contribution to the Annual Conference of the Development Studies Association; see Huq (1995b).

industrialisation. Such a claim goes against the common belief that as latecomers, developing countries are fortunate in that they have a backlog of technologies to draw upon, thus making their development process that much easier (Gerschenkron 1962). The argument goes like this: the wheel is already invented and all that is required of the developing country investors is to choose from the technology shelf. The implication would seem to be that if developing countries allow the market to guide them to the correct choice of technology, given time, all will be well.

In this article, we examine this viewpoint in the light of some contemporary evidence of technology promotion in developing countries. We then draw some lessons for developing countries in general, and for the Maghreb countries in particular.

No attempt is made here to show the link between technology promotion and economic development. It will, however, be alluded that there is 'very little disagreement about the importance of technical change for economic development and trade promotion. Virtually all economists, neo-classical, Keynesian, Marxist, Schumpeterian or whatever, accept the point that productivity growth depends very heavily on the introduction and efficient diffusion of new and improved processes and products in the economic system' (Freeman 1989: 85).

There is hardly any dispute, even from the neoclassical perspective, that the government should contribute to the development of institutions for improving markets such as technology because of the externalities involved. Markets for technology development fail because knowledge leaks (Wade 1990: 11–13). In areas such as manpower training and R&D, market failures will lead to underinvestment, thus necessitating government intervention either in terms of direct production or through the provision of subsidies.

In the next section we examine technology promotion in the context of the dynamic elements involved. The following section presents findings relating to technology promotion in three developing countries: South Korea, India and Bangladesh, referring to survey studies conducted, respectively, by Enos and Park (1988), Lall (1987) and Huq et al. (1990, 1992 and 1993). The next two sections take up the argument for the role of the state in technology promotion in developing countries and draw some lessons for the Maghreb countries. Finally some conclusions are drawn.

## The Dynamic Aspects of Technology Promotion

Economists no longer treat technological phenomena as the product of what Rosenberg (1992 and 1994) has called 'a black box'. Various studies on technology transfer were carried out at the industry level, mainly during the 1970s, with the object of identifying, from a wide spectrum of technologies, the technology most appropriate to cost-minimisation or profit-maximisation.[2] These have been criticised in particular for failing to consider the dynamic aspects of technology transfer. To achieve successful transfer, technology evaluation should go beyond the static framework of cost-minimisation and in addition give attention to the following issues (UN 1987):

- the assimilation and diffusion of new technologies in the host economy; and

- the development of indigenous capacities for innovation.

Enos and Park (1987), Dahlman *et al.* (1987), Lall (1987 and 1992) and Huq *et al.* (1992 and 1993), among others, took the wider approach in examining technology promotion in developing countries. An important feature of the dynamic approach is that the development of technological capability is viewed as a process of learning.

The process may be viewed as comprising three main stages:

Stage 1: Selection/Purchase;

Stage 2: Absorption; and

Stage 3: Diffusion.

The process of technology transfer starts but does not end with Stage 1, which is taken care of through the conventional cost-minimisation approach. Stages 2 and 3 deserve careful consideration as it is here that the dynamic aspects of the process may be captured.

*Absorption* may be viewed as the initial process of technology assimilation or 'digestion' by which users build up a thorough knowledge of the technology in question and develop capability in installing, maintaining, designing and manufacturing the equipment concerned.[3] *Diffusion* denotes the final stage when the technology is adopted by others with the help of the original recipient.

Another way of evaluating the transfer process is to identify and list the capabilities which will be developed with the full transfer of technology. Dahlman *et al.* (1987) originally suggested three such (production, investment and innovation) and, subsequently, Lall (1992) added a fourth (linkages).[4]

While these approaches greatly help us in introducing a number of the dynamic elements which could not be captured in the conventional studies of cost-minimisation, there is, however, difficulty in quantifying the level of, say, absorption and diffusion, or in measuring the various capabilities. Although there is general agreement as to the factors involved in the process, given the qualitative nature of many of the explanatory factors, including government commitment, it is not easy to extend the analysis in a quantitative manner. Moreover, if technological capability is used as a dependent variable it is not easy to quantify that variable either.[5]

Methodological problems notwithstanding, the case for understanding technology – its development, transfer and management – as a dynamic process advancing economic growth remains.

## Evidence of Technology Promotion from Developing Countries

Unfortunately not many detailed surveys of technological capability exist. In this section, we present findings that are available from three developing countries, South Korea, India and Bangladesh, with the view to drawing some lessons of experience in technological capability building.

## Evidence from Bangladesh

In Bangladesh, industrialisation has been accorded policy emphasis since the mid-1950s when, as the eastern part of Pakistan, the region was involved in the development planning exercise carried out initially under the First Five-Year Plan (1955–60) and more rigorously under the Second (1960–65) and the Third Five-Year Plan (1965–70) of Pakistan with the clear objective of making manufacturing the leading sector of the economy. After Bangladesh's independence in 1971, the target of industrialisation was eagerly adopted and it was almost taken for granted that industrialisation was just around the corner for Bangladesh and that soon all would be fine (Robinson 1974). However, after two decades of independence and a number of development plans, each emphasising industrialisation, Bangladesh's record is weak, to say the least. The share of manufacturing in GDP is still no more than 10 per cent and, if the cottage and the small-scale sector is excluded, is only 6 per cent.

For all that, the experience gained over the years is instructive as may be noted from our survey of three industries – leather, chemical fertilisers and machinery manufactures – with respect to the promotion of technology.[6]

Consider first the case of machinery manufacturing which constitutes a good part of the Bangladesh capital goods sector (Huq et al. 1993). Extensive information was collected direct from 101 sample plants from both the public and the private sector (55 small, all private; 22 medium, all private; and 24 large – 12 private and 12 publicly owned). In total, nine sub-sectors, which constitute the major part of the capital goods sector of Bangladesh, were covered.[7] Technological capability in each of the sub-sectors has been examined by viewing a number of relevant aspects, indicated below.

*Design Capability*

While a number of public sector units have obtained licences from reputable foreign companies to follow or adapt their designs, this is not generally the case in the private sector. Only in diesel engines and electrical machinery have one or two private sector units obtained foreign licences; for the rest of the private sector units, copying is a standard practice. It was, however, found that firms have acquired the capability to produce simple machinery and equipment, according to orders received from customers. So far as sophisticated machinery and equipment are concerned, these can be manufactured only in the public sector plants such as the Bangladesh Machine Tool Factory (BMTF), Chittagong Dry Dock, General Electric Manufacturing Company (GEMCO) and Khulna Shipyard. Unfortunately, some of these plants have been experiencing serious management and other constraints since their inception and at least two (BMTF and GEMCO) are almost at the point of closing down. Although production in the private engineering plants, which are mostly small- and medium-scale units, is based on copying some foreign items, the ingenuity of the skilled labour force needs to be recognised. For example, we found the private machine tools sector to be able to adapt the sizes of machine tools – simple lathes, drills, for instance – to meet customers' specifications. The same ingenuity was observed in a number of other sectors including sugar manufacturing machinery and structural engineering.

*Local Manufacturing Capability*

The local content in terms of parts and components varies widely from product to product. In the case of the private sector assembly of diesel engines, all the required parts and components are obtained from abroad. On the other hand, Bangladesh Diesel Plant, which is in the public sector, has achieved a high level of integration in the manufacture of one-cylinder engines (local content is 73 per cent), though in two-cylinder engines the local content is only 23 per cent. The case of machine tool manufacture in the private engineering plants, however, provides a positive example in that the local content is something like 85 per cent. However, as contracting out is not common in these plants, the batch size is small, thus adversely affecting both the quality and the cost of production.

*Assembling, Installation and Maintenance Capability*

High-level technological capability is, however, observed in assembly, erection and maintenance, and this is found in both the public and the private sector. Indeed, in all the nine sub-sectors studied, 100 per cent capability was observed in these three specific areas. An earlier study by

Huq and Islam (1992) on the manufacture of fertilisers in Bangladesh provides some further information on the maintenance (as well as operational) capability in this particular industry. Bangladeshi engineers were found to be able to maintain fertiliser plants, which are undoubtedly of high complexity, without experiencing serious difficulties. The example of the Fenchuganj Fertiliser Factory, the first of its kind in the country, is perhaps worth invoking here. This plant, which was supplied by Kobe Steel of Japan and started operation in 1962, had become outdated by the late 1980s and many critical parts were unavailable from outside the country, although the engineers were successfully maintaining the plant at a high level of capacity utilisation, operating for 302 days per year on average during 1985–90, against 312 as designed.

These attainments, the achievement of which falls under 'technology absorption' (Enos and Park classification, 1987), are undoubtedly fundamental to the process of developing technological capability. It is necessary, however, also to consider other key elements of the process – competence in production, investment, innovation and linkage – of which mention was made above.

*Production Capability*

Bangladesh has found it relatively easy to achieve production capability in simple products and processes, e.g., in leather manufacturing. (Huq and Islam 1990) But as regards complex products and processes, e.g., precision machine tools or fertiliser manufacturing, there has been limited success. However, simple production capability, i.e., the ability to run the plants, is found to be highly satisfactory in fertiliser manufacturing, while (contrary to the experience, for instance, of India and South Korea) it is not so for Bangladesh in precision machine tools and other sophisticated engineering products. Ease of importing the engineering items, helped by aid-finance and lack of appropriate tax and other relevant policies, have been blamed for low capacity utilisation in the engineering plants in question in Bangladesh (Huq *et al.* 1992, 1993).

*Investment Capability*

Heavy dependence on foreign aid has not helped Bangladesh in making progress in this particular aspect of technology promotion. Most often, foreign engineering and consultancy firms have been heavily involved in the supply of machinery and equipment, project design, and, at times, even construction and supervision, while local engineering and consultancy firms have remained almost neglected (Huq *et al.* 1992 1993). Furthermore, little attempt has been made to minimise project costs in new or expansion units, and this appears to apply to most of the public and the private sector plants which have often been financed with subsidised lines of credit.

## Innovation Capability

The ability to improve technology or to develop new products or processes is missing even in the leather manufacturing sector (Huq and Islam 1990), the industry which has the simplest of operations of the three surveyed. Many of the firms in this sector are even reluctant to move into high value-added products, and the government had to impose restrictions on the export of wet-blue leather to encourage further local processing of this product.

## Linkages Capability

This is perhaps the weakest area in technology assimilation in Bangladesh, thus causing failure in the diffusion of imported technologies and frustrating the deepening of the industrial sector. The study on fertiliser manufacturing provided a clear instance of total failure in this regard. The low or negligible involvement of the local engineering sector in the fertiliser plants of the country is striking, although at least one-third of the total project works of the large-scale plants (i.e., of those built in recent years) could have been completed locally (Huq and Islam 1992).

Table 1 summarises the state of technology promotion in Bangladesh in a number of sub-sectors and, as can be seen, the country has failed to make any significant progress as viewed under technology 'absorption' and 'diffusion'.

TABLE 1

TECHNOLOGY ABSORPTION AND DIFFUSION IN THE
BANGLADESH MACHINERY MANUFACTURING SECTOR

|                                       | Absorption  | Diffusion |
| ------------------------------------- | ----------- | --------- |
| machine tools production              | partial     | nil       |
| cotton textile machinery              | partial     | nil       |
| jute textile machinery                | partial     | nil       |
| leather machinery                     | negligible  | nil       |
| plastics machinery                    | negligible  | nil       |
| sugar machinery                       | partial     | nil       |
| electrical machinery and equipment    | partial     | nil       |
| manufacture of diesel engines         | partial     | nil       |
| structural engineering                | partial     | nil       |

Source: Huq et al. (1993).

## Evidence from South Korea and India

### South Korea

South Korea, which is now being considered as *Asia's Next Giant* (Amsden

1989), has achieved this status through consistent, rapid growth over the last 30 years or so. In the late 1950s the per capita income of South Korea was only just double that of Bangladesh (Khan and Hossain 1989: 7), while in the early 1990s it was over 30 times greater (World Bank 1994: 162-63). Amsden (1989) and Chang (1993), among others, strongly believe that the role of the state in South Korea has been a major factor in the transformation of the economy in such a short period, while in the case of Bangladesh, according to Khan and Hossain (1989: 3), who also believe that in a modern state the role of the government is a critical determinant of both the rate and the quality of economic growth, there was lack of 'a strong and effective government'. We present below the findings of a recent study on technology promotion and the role of the government in this regard in South Korea.

In their study on South Korea, Enos and Park (1987) have concentrated on the transfer of technology from developed countries (the USA, Japan and Germany) to the Republic of Korea. In examining the stages of the transfer, they focus on the recent acquisition of sophisticated technology by Korean companies in four selected industrial sectors: petrochemicals, iron and steel, heavy engineering goods, and textiles.

The two main stages of the transfer process, absorption and diffusion, were studied in particular detail. Table 2 summarises the level of absorption. It is apparent that 'the Koreans have entered more in the stages of construction, start-up and operation and improvement than in the earlier stages of design, and in the later stage of research and development; and that there are not great differences in participation across industries' (ibid.: 243-4). However, confining the observation to more than one incorporation of a technology (as found in three industries: petrochemicals, artificial fibres, and iron and steel), 'the general pattern is of increasing participation from earlier to later installations'. Thus, if absorption is viewed in a dynamic sense as progress from installation to capability development via technology assimilation, then all three cases demonstrate an ability on the part of the Koreans to have made effective use of the technology transfer facility.

The achievement in terms of technology diffusion is, however, much more limited, largely due to the fact that in the sample chosen by the authors, 'adoptions of imported technology have been limited ... characterised by single firms employing sophisticated technologies on a large scale' (ibid.: 224). The authors, however, do not find the limited degree of diffusion (technology adoption) very critical as, in their words, 'This was the result of deliberate action on the part of the Korean government: had the Korean government chosen to encourage the construction of small-scale plants there would have been more diffusion, but the government preferred, rightly in our estimation, to exploit the substantial economies inherent in large-scale operation' (ibid.: 244). Further they note that there 'has been the diffusion of the technology to institutions supplying resources to the adopting firm. The main supplying institution is the industry manufacturing capital goods in Korea. Encouraged by the government's policy of stimulating local production of capital goods, firms adopting foreign technology did communicate their needs and commissioned the purchase of capital goods, usually those of a simple nature but occasionally those of considerable complexity' (ibid.: 245).

The conclusions reached by the authors are revealing, especially as to the role of government in the absorption of technology. Enos and Park strongly believe that the Korean government has played a key role in the acquisition of modern techniques: 'the government assuring itself that the contracts negotiated with the foreign suppliers contained clauses relating to the acquisition of patents, designs and know-how; to the training, both abroad and on the site, of Korean engineers and managers; to the speedy replacements of expatriates; and to access to improvements in the products and processes. The government also made certain that the terms in the contracts were fulfilled' (ibid.: 229).

Being convinced that success in the absorption of foreign technology was critically dependent upon the precise terms obtained by the Korean government in its negotiations with the foreign suppliers, Enos and Park conclude that 'a major determinant of the ability of a developing country to absorb an imported technology is the preferences of its government, as reflected in the terms that it imposes upon foreign suppliers' (ibid.: 248).

*India*

In terms of per capita income, India is also a poor country like Bangladesh. Both are categorised as low-income economies (see World Bank 1994: 162) and both share the same colonial experience under British rule. However, India is more diverse – socially, economically and geographically – than Bangladesh. India has transformed the structure of her economy, the share of manufacturing in GDP being as high as 17 per cent in 1992 (World Bank: 166). India has also achieved great success in raising her gross domestic savings and investment, which stood at 22 and 23 per cent, respectively, of the GDP in 1992 (the corresponding figures for the USA are 15 and 16 per cent). Thus viewed, it may be argued that India has certainly come out of the Nurksian 'vicious circle of poverty', at least in the sense of low income leading to low savings. The task of technology promotion has been taken seriously in India and the role played by the government in this regard has been quite significant.

Lall's study (1987) on India's approach to the acquisition of technological capability by selected, large-sized, manufacturing and consultancy firms including three established industrial sectors (cement, iron and steel, and textiles) is of special interest.[8] Lall (1987: 38) refers to the three chosen sectors as 'basic industries', with well-proven technologies which exist in all newly industrialised countries. For India, these are all 'mature' industries which have been long established in the country: textiles (in its modern factory form) for over 150 years, cement and (integrated) iron and steel for about 70 years. In each of these sectors he examines the three main agents of technology promotion: manufacturers of the final product, manufacturers of capital goods used in that sector, and the consultants who provided process engineering and related services. There are 'negative as well as positive aspects of technological development in India' (Lall 1987: 227–8).

It is apparent that the Indian government, though remaining generally active in promoting technological capability, was not as supportive as was the South Korean government. According to Lall (1987: 239), 'while Indian capabilities were stimulated by policy, they were also contained by it, guided in particular directions and inhibited from being fully exploited in an efficient direction. Indian technological learning was not fully stretched: it

TABLE 2

ABSORPTION OF FOREIGN TECHNOLOGY BY KOREAN ENGINEERS (ACCORDING TO THE STAGE OF THE PROCESS IN INCORPORATION)

| Case | Stage in the Process of Incorporating the Technology | | | | | | |
|---|---|---|---|---|---|---|---|
| | Planning and Negotiation | Process Design | Equipment Design | Construction | Start-up and Operation | Improvement | R&D |
| **Petrochemicals** | | | | | | | |
| Ulsan plant (1945-85) | s | o | o | s | s | x | o |
| Yeocheon plant (1975-85 | s | s | s | s | s | x | s |
| | | | | | | | |
| **Synthetic fibres** | | | | | | | |
| Taegu plant | | | | | | | |
| Nylon line 1 (1960-85) | s | o | o | s | s | s | o |
| Nylon line 5 (1970-85) | s | s | s | s | s | s | s |
| Gumi plant | | | | | | | |
| Nylon line 3 (1983-5) | x | x | x | x | x | x | x |
| | | | | | | | |
| **Diesel engines** | s | o | o | s | s | s | o |
| | | | | | | | |
| **Iron steel** | | | | | | | |
| 1st stage (1965-85) | s | o | o | s | s | s | o |
| 2nd stage (1974-85) | s | o | o | s | s | x | o |
| 3rd stage (1976-85) | s | o | s | s | s | x | s |
| 4th stage (1979-85) | x | x | x | x | s | x | s |

Key: o = no Koreans participating; s = some participation; x = all Koreans

Source: J.L. Enos and W.H. Park (1988: 243).

was, on the contrary, stunted and deformed, reaching an artificial limit long before it need have done.

Thus, in the final analysis, it does appear that 'an overwhelming portion of the blame for failures of technologies effort in India was economic: and *can be traced directly or indirectly to economic policies pursued by the government*. Some of its achievements have also resulted from these policies. It is likely, however, that these achievements would have been more weighty and socially beneficial had a different set of policies permitted the same talents to be deployed to different ends' (Lall: 228).

It is true that there were failures, but such instances of failure are perhaps unavoidable. As Lall (1987: 240) admits, 'Even technologically advanced countries often go wrong in their technology policies (look at the UK or France), though they all feel that *some* interventions are needed to face the competitive challenges thrown up by the current technological revolution.'

## Supportive Role of the State

The survey of experience, though limited to only three selected countries, suggests that the question of technology promotion in developing countries is far from simple. Given the difficulties in the identification/ purchase stages, the availability of technologies in the developed countries does not guarantee late-comers that, by depending on market forces, they will be able to select cost-minimising alternative, far less achieve technology absorption and diffusion – two important stages of technology promotion where market failure calls for government intervention, as mentioned earlier. Thus one can see why Amsden (1989: 13) criticises Gerschenkron for taking a simple view that backward countries are fortunate that they have a backlog of technologies to draw upon. According to Amsden, 'Gerschenkron failed to give equal weight to the proposition that the more backward the country, the harsher the justice meted out by market forces.'

In order to achieve and maintain competitiveness, a country needs to develop general technological capability, as perceived by Frederich List (1841) over a century and a half ago in regard to Germany. As Freeman (1989: 97) has put it: 'it is the national system of innovation which is decisive, not the particular range of products. Universities, research institutions, technological infrastructure, industrial training systems, information systems, design centres and other scientific and technical institutions provide the essential foundation which alone make possible the adaptation to structural change in the economy associated with changes in techno-economic paradigm.' Indeed, it is the capability to *use* new technologies which is paramount, not the availability of these technologies in the world.

Of the three countries surveyed, it is apparent that South Korea has consistently provided a supportive state role in technology development. Such a role, according to Enos and Park, has proved essential and they conclude that: 'There is no stage in the process of incorporating an imported technology that a conscientious and patriotic government should neglect' (Enos and Park: 257).

In the case of India, the state's contribution was a mixture of promotion and obstruction. The promotion of technological capability in India, as Lall (1987: 239) points out, has been 'stimulated by (government) policy'. However, there were obstructions resulting from 'economic policies pursued by the government' which in some way limited the achievements (ibid. 228).

In the case of Bangladesh, the role of the state has been of an obstructionist rather than a supportive nature (Khan and Hossain 1989, Huq 1995a).[9] The obstructionist role has obviously not helped. For instance in the case of the development of the Bangladesh capital goods sector, Huq *et al.* (1993, 126) intimate: 'There is a serious contradiction in Government policy towards the development of machinery manufacturing in Bangladesh. Huge installed capacity, built systematically over a period of 20 years, in various public sector engineering plants ... remains very much underutilised as the products which could be manufactured in most of these plants are being imported liberally. ... The private sector units also experience lack of domestic demand, mainly because of import preference by the customers. Tax anomalies have contributed to a great extent in making imported machinery and equipment (complete units) cheaper than locally made comparable items.'

To be supportive, governments in developing countries must act positively to create the right environment: 'they must create the supply of technical manpower to assimilate technological development, and they must set the right environment for their industries to develop the requisite capabilities ... specific policies have to be implemented on the extent of protection, domestic competition, imports of technology, in-house R&D, the nature and amount of foreign investment, the S&T infrastructure, and all other things that influence learning and production efficiency' (Lall 1987: 240–41).

The learning process in technology acquisition perhaps needs to be emphasised. Even if government intervention succeeds, through subsidies, for instance, in making manufacturing activity profitable, there is no guarantee that those with capital will, or can, invest in manufacturing. A number of other conditions, including the availability of technical personnel, need to be satisfied. The following observation by Amsden in the case of South Korea is pertinent: 'Once the entrepreneurs recognised that government subsidies could make manufacturing activity profitable, and *that Korean engineers could build ships that floated* and steel that bore weight, they increasingly turned their attention away from speculating toward accumulating capital' (Amsden 1989: 23, emphasis added).

It is perhaps in order to mention that the recent emphasis on liberalisation has done no good to technology promotion in developing countries. Fortunately, the argument has not diverted the attention of countries such as India and South Korea which, because of their reasonable (or in the case of South Korea, highly respectable) level of domestic savings, could withstand the pressure from outside, including that from the World Bank and the IMF. But low-income countries such as Bangladesh, which have remained heavily dependent on foreign aid for their survival, have found it difficult to withstand that pressure and, in the process, have had to abandon any serious state attempt at technology promotion (Huq 1994). In the case of Bangladesh, the lack of a supportive state role has proved disastrous, to say the least, as, on the one hand, the huge installed capacity in the capital goods sector remains idle or highly underutilised and, on the other, as mentioned earlier, machinery and equipment which could be produced in many of these plants is being imported liberally, partly following the drive of the country towards liberalisation and partly reflecting the high dependence of the country on foreign aid for its development. The failure to understand the mechanics of technology promotion should, therefore, provide an important explanation for low industrialisation and underdevelopment in developing countries.

**Lessons for the Maghreb Countries**

According to the World Bank's classification, the three core Maghreb countries (Algeria, Morocco and Tunisia) belong to the group of lower middle income economies (World Bank 1995: 162–3). Except in Algeria which in 1993 had only 11 per cent of GDP in manufacturing (down from 15 per cent in 1970) and a negative annual average growth rate of 2.2 per cent during 1980–93 (perhaps largely due to political troubles), the Maghreb has achieved a reasonable level of manufacturing growth, as may be seen from Table 3.

The promotion of technological capability, though limited, looks promising by the standards of other African countries. There is evidence of an indigenous capital goods sector in the Maghreb and, in the case of Algeria, it is led by agriculture. As far as Morocco and Tunisia are concerned, there is evidence of an increase in exports of goods produced by the machinery and the transport equipment sector. As a percentage of total exports, in Morocco this sector had a share of 6 in 1993 compared to the corresponding share of only 1 in 1970. The respective figures for Tunisia were 10 and 0 per cent (World Bank 1995). The role of the state has featured prominently in the progress so far achieved, especially as until the early 1990s these countries were most often pursuing, at times rather vigorously, the import substitution strategy.

However, with the recent emphasis on liberalisation and privatisation, there is a danger that insufficient attention may be paid to the externalities which are inherent in technology promotion. There is also evidence that in all the three Maghreb countries the installed industrial capacity is becoming obsolete and technically inefficient (Djeflat 1994). An immediate reason for this is the acute foreign exchange constraint which inhibits the process of technology transfer. Beyond that, however, is the larger issue of lack of indigenous capability for innovation. Government policy on innovation is expressed in the form of R&D financing, but because R&D activities are remote from industry, their innovation effect has been limited in all the three countries. In recent years, policy concern with structural adjustment in the region appears to have relegated the issue of technology promotion through innovation to a secondary position. Indeed, the trend in Morocco has been worrying, in that the wholesale adoption of structural adjustment policies has resulted in the 'deskilling' of the labour force, increasing the unemployment rate of the highly educated and retrenching on programmes that are supportive of the development of the S&T and R&D capability of the country (Lehlou 1994).

TABLE 3

GNP PER CAPITA IN US $ AND THE MANUFACTURING SHARE OF GDP
AND ITS GROWTH IN THE MAGHREB COUNTRIES

|  | GNP per capita | Share of manufacturing in GDP | Average annual growth in manufacturing (%) | |
|---|---|---|---|---|
|  | (US$), 1993 | (%), 1993 | 1970–80 | 1980–93 |
| Morocco | 1,041 | 18 | 3.9 | 7.0 |
| Tunisia | 1,720 | 19 | 6.6 | 3.5 |
| Algeria | 1,780 | 11 | 7.6 | -2.2 |

Source: World Bank, World Development Report 1995, pp.162–7.

It is highly unlikely that, given the externalities involved, there will be any rapid development of the capital goods sector in the Maghreb countries in an environment of free trade as is implied in the liberalisation approach. The role of the state also needs to be emphasised in other areas of technology promotion such as promotion of R&D initiatives in collaboration with industry, negotiations with foreign suppliers of machinery and equipment, licensing agreements, and even in promoting exports which will help in enabling the domestic manufacturers to reap the benefit of scale economies.

## Conclusion

The fact that there are already technologies which the developing countries can draw upon is not enough to ensure technology absorption and diffusion. For successful technology transfer to take place (i.e., for the promotion of technological capability), the developing country concerned is required to go beyond the initial stage of importing technology. More and more emphasis must be put on the ability to assimilate, use, adapt, or create technology.

Given the externalities arising from technology promotion and the failure of the market to internalise these externalities, the importance of the supportive role the state can play in this respect cannot be overemphasised. Government involvement is reflected in various ways – tariff policy, technology transfer negotiations, aid negotiations, management of public sector projects, credit policy towards the private sector, export policy, R&D support and manpower development. Government commitment to technology promotion needs to be reflected in all of these. The findings from the three Bangladesh industry studies (Huq et al. 1990, 1992, 1993) provide evidence of lack of progress in technology promotion largely because of the absence of government commitment. In the case of South Korea (as observed by Enos and Park 1987), by contrast, the government has played a supportive role: 'There is no stage in the process of incorporating an imported technology that a conscientious and patriotic government should neglect (ibid.: 257).

In conclusion, for technology promotion, the support of the state needs to be unwavering as in the case of South Korea. State commitment in the face of policy constraints is likely to yield only partial success, as evidenced in the case of India. In an obstructionist policy regime, as in Bangladesh, failure in technology promotion may be expected to result. For the Maghreb countries, as for developing countries in general, it may be concluded that, given the externalities involved, a supportive role of the state will be required for technology promotion now that a policy framework which advocates the liberalisation of the economy has been adopted.

## NOTES

1.  Contributors to the topic include Pickett (1975), Rahim (1979, 1981), Teitel (1980), Westphal (1982), Stewart (1984), Pack and Westphal (1986), Dahlman *et al.* (1987), Enos and Park (1987), Forsyth (1987), Lall (1987, 1992), Nelson (1987), Freeman (1989), Enos (1991), Huq *et al.* (1992, 1993) and Cooper (1994).

2.  For example, a number of industry studies were carried out at the David Livingstone Institute of Strathclyde University with the title of 'Choice of Technique in Developing Countries', under the editorship of Eric Rahim. See, for example, Keddie and Cleghorn (1980) and Huq and Aragaw (1981).

3.  See Huq *et al.* (1992 and 1993) for some in-depth evaluation of technology absorption in the context of fertiliser and machinery manufacturing in Bangladesh by viewing some relevant aspects such as designing, local manufacturing, assembling, installation and maintenance capabilities.

4.  *Production capability*, needed to operate productive facilities, is reflected in productive efficiency and in the ability to adapt operations to changing market circumstances; *investment capability*, needed to establish new productive facilities and expand existing facilities project designs to suit the circumstance of the investment; *innovation capability*, needed to create new technology, is reflected in the ability to improve technology or to develop new products or services that better meet specific needs; and *linkages capability* is reflected in the ability to transmit information to, and from, component or raw material suppliers, subcontractors, consultants, service firms, and technology institutions.

5.  See, for example, Huq *et al.* (1993) who make an attempt to apply a regression model to determine the explanatory variables of technology promotion in the Bangladesh machinery manufacturing sector.

6.  The study 'Technology Transfer to Bangladesh', which was conducted at the Bangladesh Institute of Development Studies and in which the author was closely involved, was carried out during 1988–91, when three industry sub-sectors were individually investigated. See Huq and Islam (1990), Huq and Islam (1992) and Huq, Islam and Islam (1993).

7.  The sectors covered are machine tools, cotton textile machinery, jute machinery, leather machinery, plastics machinery, sugar machinery, electrical machinery and equipment, diesel engines and structural engineering.

8.  He took a sample of 19 large firms: 14 manufacturing firms and five consultancies.

9.  According to Khan and Hossain (p.5): 'In Bangladesh successive regimes have been preoccupied with setting up arrangements for their own survival. They were not strong enough to impose a coalition among the often contending economic forces – the actual and potential entrepreneurs -- and subject them to a set of rules of the game whose continuity would gradually come to be accepted.'

## REFERENCES

Amsden, A. (1989), *Asia's Next Giant: South Korea and Late Industrialisation*, Oxford University Press, New York.

Chang, H. (1993), 'The Political Economy of Industrial Policy in Korea', *Cambridge Journal of Economics* , Vol.17.

Cooper, C. (1994), 'Technology Policy and Industrialisation Policy in the Global Economy', *Science, Technology and Development* , Vol.12, Nos.2/3.

Dahlman, C.J., B. Ross-Larson and L.E. Westphal (1987), 'Managing Technological Development: Lessons from the Newly Industrialising Countries', *World Development,* Vol.15, No.6.

Djeflat, A. (1994), 'Strategies for Science and Technology-based Development in the Maghreb', paper presented at the MAGHTECH'94 conference, Sfax, Tunisia (7–9 Dec. 1994).

Enos, J.L. and W.H. Park (1988), *The Adoption and Diffusion of Imported Technology: the Case of Korea*, Croom Helm, London.

Forsyth, D.J.C. (1987), *Technology and Development: a Manual for Policy Assessment*, ILO,

Geneva (mimeo).

Freeman, C. (1989), 'New Technology and Catching Up' in C. Cooper and R. Kaplinsky, *Technology and Development in the Third Industrial Revolution*, Cass, London.

Gerschenkron, A. (1962), *Economic Backwardness in Historical Perspective*, Harvard University Press, Cambridge, MA.

Huq, M.M. and K.M.N.Islam (1990), *Choice of Technology: Leather Manufacturing in Bangladesh*, University Press, Dhaka.

Huq, M.M. and K.M.N. Islam (1992), *Choice of Technology: Fertiliser Manufacture in Bangladesh*, University Press, Dhaka.

Huq, M.M., K.M.N. Islam and N. Islam (1993), *Machinery Manufacturing in Bangladesh: an Industry Study with Particular Reference to Technological Capability*, University Press, Dhaka.

Huq, M.M. (1994), 'Technology Transfer to Bangladesh: Aid-dependence and Failures in Technology Acquisition', *Science, Technology and Development*, Vol.12, Nos.2/3.

Huq, M.M. (1995a), 'Industrialisation in Bangladesh: the Need for Supportive Government Role', Discussion Paper No.2 under the Strathclyde–BIDS Series on *Industrialisation in Bangladesh*, Department of Economics, University of Strathclyde, Glasgow.

Huq, M.M. (1995b), 'Technology Promotion, the State Role and Developing Countries', paper presented at the DSA Annual Conference, University of Dublin.

Khan, A.R. and M.Hossain (1989), *The Strategy of Development in Bangladesh*, Macmillan, London.

Lehlou, M. (1994), 'Systéme Educatif, Enterprises et Difficultés de la Transition au Maroc', paper presented to MAGHTECH'94, Sfax, 7–9 Dec.

Lall, S. (1987), *Learning to Industrialise: the Acquisition of Technological Capability by India*, Macmillan, London.

Lall, S (1992), 'Technological Capabilities and Industrialisation', *World Development*, Vol.20, No.2.

List, F. (1841), *The National System of Political Economy* (English translation, 1904), Longmans, London.

Nelson, R.R. (1987), 'Innovation and Economic Developments: Theoretical Retrospect and Prospect' in J. Katz (ed.), *Technology Generation in Latin American Manufacturing Industries*, Macmillan, London.

Pack, H. and L.E.Westphal (1986), 'Industrial Strategy and Technological Change: Theory versus Reality', *Journal of Development Economics*, Vol.22, No.1.

Rahim, E. (1979), 'Editorial Introduction', in J. Keddie and W. Cleghorn, *Brewing in Developing Countries*, Scottish Academic Press, Edinburgh.

Rahim, E. (1981), 'Editorial Introduction' in M.M. Huq and H. Aragaw, *Choice of Technique in Leather Manufacture*, Scottish Academic Press, Edinburgh.

Robinson, E.A.G. and K. Griffin (1974) (eds.), *The Economic Development of Bangladesh with a Socialist Framework*, Macmillan, London.

Rosenberg, N. (1982), *Inside the Black Box: Technology and Economics*, Cambridge University Press, Cambridge.

Rosenberg, N. (1994), *Exploring the Black Box: Technology, Economics and History*, Cambridge University Press, Cambridge.

Stewart, F. (1984), 'Facilitating Indigenous Technical Change in Third World Countries' in M. Fransman and K. King (eds.), *Technological Capability in the Third World*, Macmillan, London.

Teitel, S. (1984), 'Technology Creation in Sei-industrial Economies', *Journal of Development Economics*, Vol.16, No.1, pp.39–61.

United Nations (1987), *Transnational Corporations and Technology Transfer: Effects and Policy Issues*, Centre on Transnational Corporations, New York.

Wade, R. (1990), *Governing the Market: Economic Theory and the Role of Government in East Asian Industrialisation*, Princeton University Press, Princeton.

Westphal, L. (1982), 'Fostering Technological Mastery by Means of Selective Infant-Industry Protection' in M. Syrquin and S. Teitel (eds.), *Trade, Stability, Technology, and Equity in Latin America*, Academic Press, New York.

World Bank (1994), *World Development Report 1994*, Oxford University Press for the World
    Bank.
World Bank (1995), *World Development Report 1995*, Oxford University Press for the World
    Bank.

# SUMMARY ARTICLES

# Summary Articles

## Technological Innovation and Its Socio-organisation: Impact on the Textile Sector in Tunisia

In the course of technological progress, the several socio-professional categories of the labour force develop different attitudes. This article analyses these with particular reference to the case of the textile sector in the region of Monastir in Tunisia. The groups of workers investigated (1,500 in the sample), including workers and managers, are at one in their attitude of mistrust towards technological innovation. This climate of mistrust is reflected through conflicts of roles, status, objectives and power. The article looks at the introduction of new technologies to the textile industry and puts forward suggestions with the view to enhancing the flexibility and adaptation of the organisation and adequate choice of technologies.

HABIB AFFES
*Faculté des Sciences Economiques et de Gestion of Sfax, Tunisia*

## Training Motivation and Information: Three Essential Ingredients for Development

Development strategies in the last three decades in Algeria have relied heavily on material investment and neglected to a large extent investment in human capital, in spite of the huge budget allocated to education and training. Numerous problems have resulted from this situation, one of which relates to the linkage between university output and industry needs. This article analyses some of the problems which the education system faces and argues that three policies need to be conducted simultaneously: restructuring of the system, increased motivation and the adoption of a new information approach.

M. BENHAMADI and Y. BAHAYOU
*Centre d'Etudes et de Recherche sur l'information Scientifique et Technique (CERIST)*

The articles summarised here are published in full in French in the proceedings of the MAGHTECH'94 conference, *Science, Technologie et Croissance au Maghreb*, edited by A. Djeflat and R. Zghal (1996) Biruni, Sfax, Tunisia, 279 pp.

## Industrial Performance through the 'Just-in-Time' Principle

Strategies for improving the economic efficiency of industries would require, *inter alia*, that production instruments be adapted to the rapidly changing conditions of market demand. Among these, three instruments have been introduced: the 'just in time', total quality management and the computer-integrated manufacturing system. This evolution reflects changes in the organisational principles, in the level of involvement of men and the utilisation of new technologies. This article concentrates on the introduction of the 'just-in-time' principle adapted from the Japanese system to a Tunisian company (Vélo-Embrayage-Tunsie) and tries to assess the impact on performance during the period 1982–92.

BEN ALAYA LOTFI
*Faculté des Sciences Economiques et de
Gestion de Sfax, Tunisia*

## Role of Culture and Humanities in the Training of Engineers in Tunisia.

The training of engineers is characterised by heavy inputs of science and technology leading to the production of qualified personnel but lacking in capacity in terms of communication and social integration. Young students, because of the syllabuses on which their education is based, tend to be detached from the reality of their own society and come out of schools, colleges and universities too ill-equipped to manage problems they will encounter in their work environment. This can be a major problem regarding the effectiveness of locally-trained engineers. There have been recent attempts to tackle this problem through the introduction of new syllabuses in the training system. This article looks at these attempts and tries to assess how effective they can be in helping to increase the abilities of engineers to communicate more efficiently and to be more integrated into the broader socio-economic environment.

HAMED BEN DHIA
*Ecole Nationale des Ingenieurs de Sfax, Tunisia*

## The Issue of Quality and Its Requirements in the Tunisian Industry: a Case Study

The strategic behaviour of enterprises cannot be isolated from the constraints of their environment, notably the political and economic aspects of it. The lifting of protectionism has brought pressure to bear on firms operating in the framework of the global economy to adopt a new logic based on quality rather than quantity.

However, the experience of advanced countries, notably in Europe and America, has shown that the shift towards the quality principle is not an easy option for firms inasmuch as it may cost three times more than it can produce in terms of profitability. This article looks at a sample of 39 French firms where the principle of quality was introduced in order to examine the approach used with a view to assessing the 'quality policy' used by Tunisian firms with the support of the government.

RYM BOUDERBALA
*Faculté des Sciences Economiques et de Gestion de Sfax, Tunisia*

## The Relationship between the University, Research and Enterprise: towards a New Paradigm of Communication

Through its models and conceptual tools, communication theory may be applied in many areas owing to its paradigmatic dimension. It may be used in particular in modelling the relationship between the university, research and the productive sector.

In spite of its narrow character, this modelling operation of a complex phenomenon makes its possible to assess this kind of relationship. Thus the proposed model works according to a network of three members using channels and liaisons. This network allows all types of communication, including pedagogical, scientific, technical, institutional and public relations, provided that each member develops a capacity to manage the flows, the liaisons and the information stock. The article examines in detail these processes and applies them to the Algerian situation with the objective of identifying the problems associated with the relationship between university research and the experience of enterprises.

DAHMANE MADJID
*Centre de Recherche sur l'information Scientifique et Technique (CERIST), Algeria*

## Technological Paradigms and Work Organisation: a Survey of Some Moroccan Firms

Most industrial small- and medium-scale enterprises (SMEs) organise work according to the Taylorist way. The scientific principles underlying this approach are badly grasped by entrepreneurs. Small firms in Morocco tend to make extensive use of labour, while medium-sized firms tend to use equipment more intensely. Neither group seems to comply, however, with the Taylorian principles for increasing productivity. This article tries to analyse the complex link between new technologies and labour in Moroccan firms and why the paradigms associated with new technologies are not always well grasped locally.

NOURREDINE EL AOUFI
*University of Mohammed V of Rabat, Morocco*

## R&D Requirements and their Financing in the Tunisian Agricultural Sector

The food needs of Tunisia cannot be entirely satisfied by its current system of production. The introduction of new techniques into the agricultural sector might help to overcome this problem of shortfall in production. Local production capability exists but is badly lacking in management, adequate financing and a clearly defined strategy. This article looks into all these issues by referring to experiences in other parts of the world namely the land-grant system in the USA and to theories such as the endogenous growth model and the balanced financing (endogenous and exogenous) approach.

ANIS EL-BORGI
*Faculté des Sciences Economiques et
de Gestion de Sfax, Tunisia*

## The State of National Research in the Field of Employment in Morocco

In this article the author undertakes an evaluation of the research work conducted in the field of employment in Morocco. This research is made necessary by the application of the structural adjustment programme and its effects on employment in particular. Three major approaches are identified and examined: the approach which emphasises economic analysis, the approach which puts the emphasis on social integration, and finally the institutional approach. This review will help to identify the strengths and weaknesses of each one and draw better prospects for the future.

DRISS GUERRAOUI
*University of Mohammed Ben Abdallah of Fez, Morocco*

## The Training–Employment Relationship and Technological Challenges in the Advanced Economies: What Lessons for the Maghreb Countries?

The relationship between employment and training raises many issues when considered in the context of contemporary economic and social changes in developing countries. Neo-classical theory and particularly the theory of human capital have tried to set the theoretical bases to the inequalities in terms of salaries in the labour market. Education and training have thus become investments based on the criterion of both economic and social logic. This article looks at adult continuous training in France and assesses what impact technological changes may have on it. It also makes an attempt to draw lessons for the Maghrebian countries.

MALIK MÉBARKI
*University of Science and Technology of Lille I, France*

## The Technological Dimension in the Financing of Algerian Public Enterprises

Since the launching of economic reforms in Algeria in 1989, the government has been trying to improve the economic and financial performance of public sector enterprises, with the view to enhancing their competitiveness and hence their ability to participate in the world market, earning foreign exchange which the country badly needs. The technological dimension of this process is important. However, it appears to be neglected. This article looks at the approaches used to analyse the incorporation of the technological dimension into the process. In this respect it adopts a broad definition of technology, including managerial, financial and technical know-how.

ABDELHAMID MEZAACHE
*Financial economist and consultant, Algiers, Algeria*

## Technological Choices and Economic Constraints on the Building Industry in Algeria

For two decades, Algeria has had access to important oil surpluses, a great part of which has been devoted to investment and development projects. Investment in industry benefited from massive imports of technology. This was induced by the growing demand particularly for housing. The imports included a variety of technologies related to the field of construction. This article assesses the experiences of technological choice, analyses the relative weight of the economic factors which determined most of these choices and looks into the future technological prospects of the construction sector.

FAROUK TEBBAL
*International consultant and former Minister of Housing of Algeria*

## Maintenance Policy and Technology Transfer Requirements and Economic Reforms in Algeria

Maintenance has long been considered as a negligible function in the Algerian industry. It usually takes the forefront when machines and equipment break down and the production process is hampered. However, some studies of the textile sector have shown that it may provide an important basis for technological mastery and technology transfer. While bureaucratic constraints resulting from the planned economic system left little scope for the public enterprise to incorporate maintenance into its technology strategy, the new reform programmes open up prospects by liberalising the system and making the enterprise more autonomous. This article looks into these issues and probes the possibility of extending the experience to other sectors.

RACHID TANDJAOUI
*Deputy General Manager of SIMAC*
*(a private enterprise in Algeria)*

## Capital Goods Sector and Technology Transfer Dynamics in Algeria

The role of the capital goods sector is often neglected when technology transfer dynamics are examined. Yet many theories in the 1970s have put the emphasis on this sector as part of the broad strategy of industrialisation in developing countries. In Algeria this sector received massive investments during the two four-year plans. The sector is heavily dependent on foreign technology. Looking more specifically at the railways industry, the article analyses the policies and terms of technology transfer and accumulation and argues that a regional policy has a better chance to succeed in mastering technology than a country-based policy which is bound to be market constrained.

KAMEL BEHIDJI
*Deputy Director, ENCC*
*(The National Enterprise for Heavy Metal Frames in Algeria)*

# Index

www.ingramcontent.com/pod-product-compliance
Ingram Content Group UK Ltd.
Pitfield, Milton Keynes, MK11 3LW, UK
UKHW020431010325
455677UK00029B/1099